AGE AS AN EQUALITY ISSUE

Until recently, age discrimination attracted little social opprobrium. However, ageism has been thrust onto the equality agenda by the spectre of an ageing population. This has led to a range of policies on 'active ageing.' Most importantly, legally binding legislation prohibiting age discrimination in employment will need to be in place by 2006. Remarkably little attention has been paid to the key issues. To what extent is age inevitably linked with declining capacity? What are the central aims of a policy on age equality, and how can these be realised in law? How should law and policy address age discrimination in health, education and employment? What lessons can be learned from the US and Europe? And should young people be dealt with in the same way as older people?

This book answers these questions in a series of chapters by experts from a wide range of disciplines. It begins by examining the nature of the ageing process and then turns to a detailed analysis of the concept of age equality. In the light of this analysis, the following three chapters critically assess employment, education, and health. A separate chapter is devoted to discrimination against children. The last two chapters consider the experience in the US, and other European countries.

Age as an Equality Issue

Edited by
SANDRA FREDMAN
Exeter College, Oxford
and
SARAH SPENCER
Institute for Public Policy Research

·HART·
PUBLISHING
OXFORD AND PORTLAND OREGON
2003

Hart Publishing
Oxford and Portland, Oregon

Published in North America (US and Canada) by
Hart Publishing c/o
International Specialized Book Services
5804 NE Hassalo Street
Portland, Oregon
97213-3644
USA

Hart Publishing is a specialist legal publisher based in Oxford, England.
To order further copies of this book or to request a list of other
publications please write to:

Hart Publishing, Salter's Boatyard, Folly Bridge,
Abingdon Road, Oxford OX1 4LB
Telephone: +44 (0)1865 245533 or Fax: +44 (0)1865 794882
e-mail: mail@hartpub.co.uk
WEBSITE: http//www.hartpub.co.uk

British Library Cataloguing in Publication Data
Data Available
ISBN 1–84113–405–8 (hardback)

Typeset by Hope Services (Abingdon) Ltd.
Printed and bound in Great Britain on acid-free paper by
Biddles Ltd, www.biddles.co.uk

Contents

About the Contributors

Colm O'Cinneide is a Lecturer in the Law Faculty at University College London.

Sir John Grimley Evans is Professor of Clinical Geratology, University of Oxford, and Fellow of Green College, Oxford.

Sandra Fredman is Professor of Law, Oxford University and a Fellow of Exeter College.

Lawrence M Friedman is Marion Rice Kirkwood Professor of Law at Stanford University, California, USA.

Bob Hepple QC is Master of Clare College and Emeritus Professor of Law in the University of Cambridge.

Jonathan Herring is a Fellow in Law of Exeter College, Oxford.

Janice Robinson is Director of Health and Social Care, King's Fund.

Tom Schuller is Dean of the Faculty of Continuing Education and Professor of Lifelong Learning at Birkbeck, University of London.

Sarah Spencer is a Senior Associate at the Institute for Public Policy Research, Chair of the Equality and Diversity forum and Visiting Professor, Human Rights Centre, University of Essex.

1

Introduction

SANDRA FREDMAN AND SARAH SPENCER

AGE DISCRIMINATION IS a relative newcomer to the equality arena. While discrimination on grounds of race or sex has been prohibited for nearly three decades, deep seated inequalities on grounds of age, whether in employment, health care, social services or education, have been accepted as natural or appropriate.

With the coming of the new millennium, this has begun to change, prompted primarily by an increasing recognition of the Europe- wide trend towards an ageing population. Life expectancy both at birth and at retirement age continue to lengthen and fertility rates remain very low. Europeans live longer but have far fewer children and grandchildren to replace them than previous generations. The result is that in less than 15 years, the number of Europeans in the 20–29 age band will fall by 20 per cent, the number in the 50–64 age group will increase by 25 per cent and the number of people aged 80 and over will increase by 50 per cent. By 2015 one-third of those of working age will be 50 years and over. At the same time, people are retiring earlier. The period of retirement is therefore elongated from both ends: people are retiring far earlier and living far longer.

Concerns with the ageing population have led to important new policy developments. With the economic upturn and consequent skill shortages, employers have begun to look to the older age group as a source of labour. The European Commission has recently pinpointed ageing as one of the six common challenges to sustainable development. As a result, the European Employment Strategy specifically refers to policies on active ageing in the guidelines to member states. EU member states are now taking steps to strengthen cooperation on ageing issues in government spending, employment, pensions and health care.

'Soft' law initiatives such as these are now hardening into legally binding prohibitions. Most importantly, an EU Directive of 2000,[1] establishing a general framework for equal treatment in employment and occupation, requires member states to introduce legislation prohibiting discrimination on grounds of age in employment and training by 2006 (hereafter, the 'framework directive'). In Northern Ireland, public authorities already have a duty to promote equality of

---

[1] Council Directive 2000/78/EC establishing a general framework for equal treatment in employment and occupation.

opportunity on grounds of age.[2] In addition, formal policies to end age discrimination are now being actively pursued within health and social services

Despite the gathering momentum towards reform, there is still little consensus on the meaning of equality in the context of age and how can it be achieved. It is these issues which the chapters in this book aim to elucidate. As well as demonstrating the patterns and incidence of age-based inequality, the book aims to provide a conceptual framework for understanding age equality. It also goes further, and suggests key policy directions in crucial contexts such as employment, education and health care. In addition, by providing a comparative perspective, the book casts further light on positive and negative aspects of different legislative strategies as experienced by other countries.

In chapter two, Sir John Grimley Evans examines the myths and realities of the ageing process itself. Many processes, he argues, are mistakenly associated with ageing, and these need to be distinguished from true ageing. Thus the population of older people might appear to have different characteristics from younger people, but this is not because of their age but because of selective survival rates or cultural changes over time. For example, older people appear to learn more slowly, but this is often because educational techniques are adapted to the prime age culture, rather than to the culture they were familiar with. Older people may also appear to be less functional because they face more difficult challenges than younger people. In particular, less appropriate health care is often provided for older people. True ageing processes, by contrast, are a result of a complex interaction between intrinsic or genetic factors, and extrinsic or environmental factors. The result is that generalisations about older people are inevitably inaccurate and often prejudicial. Individuals, he argues, must be considered according to their individual characteristics, rather than their age.

These insights reveal two common but damaging misapprehensions: that increased longevity will necessarily increase health care costs, and that health care is necessarily ineffective in later life. Longevity achieved by the right mechanisms, he argues, will reduce costs of care in later life. Similarly, health care which is appropriately targeted at the individual's needs is likely to provide commensurate or even greater benefits to older than to younger people.

It is clear from the above discussion that not all distinctions on grounds of age are discriminatory. How then do we demarcate legitimate distinctions from those which should be prohibited? This requires a clearer understanding of the meaning of equality in respect of age, and how this can be achieved. It is this question which is the focus of chapter three. In this chapter, Sandra Fredman argues that equality is not a unitary concept but can be defined differently depending on what aims and objectives are identified. The chapter examines the major existing conceptions of equality and their relationship with age, beginning with the basic principles that likes should be treated alike and that individuals should be treated according to their merit, and moving on to more

---

[2] Northern Ireland Act 1998, s 75(1)(a).

searching notions such as equal opportunity, equal results and equal need. While each of these notions is capable of making some contribution, the chapter concludes that all are problematic in their own way.

Instead Fredman argues that in the context of age, the central aim of equality should be to facilitate equal participation of all in society, based on respect for the dignity of each individual. This draws directly on the newly adopted EU Charter of Fundamental Rights which proclaims the right of the elderly 'to lead a life of dignity and independence and to participate in social and cultural life'.[3] Dignity is not an individualistic or abstract notion but is firmly grounded in the notion of community and social participation. It also entails the facilitation of effective choice. For example, equality in health care requires that individuals be given a range of choices, not that decisions be made for them. As Grimley Evans argues, quality adjusted life years are valid techniques for helping an individual decide which treatment he or she should choose. But they should not be used to decide for a person which of their ailments should be treated.

It is crucial, however, that the ability to exercise choice is genuine. This requires measures to be taken to ensure that people of all ages have real choices, and are genuinely able to pursue those choices. This is a potentially radical approach, which requires active measures. Not only should age barriers be removed. In addition, positive provision should be made, including the adjustment of pension schemes, the introduction of flexible working, the adaptation of transport and housing, the appropriate allocation of health care resources and information and the provision of age-appropriate lifelong learning. For example, for older people the choice to continue to live at home may only be a genuine one if there is assistance in modernising or adapting housing. Many older people live in houses which are poorly insulated and dilapidated. The debilitation caused by cold, hunger and financial anxieties in themselves significantly limit older people's ability to make meaningful choices.

The chapter also considers what limits on equality are justifiable. The common argument that older people have had a 'fair innings' is rebutted. More attention needs to be given, however, to the argument that equality is costly, both to individual employers and on the macro-economic level. This argument demands a complex response. As a start, it can be shown that there are many ways in which age equality is good for business. It opens up a wide pool of talent from which employers can draw, and yields a diverse workforce with a range of skills and experiences. Similarly, age equality can save public money. The money spent, for example, in giving greater educational opportunities to older people ultimately saves money by opening up opportunities for older people to continue in paid work, to participate in unpaid caring or voluntary work and to take more care of their own health and finances. The money spent in health care aimed at greater independence and autonomy of older people saves costs to the social services as a whole and to individual carers.

---

[3] Art 25.

This is not to deny that there may be net costs associated with age equality. However, as Robinson argues in chapter five, in making the calculation it is important to take into account the costs of age inequality. As Robinson shows, the costs of age discrimination are currently paid by older people themselves, who experience avoidable pain and misery, disability and premature death by being denied access to timely treatment, care and support. The costs also fall on families who take on the responsibility of caring for older relatives who are ill or disabled. Costs saved in the health sector also clearly fall on other sectors, notably on local authority social services responsible for financing long-term care, and on the social security budget used for funding disability benefits and care allowances.

The real question then becomes not what is the cost of age equality, but how should the cost be equitably distributed among the three main possible cost-bearers: employer, the state and the individual or the family. The chapter argues that ultimately the movement towards age equality rests on the ethical arguments identified, rather than its cost-effectiveness. Certainly, the more evidence that such equality also furthers business and macro-economic interests, the better. Where there is a real cost, however, the solution must be addressed holistically, moving in favour of a fair distribution of costs between individual, employer and state, and with proper regard for the basic individual right to age equality, rather than assuming that shifting the cost away from the employer is the only dimension of justification needed.

The following chapters flesh out these themes in the specific contexts of employment, health care and education. In chapter four, Bob Hepple shows that older people become detached from the labour market for a variety of reasons, including negative stereotypes of older people, the achievement of downsizing by offering older workers attractive redundancy packages, and the perception that age discrimination is legitimate because it is not unlawful. He argues that action against age discrimination in employment should be an essential aspect of UK employment policy. Such a policy should aim to increase the participation of people aged over 50 in the labour force; to reduce youth unemployment; and to promote a skilled, trained and adaptable labour force.

Translating this into legislative terms, Hepple argues that the acceptable justifications for limiting equality need to be closely specified in legislation, rather than left as a general defence. In the context of employment, this should take the form of a list of specific exceptions to the principle of equal treatment. Such a list should include, for example, minimum age requirements for training or employment or employment benefits, maximum age requirements based on the training requirements of the job, and positive action to promote the integration of older and younger people or to ensure their protection.

Chapter five is concerned with health and social services. Janice Robinson shows that there is a substantial body of evidence indicating that older people experience age discrimination in health care. Such discrimination is regarded as unacceptable by the current Labour Government, whose National Service Framework for Older People requires health and social care agencies 'to root out age discrimination'. However, Robinson argues, scrutinising health and social care in order to identify age discrimination is a complex and contentious process. Age-based differences in the organisation and delivery of care are not necessarily discriminatory, and it can be difficult to distinguish between those policies and practices that disadvantage older people and those that do not. For any real progress to be made in eliminating age discrimination, people involved in scrutinising services will need a good understanding of what age equality in health and social care means. Yet, as this chapter shows, there is considerable uncertainty and confusion among service staff who are held responsible for ensuring that their services do not discriminate against older people.

An even more complex pattern emerges in the context of education. In chapter six, Tom Schuller shows that demonstrable inequalities exist in the age distribution of education, in almost every form. In absolute terms, although older people's access to education has improved in some respects over the last decade, their opportunities relative to those of younger generations have not. Three particular aspects of inequality are identified in relation to education: the massive systemic bias in favour of youth; issues to do with intergenerational relations; and cumulative inequality. Older people get less access to education compared with younger generations; and inequalities within age groups are reinforced over time. The key to achievement of greater equality, he argues, lies in shifting the overall basis of educational policy towards a broad vision of lifelong learning.

All these chapters emphasise that action against discrimination cannot rely solely on voluntary and other promotional measures, but must be supported by legislation. Hepple argues that an effective, efficient and equitable regulatory framework should be set in place, aimed at encouraging personal responsibility and self-generating efforts to promote age equality at work. Similarly, Robinson maintains that legislation is needed to increase the motivation of staff to organise and deliver their services in a way that does not disadvantage older people. It is also needed to strengthen the ability of older people and others working in their interests to challenge discriminatory practice and to seek redress. Schuller takes a somewhat different position. He advocates an entitlement to an education grant for everyone who reaches their fiftieth birthday, weighted in favour of those who have had no post-secondary education. This, in his view, would be more constructive in changing patterns of demand and supply than the threat of litigation. However, he emphasises that placing the primary emphasis on changing overall education policy to make it lifelong does not mean that legislation on discrimination is inappropriate. On the contrary, much of the argument above suggests that measures in relation to education should be part of the wider move on age discrimination.

Similarly, the authors are all in agreement that to achieve age equality it is not sufficient to prohibit discrimination only in employment and training, as is being currently proposed, following the contours of the EU Directive. To achieve age equality in this sense requires legislation which extends beyond the labour market to all aspects of civic life. The causes and symptoms of the problem permeate an area well beyond the employment relationship and can only be effectively dealt with by recognising the interaction of a series of different elements. The focus on employment places a burden on employers which they cannot be expected to discharge unless corresponding duties are placed on providers of education, health care and transport.

There is similar agreement that it is not sufficient to rely on an individual litigation model, which means that the law can only respond in a piecemeal fashion to a particular individual dispute. Not only does this lead to haphazard reactions, it also limits change to the provision of retrospective compensation to individuals, rather than ensuring institutional change.

Far more appropriate is a proactive method, based on a positive duty to promote age equality, which facilitates a systematic and strategic approach, in which employers, the state and other bodies participate actively in resolving the problem. In the context of employment, the content of the positive duty is already well formulated in the Code of Practice on Age Diversity. What is lacking is a sufficient method of enforcement. Similarly, Robinson shows that conventional anti-discrimination legislation is not likely to be effective in combating ageist practices in health and social care. There is a strong argument for creating new laws that place a duty on health and social care agencies to promote age equality and that requires them to demonstrate that they do not discriminate unlawfully against anyone on grounds of age. Hepple therefore argues that a duty on public authorities to have due regard to the promotion of equal opportunities should include age. Effect should be given to this through the normal systems of best value reviews, audits and inspections. That is not to say that legislation by itself will achieve greater age equality. As Robinson argues, education and training of staff will also be needed to change hearts and minds.

Most challenging and controversial is the question of mandatory retirement ages. Instead of either an outright prohibition of all mandatory retirement ages, or outright permission to continue these, Hepple advocates a third option. This would permit a contractually agreed mandatory retirement age that is linked to the age of admission to an occupational pensions scheme which has been approved under pensions legislation. This could be said to further the legitimate aim of encouraging planning of retirement as a form of deferred compensation. Where there is no informed consent and no occupational pension, the employer would have to justify the mandatory retirement in the factual circumstances of the case. The provisions of the Employment Rights Act that exclude the right to claim unfair dismissal or redundancy after the normal retirement age, should be repealed.

Thus far, the discussion has focused on older people. In fact, however, any new legislation must cover the whole age range. In chapter seven, therefore, Jonathan Herring examines the role of equality in relation to children. Children pose a specific challenge, to achieve the appropriate balance between giving children the right to decide for themselves, and giving adults the responsibility for taking decisions as to what is in children's best interests. As Herring shows, the debate is no longer over whether children have any rights, but rather whether there is any justification for denying children all the rights that are available to adults, and particularly whether children should have the right to autonomy, including the right to make mistakes. Herring acknowledges that, in the light of widespread child poverty both in Britain and elsewhere, this focus on autonomy has somewhat skewed the debate. However, this is the key issue which has distinguished different academic approaches.

At one end of the spectrum are the paternalists, who argue that the law should do all it can to promote the well-being of children. This means that decisions for children should be taken by others: primarily their parents, except where parents themselves might cause significant harm, in which case the responsibility lies in the courts. At the other end of the spectrum are the child liberationists, who argue that children should have equal rights to adults, including the rights to vote, determine their own education, engage in sexual activities and use drugs. A third position attempts to balance rights to autonomy with protection. On this view, children have an interest in being able to make decisions for themselves, unless such a decision would undermine their basic physical, emotional or intellectual interests, or their opportunity to develop all their potential so as to enter adult life with the least risk of being detrimentally affected by avoidable prejudices incurred during childhood. Herring himself argues for a different view. Instead of relying on the differences between adults and children in order to justify a different legal regime for children, he argues a better approach would be to recognise that adults can be similar to children in terms of vulnerability and dependence. Therefore, the structure of rights themselves needs to be scrutinised: if children need 'protection' from certain sorts of rights, perhaps adults do too. Thus, he concludes, a stronger case for equality of rights can be based on recognising the dependency and vulnerability of adults, rather than seeking to prove the competence and self-sufficiency of children.

Although legislation against age discrimination is a newcomer in Britain, other jurisdictions have lengthy experience. Laurence Friedman gives a valuable insight into 35 years of experience of such legislation in the US. The United States Congress passed the Age Discrimination in Employment Act in 1967, only three years later than the Civil Rights Act which, among other things, outlawed race and sex discrimination on the job. Employers are not allowed to discriminate in hiring, firing, or conditions of work. The law also outlaws discriminatory job advertisements; discrimination in pay, and in use of company facilities. Federal law is bolstered by state legislation, where age discrimination laws are almost universal.

Several important aspects of the US law should inform the domestic debate. The first concerns the role of the equality commission. A burning issue in current debates in Britain is whether there should be a single equality body administering all strands of equality law. Hepple in chapter four argues forcefully for such a body. In the US, the federal law is administered by the Equal Employment Opportunity Commission (EEOC), a federal agency, which also has responsibility for job discrimination on the basis of race, sex, religion and the like. As Friedman shows, a person who thinks he or she is a victim of age discrimination can file a complaint with the EEOC, which will investigate the claim. If it decides there is some substance to the complaint, it will try to work things out with the company. If this attempt at conciliation and settlement fails, the EEOC can either take the case to court itself; or, in cases where it chooses not to, it can give workers so-called 'right-to-sue' letters, and let them go to court on their own.

The second aspect of US age legislation which is highly relevant to the domestic debate concerns its scope. Notably, the US age legislation is confined to employment, as compared with the 1964 civil rights law, which covers public accommodations, housing, and education as well. It is also about older workers exclusively, its scope beginning at 40, and is based on conventional litigation models. These limitations contribute significantly to the way in which the Act has operated. As Friedman shows, most plaintiffs in age discrimination lawsuits have been white males in high-paying, high-status jobs. This experience underscores the point made in all the previous essays: namely, that legislation developed in the domestic law should not be confined to employment, and it should not rely wholly on an individual litigation model of enforcement.

The US case law has also been dominated by complaints about job termination rather than about a failure to hire, which had originally been thought to be the main target of the legislation. Indeed, Friedman notes, age discrimination law has become a law about wrongful discharge. In the UK, the fact that there is a well established remedy for unfair dismissal should avoid this particular problem arising; but only if the current exemption from employment rights for those over 65 is withdrawn.

Of equal importance is the need to look to our EU partners, who like the UK are bound to implement legislation forbidding age discrimination in order to comply with the EU Framework Directive. In his chapter Colm O'Cinneide assesses the current situation in a number of European countries, with particular emphasis on the relevant Finnish, Dutch and Irish legislation, to determine what useful lessons can be drawn. He contrasts 'minimalist approaches', or ad hoc responses to particular labour market problems with limited scope and many exceptions, with approaches which see age discrimination as a fundamental right. Such an approach recognises age discrimination as on a par with other forms of discrimination. It therefore prefers a more intrusive standard of review, particularly in respect of justification, and affords age equality legislation a wide scope (in particular extending it to goods and services).

There has been as yet a limited response to the requirements of the Directive throughout much of the EU but Finland, The Netherlands and Ireland have all implemented or are in the process of implementing comprehensive age discrimination codes founded upon a discrimination law model rather than a labour market regulation model. They offer the most valuable comparative experience for the UK, particularly in respect of specific issues, such as the age span of the legislation, the approach to retirement, the way in which exceptions are formulated and the enforcement procedures.

O'Cinneide argues that in framing legislation to comply with the Directive, the UK could follow The Netherlands, which makes full use of the exceptions permitted in the Directive, and, like the Directive, confines itself to employment-related activities covered in its limited scope. Alternatively, the UK could follow the Irish model which has taken a far more robust rights-based approach. Most importantly, the Irish legislation goes beyond employment and covers education, health and access to goods and services. The Irish experience, he concludes, demonstrates that extending the scope of age legislation to these areas can produce real results in combating in-built age prejudice. The experience of other jurisdictions also demonstrates the need for strong enforcement. Most relevant is the Irish Equality Commission, which has jurisdiction over all the grounds of discrimination, including age, and already has a record of vigorous promotion of age equality.

Most of the chapters in this book were presented at a series of seminars organised by the Institute for Public Policy Research (IPPR), and a conference with University College London (UCL), in conjunction with the Nuffield Foundation. The chapters, and the book as a whole, have benefited enormously from the interchanges with the seminar participants who had expertise in a wide range of areas, and were able to contribute valuable insights. The editors are indebted to the Nuffield Foundation for its support in running these seminars and acknowledge with thanks the contributions of the seminar participants, and of Patrick Grattan, Tessa Harding, Peter Robinson, Dominic Johnson and Gerison Lansdown who, with some of the authors in this book, were members of an advisory group to the project whose contribution to its analysis was invaluable. Many thanks are also due to Matt Gill at IPPR for bringing the participants together, to Meghna Abrahim for Research Assistance, to Lisa Penfold at UCL, to Jayna Kothari, for her able assistance in editing the book and to Richard Hart, for his support, enthusiasm and patience.

2

Age Discrimination: Implications of the Ageing Process

JOHN GRIMLEY EVANS

THIS CHAPTER EXAMINES attitudes to human ageing and the human aged. Although the discussion focuses on health, many of the issues which arise in the context of health care are directly or indirectly applicable in other contexts, notably those of employment and social policy. While from one perspective the demographic challenge of the next 30 years can be seen to lie in the increasing numbers of older people; from a different perspective, the challenge arises from the diminishing numbers of people of working age.

THE NATURE OF HUMAN AGEING

Ageing is characterised biologically as loss of adaptability of individual organisms as time passes. It is revealed in a rise of mortality rates with age. In the human species, mortality rates fall from infancy to a low point around the age of 11 or 12. Senescence (ageing) then becomes manifest and death rates rise progressively into old age.

True ageing comprises differences that have come about because older people have changed from how they were when they were young. However, these processes have to be distinguished from other sources of differences between young and old that are not due to ageing but frequently mistaken for it. There are three such 'non-ageing' processes. First, the differences between young and old might be due to selective survival, rather than age. Secondly, the apparent differences might arise because of the effects of considering two cohorts which are not truly comparable, because they have lived in different periods, and subject to different cultural influences. Thirdly, the difference might be due to the fact that older people face greater challenges than younger people. Each of these processes will be described.

The chapter then turns to 'true' ageing. In this context, a distinction is drawn between 'primary' and 'secondary' ageing. Primary ageing can be 'intrinsic', due to genetic features; or 'extrinsic' relating to lifestyle and environment. Secondary ageing reflects adaptations to the consequences of ageing. Such adaptations can be specific to individuals, or generalised across the human species. Thus secondary ageing will be considered both from the individual perspective and from that of the species. Each of these processes is considered in detail below.

The table sets out a structure for the differences between young and old people.

Table 1: *Differences between Young and Old People*

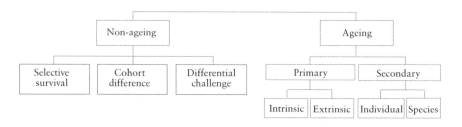

'Non ageing' processes

The first type of difference between young and old that is not due to ageing but frequently mistaken for it is known as 'selective survival'. Selective survival arises because those who survive to the ninth or tenth decades of life are a small minority of those born at the same time but who died at earlier ages. Selective survival factors include genes, some related to susceptibility to specific diseases such as coronary disease or diabetes. Scientists are searching for other genes, sometimes referred to as Longevity Assurance Genes (LAGs) that control basic ageing processes at cellular or organismic level. Other selective factors for survival are to be found in environment and lifestyle. Social class, education, intelligence, smoking, exercise and alcohol use, are all relevant. There is also evidence that personality may be important; older people who insist on remaining in command of their lives, even at the risk of being considered bad patients or crotchety, seem to survive longer than the more complaisant. Thus, certain characteristics might be more frequent or pronounced in very old people not because they have come on with age, but because only people with such characteristics have survived to old age.

The second type of difference between young and old that is not due to ageing but frequently mistaken for it, is due to cohort phenomena. Cohort phenomena are consequences of the different experience of people born at different times. These may reflect biological influences such as maternal health or infant nutrition; they may also reflect generational differences in education and lifestyle or traumatic experiences such as warfare or famine. Cohort phenomena can affect physical health and survival but have also been demonstrated in psychological functioning. People born 70 years ago were educated and acculturated in a world very different from the one surrounding people born today.

Most importantly, children are taught how to learn, and they were taught differently in previous generations. Failure to appreciate cohort differences can lead to older people being thought inefficient at learning new technologies or industrial processes. Older people can be as readily retrained as younger for most new technologies, if culturally appropriate techniques of training are used.

The third type of difference between young and old that is not due to ageing but frequently mistaken for it is caused by differential challenge. Differential challenge is a serious social problem. Ageing as loss of adaptability can only be fairly assessed if the same challenge is offered to individuals of different ages. In practice society is organised so that all too often we present older people with more severe challenges than face the young and then attribute their poorer outcome to ageing rather than the fact that we have loaded the dice against them. In the 1970s the classic example of this in the UK was the poorer quality and colder housing in which, partly as a consequence of social policy, poorer old people lived. This was a contributor to the higher incidence of overt hypothermia and of winter non-hypothermic deaths in older people.

In present day UK a major problem of differential challenge lies with the poorer quality of health care provided for older people. In some instances this is due to overt policy; one example is the existence of parallel but differently endowed acute general medical and geriatric services to be found in parts of the UK. A new development is to be government policy, as expressed in the National Service Framework, to limit the access of older people—on the basis of their age—from acute hospitals and sideline them to cheaper 'intermediate care' facilities. There is also irrational practice and policy for admission policies to coronary or intensive care units, and in the deployment of therapeutic preventive interventions. At local levels there are no adequate safeguards in the National Health Service to identify and eradicate ageist practice as distinct from explicit ageist policy. These issues are elaborated further in chapter five.

True ageing

These 'non-ageing' processes should be distinguished from true ageing, which, as we have seen, comprises differences that have come about because older people have changed from how they were when they were young. True ageing itself consists of different types of process. A distinction should be drawn between primary ageing and secondary ageing.

Primary ageing comes about through interactions between extrinsic factors in lifestyle and environment with intrinsic (genetic) factors. Some of these interactions may be very specific. Cigarette smoking does not affect everyone in the same way. Genes determine whether cigarette smoke will be metabolised into carcinogens. Similarly, genes determine whether an excess of sodium in the diet will cause a rise in blood pressure. Other interactions may be more general; for example, moderate exercise has beneficial effects on several physiological functions. It strengthens bones as well as muscles, improves coordination, prevents obesity and helps to keep the heart and arteries healthy.

Extrinsic factors in ageing are detectable by epidemiological methods comparing the ageing experience of people living in different ways or in different environments. In addition to the changing incidence of specific age-associated diseases, the more general impact of extrinsic ageing factors has become apparent in recent trends in the United States where disability levels among older people have been falling since the 1980s. Periodical surveys of health and fitness have been carried out on samples of the national population in the US since 1982. Over this period Americans have been living longer and there has been an increase in the numbers of people aged over 65 years. But this has not been accompanied by a massive increase in the numbers of disabled people because older people there have been becoming fitter and healthier. There are now two million fewer people aged over 65 with significant disability than would have been expected on the basis of the 1982 figures.[1]

Intrinsic ageing has been a biological enigma since natural selection was recognised in the nineteenth century as the fundamental process of evolution. There appears to be a paradox in that one might expect 'selection of the fittest' gradually to abolish ageing. The longer individuals live, the greater the sum of their lifetime opportunities for passing their genes into succeeding generations. Part of the explanation for the paradox is that even without ageing no individual would live forever. Sooner or later death would strike, from disease, accident, famine, predation, or warfare. There would be few individuals surviving to reproduce in old age so natural selection has nothing to work on. In particular, genes that manifest deleterious effects, but only in later life, would not be weeded out by natural selection. Their effects will only become apparent when a species finds itself in an environment in which it lives longer than it could in the environment in which it evolved. Modern civilisation for humans, and zoos for other animals, will uncover late life problems that never emerged in the wild a quarter of a million years ago.

This is only part of the story, however. The more fundamental basis of intrinsic ageing has been elucidated by Kirkwood in his disposable soma theory.[2] This proposes that essential genes pacing the ageing process are those determining the efficiency of damage control (by prevention, detection, repair and replacement). An organism evolves an optimal balance between investment in damage control to ensure longevity and investment in reproduction to contribute genes to succeeding generations. In dangerous environments, where life will be short anyway, the evolved optimum is for little investment in longevity but a high reproductive rate. In less dangerous environments, it may be worth having a

[1] KG Manton and X Gu, 'Changes in the prevalence of chronic disability in the United States black and nonblack population above age 65 from 1982 to 1999' *Proc Natl Acad Sci USA* (2001) 98(11), 6354–59.

[2] TBL Kirkwood and MR Rose, 'Evolution of Senescence: Late survival sacrificed for Reproduction' *Phil Trans R Soc Lond B* (1991) 332, 15–24.

longer life with a lower but more efficient reproductive rate. In a safe environment, breeding seasons matching births to food supplies and parental care to ensure the survival of offspring to their own reproductive maturity will be good investments. Kirkwood has shown however that in terms of evolutionary fitness the maximal investment in damage control and longevity will always be less than necessary totally to abolish the accumulation of biological damage manifesting as ageing. The history of our own species is of a massive lengthening of maximum lifespan but we still accumulate damage that manifests as loss of adaptability as time passes.

Secondary ageing can be distinguished from primary ageing. Secondary ageing reflects the adaptations of individuals or the human species to the consequences of loss of adaptability with ageing. Thus, secondary ageing should be considered both from the individual perspective and from that of the species. For individuals secondary ageing is most prominent in the behavioural and psychological fields. We give up hazardous sports in early adult life when our ability to get out of dangerous situations no longer matches our propensity for getting into them. Obsessional behaviour and systematic note taking in middle life compensate for a memory whose reach begins to exceed its grasp.

At a species level the female menopause is an evolved adaptation to the increasing risks, ineffectiveness, and biological costs of reproductive activity in the female. In the context of a species with a family and tribal organisation and a cumulative culture based on speech, there came a point in a woman's life when in terms of getting her genes into succeeding generations, the variable on which evolution works, it was better for her to give up increasingly dangerous and ineffective attempts to produce children of her own containing 50 per cent of her genes, and instead to contribute to the survival of her grandchildren each containing 25 per cent of her genes.

Individual Trajectories of Ageing

The pattern of *ageing* as revealed in population statistics does not take these various differences into account and therefore does not give an accurate picture. These statistics are corrupted as we have seen by *cohort effects*, in that they show the effects of the different experience of people born at different times. The pattern of ageing is also affected by *secular effects*. People aged 65 now inhabit a different world from people who were 65 twenty years ago. Mathematically it may not be possible to dissect these three components (namely, true ageing effects, cohort effects and secular effects) from population statistics. Longitudinal studies in which individuals are followed through their ageing processes are affected by secular changes and may mislead if results from different individuals are aggregated.

Not surprisingly an important aspect of human ageing is an increase in interindividual variance. As individuals, we start at different functional levels, we age at different rates, and different things happen to us along the way. It is even less justifiable to make generalisations based on average levels of function about 'the elderly' than it is about 'the young'. The increase in variance comes about because some people change while others do not. There will be individuals in their eighties functioning well within the normal limits for people of 30.

In mental functioning a significant part of the average decline with age is produced as an increasing proportion of individuals enter their period of 'terminal drop' in which mental function deteriorates rapidly in the year or two before death. Those survivors not in this phase are typically functioning as well as ever and it is unjust to assume that they are sharing the fate of their fellow members of their age group. Geratological science demonstrates that individuals must be assessed as individuals and not assumed to possess the average properties of their age group.

Another source of unpredictability in later life are differences in the average ageing trajectory of different physiological and psychological functions. Some physiological functions typically show decrements early in adult life; others not until later. In the psychological sphere 'fluid' intelligence tends to show earlier and more marked changes than 'crystalline' intelligence. In crystalline intelligence we apply previously learned techniques to a problem—for example we recognise how to reduce a problem to a quadratic equation and remember where to find the equation for solving it. Fluid intelligence involves the solving of problem of a type we have not met before. It may require 'lateral thinking' or the invention of some entirely new approach.

IDEOLOGY

Value-free science is an illusion. The questions one identifies as needing answers and the evidence one accepts as relevant reflect one's ideological framework. Ideology is the set of primary values from which principles of ethical behaviour are derived. Being primary, ideologies are in a sense necessarily arbitrary; examples have arisen from apophanous experiences on the road to Damascus or under a Banyan tree or through the vengeful broodings of Marx and Hitler. Individual choice of ideology is a matter of life experience, psychology and psychopathology.

It is however of evolutionary advantage for societies to have collective ideologies since successful living together in a nation or a wider community requires there to be rules of behaviour and relationships between individuals that are generally understood and generally obeyed. Some nations have their ideologies set out in a formal constitution; one example underlines the primary nature of the ideology in proclaiming its assumptions as 'held' to be 'self-evident'. In the UK we have no written constitution and have to deduce our ideology from our history, and the language common to our political parties. Since 1534 the ideology of our society has evolved towards respect for the uniqueness and inherent value of individuals, and their right to live their lives according to their own rules in so far as they do not infringe similar rights of others. This view of an ideal society was explicitly expounded by JS Mill[3] in his essay on liberty. Matthew Arnold put a gloss on Mill with a comment that modern legislators might have read with benefit. A healthy society, said Arnold, is not based upon rights but upon duties; no one should expect to have rights without duties and the rights of an individual arise from the duties of other individuals towards him or her.[4] If we accept this view of British society (would any politician deny it?) certain implications arise for the duties of the NHS and those who work in it. This can be summarised in what may be called the three principles of equity.

1. Equity in health care requires equal care for equal need.
2. Need is defined in terms of the capacity to benefit.
3. Benefit is to be assessed by the recipient rather than the purveyor of health care.

Individual lives are incommensurable since each can be valued only by the person living it and there is no way in which different lives can be brought to a common measure. It is no business of the British state to determine that the lives, and desire for life, of some citizens are worth more or less then the lives, and desire for life, of others. Devices such as quality-adjusted life years are valid techniques for helping an individual decide which of a range of treatments he or she might require for a particular affliction, but must not be used to directly or indirectly decide which persons' afflictions should be treated. There is no doubt that quality-adjusted life years are being employed in the latter improper fashion in policy making. The recent target set by the National Service Framework for Older People for limiting the emergency admission of old people to acute hospitals would quite properly have provoked a riot had it been applied to members of ethnic minorities, to women or to the lower social classes. While ideology is necessary to generate ethics, ethics do not find their way into law if unethical behaviour suits the interest of politicians. In health care the central issue is whether the NHS should be seen as a public health device to improve the health of the populace so that they may better serve the uses of the state, or as a service to help individual citizens pursue their own life goals as Mill would have prescribed.

Costs and Effectiveness of Care in Later Life

The loss of adaptability with ageing gives rise to two common misapprehensions damaging to older people: that increased longevity will necessarily

---

[3] JS Mill, *On Liberty* (London, John W Parker and Son, West Strand, 1859).
[4] M Arnold, *Culture and Anarchy* 1869 (ed JD Wilson) (Cambridge University Press, 1932).

increase health care costs, and that health care is necessarily ineffective in later life. Longevity achieved by the right mechanisms will reduce costs of care in later life.

Postponement as Prevention

One of the consequences of ageing as loss of adaptability is that the older we are when a potentially disabling disease such as coronary heart disease or stroke falls, the more likely we are to die rather than to linger in a disabled state. This biological fact means that policies that delay the onset of disability will reduce the time victims spend in a disabled state and the associated costs of care. The recent reductions in rates of disability at older ages in the US mentioned above suggest that this is already happening there and so could be made to happen elsewhere.

Cost of Living is Largely Cost of Dying

As is well known the average cost of healthcare per head is U-shaped with costs high in infancy, low in early and middle adult life but rising again into old age. Peter Zweifel, a Swiss economist has shown in longitudinal studies of cohorts that the expensive aspect of health care in later life is not living but dying.[5] The great majority of health care costs we incur are in the last few months of life whatever the age at which we set about dying. Average costs of health care rise in later life because a higher percentage of people in later ages are going through the business of dying. Furthermore, the costs of dying in later life are less than those of dying earlier, not least because of the expensive but often predictably futile care that is thrown at younger people with fatal disease. The longer we delay the onset of fatal disease the cheaper the business of dying.

Effectiveness of Health Care in Later Life

Many medical treatments, therapeutic and preventive, act by reducing the probability of an undesirable outcome by a percentage that is constant across different levels of background risk. Since background risk increases with age, that percentage benefit translates into a higher proportion of individuals benefiting from treatments at older than at younger ages. In other words, treatments are more cost-effective if given to older than to younger people, provided you regard people as people and not merely as collections of potential life-years. This has been shown for the treatment of high blood pressure, for the use of

---

[5] P Zweifel, S Felder and M Meiers, 'Ageing of Population and Health care Expenditure: A Red Herring?' (1999) *Health Econ* 8(6), 485–96.

beta-blockers, statins and ACE inhibitors after heart attacks and for anti-platelet agents in the secondary prevention of stroke.[6]

It is important to bear in mind that we give such treatments not just to prevent death but to prevent recurrence of disabling conditions such as stroke or myocardial infarction which threaten misery for the victim and costs for the health care services. Withholding therapeutic or preventive care from older people is unlikely to save money in an economic sense; though it may serve political ends by shifting the costs between budgets.

Need to Identify Individual Determinants of Outcome

Not all treatments have good results with older people. In particular, physiologically challenging surgical treatments probe the adaptability of the patient. Research from the US has shown however, that for suitably selected older people, major surgery, such as open heart operation, can be associated with acceptable levels of risk for people in their eighties and older.[7]

Age is a number derived from a birth certificate and cannot be a cause of anything (apart from prejudice). Poorer outcomes from health care interventions, where these are not attributable to poorer treatment, are due to physiological impairments that may or may not be present in a particular individual even if the probability of their presence, when nothing else is known about the individual, rises with his or her age. If one knows enough about the physiological condition of the patient, age should drop off the end of the predictive equation for outcome. This has been most closely achieved in the field of intensive care and the work of Knaus[8] who found that when everything that is known physiologically about an intensive care patient is fed into a predictive equation, age

[6] A Amery et al, 'Mortality and morbidity results from the European Working Party on High Blood Pressure in the Elderly trial' *Lancet* (1985) i, 1350–54. Antiplatelet trialists' collaboration. Secondary prevention of vascular disease by prolonged antiplatelet treatment. *Brit Med J* (1988) 296, 320–31.

Gruppo Italiano per lo Studio della Sopravvivenza nell'infarto Miocardico. GISSI-3: 'Effects of lisinopril and transdermal glyceryl trinitrate singly and together, on 6-week mortality and ventricular function after acute myocardial infarction' *Lancet* (1994) 343, 1115–22. D Hunt, P Young, J Simes, W Hague, S Mann, D Owesnby, G Lane, and A Tonkin, for the LIPID investigators. 'Benefits of pravastatin on cardiovascular events and mortality in older patients with coronary heart disease are equal to or exceed those seen in younger patients: results from the LIPID trial' *Ann Intern Med* (2001) 134, 931–40.

HM Krumholz, MJ Radford, EF Ellerbeck, J Hennen, TPPM Meehan, Y Wang and SF Jencks, 'Aspirin for secondary prevention after acute myocardial infarction in the elderly: prescribed use and outcomes' *Ann Intern Med* (1996) 124 (292) 298. The Norwegian Multicenter Study Group, 'Timolol-induced reduction in mortality and reinfarction in patients surviving acute myocardial infarction' *New Engl J Med* (1981) 304(14), 801–07.

[7] CJ Mullany, GE Darling, JR Pluth, TA Orszulak, HV Schaff, DM Ilstrup, and BJ Gersh, 'Early and late results after isolated coronary artery bypass surgery in 159 patients aged 80 years and over' *Circulation* (1990) 82 (Suppl IV), IV–229–IV–236.

[8] WA Knaus, DP Wagner, EA Draper, JE Zimmerman, M Bergner, PG Bastos, CA Sirio, DJ Murphy, T Lotring, A Damiano and EH Harrell, 'The APACHE III prognostic system. Risk prediction of hospital mortality for critically ill hospitalised patients' *Chest* (1991) 100, 1619–36.

accounts for only 4 per cent of the variance in outcome. We have grown so inured to using a patient's age as an excuse for laziness in investigating him or her properly that we have failed to build into our scientific paradigms proper identification of the true physiological determinants of outcome. Evidence-based medicine and large randomised controlled trials have exacerbated this problem by focusing on average outcomes in an essentially collectivist model of healthcare. This highlights a serious gap in research strategy.

Furthermore, when groups of patients with higher than average risks of undesirable outcomes are identified, the normal response is not to withhold care but rather to rationalise and intensify it to improve outcomes. An American study found that if older patients with trauma were monitored earlier and more invasively with the aim of compensating for age associated impairments in homeostatic mechanisms, this resulted in better outcomes.[9] The alternative approach is represented by a group of orthopaedic surgeons who developed a predictive index of outcome for older people with proximal femoral fracture and proposed withholding treatment from high-risk patients.

FINAL COMMENT

Ageist prejudice is deeply entrenched and widely pervasive in British society. It is treated as in some way 'natural', even by many older people. Whatever their political rhetoric, governments exploit ageism to subsidise the affluence of more favoured social classes. Ageism is however as great an affront to the supposed values of our society as is sexism or racism.

[9] TM Scalea, HM Simon, AO Duncan, NA Atweh, SJA Sclafani, TF Phillip and GW Shaftan, 'Geriatric blunt multiple trauma: Improved Survival with Early Invasive Monitoring' *J Trauma* (1990) 30, 129–134.

3

The Age of Equality

SANDRA FREDMAN*

WHEN DOES DIFFERENTIAL treatment on grounds of age constitute discrimination? And should such discrimination be prohibited by law? Unlike race or gender, age does not define a discrete group. We have all been young, and we will all, if we are fortunate, become old. Thus, the basic opposition between 'self' and 'other' which marks much of racism and sexism is not present in the same way. Yet detrimental treatment on grounds of age is widespread. Older people in particular, are subject to stigma, prejudice and social exclusion. The very old are too often also the poorest in society, and some are vulnerable to abuse. This is not to say that it is always invidious to classify groups according to age. It may be perfectly legitimate to set a minimum age for voting rights, or entry to the job market, or eligibility for pension benefits. Equally, it may be necessary to take measures which are specifically geared to the needs of particular age groups. Do these measures advance equality or obstruct it? To answer these questions requires a deeper understanding of the meaning of equality itself.

It is this which is the task of this chapter. Despite the newly popular rhetoric of 'ageism', 'age diversity', 'age discrimination' and 'equality', there is surprisingly little consensus as to the aims or indeed the meaning of these notions. I argue that the central aim of equality should be to facilitate equal participation of all in society, based on equal concern and respect for the dignity of each individual. Although age raises many distinctive problems, it is nevertheless possible to draw on the experience of existing anti-discrimination legislation to fashion an appropriate legislative mechanism to advance equality defined in these terms. Central to this is a holistic approach, extending beyond the labour market to all aspects of civic life. The causes and symptoms of the problem permeate an area well beyond the employment relationship and can only be effectively dealt with by recognising the interaction of a series of different elements. Also crucial is a proactive strategy, based on the positive promotion of equality, rather than relying solely on reacting to individual complaints. An individual complaints-led model means that the law can only respond in a piece-meal fashion to a particular individual dispute, leaving the main burden of reactive change on the

* I am indebted to Bob Hepple, Sarah Spencer, Tessa Harding, Gerison Landsdown and Patrick Gratton for their valuable input in the preparation of this paper. I owe especial thanks to my research assistant, Meghna Abraham.

respondent, usually the employer. A proactive method, by contrast, facilitates a systematic and strategic approach, in which employers, the State and other bodies participate actively in resolving the problem.

I begin by sketching the main problems and perspectives which arise in respect of age, both socially and legally. I then consider potential aims and objectives of equality as well limits of equality. In the final section, I deal briefly with the ways in which these ideas can be translated into particular legislative forms.

PROBLEMS AND PERSPECTIVES

Background

Until very recently, discrimination on grounds of age attracted little social opprobrium. Images of older people as dependent, burdensome and of no further use to society provided support for detrimental practices, such as early retirement and redundancy, rationing of health care, poorer quality social services, and social exclusion. Similarly, detrimental treatment of young people is frequently justified as being in their 'best interests'. Lawful parental chastisement, exclusion from the minimum wage and lack of participation in decision-making on issues closely affecting their lives are just a few examples.

In the past decade, this complacency has been exploded by a complex compound of demographic and labour market factors. Advances in medical science have substantially improved average longevity, while fewer babies are being born. At the same time, recession was deliberately managed by shedding older workers. It is now relatively unusual for people to remain in employment up to retirement age. Thus, the period of retirement has been elongated from both ends: people are retiring far earlier and living far longer. The ageing population is perceived as a problem both for governments and business. Governments, concerned to limit social spending, have begun to promote policies of 'active ageing'. With the economic upturn and consequent skill shortages, employers have begun to look to the older age group as a source of labour.

This convergence of business, macro-economic and social policy objectives has created a sunny climate of change. The non-binding Code of Practice on Age Diversity in Employment was quickly superseded by the stronger EU Framework Directive, which requires legislation outlawing discrimination on grounds of age in employment.[1] In Northern Ireland, public authorities have a duty to promote equality of opportunity on grounds, *inter alia*, of age.[2] Other jurisdictions have also addressed age discrimination. In the US, the Age

---

[1] Council Directive 2000/78/EC establishing a general framework for equal treatment in employment and occupation.

[2] Northern Ireland Act 1998, s 75(1)(a).

Discrimination in Employment Act 1967 (ADEA) outlaws discrimination on grounds of age in employment against workers over 40. Legislative provisions on age discrimination are in place in various countries including Israel, Finland, Australia and New Zealand. The South African Constitution and the Canadian Charter of Rights and Freedoms include age as a ground of discrimination. Perhaps the most detailed provisions in Europe are found in the Irish Employment Equality Act 1998 which prohibits age discrimination in employment against workers aged 18–65.[3]

This brief description suggests that the impetus to introduce age discrimination legislation is fuelled by largely utilitarian considerations. It is crucial, however, that such considerations do not obscure the concerns with individual justice and social equity which should underpin the move to eliminate age discrimination. A reversal of labour market conditions or a change in the demographic pressures to a situation which is again unfavourable to older people, should not in themselves be sufficient to trump the claims of individuals. Nor should the focus be entirely on older people. The problems of an ageing population have tended to eclipse issues affecting younger people and children.

Equality can only be understood in the context of the social conditions it aims to address. The remainder of this part therefore consists of a sketch of the problems which any age discrimination legislation would be expected to deal with. At first glance, it might appear that there is no unifying theme, but instead a cluster of discrete issues. Age-related issues which arise in employment appear to be quite different from those in health care, which differ in turn from education, social security and other public functions. For example, it could be argued that the chief aim of equality legislation in the employment field is to free the labour market from prejudicial and unsupported assumptions about the capability of a worker based on his or her age, so that the best person can be selected, promoted or retained. By contrast, the issues which arise in health care do not concern the relationship of age to capability, but instead the appropriate response, given limited resources, to the needs of individuals. Similarly, the dilemmas and difficulties faced by younger people appear to be qualitatively different from those of older people. However, it will be argued here all these aspects are in fact closely interrelated. An effective response to one issue, such as employment, requires action in several different areas, including health, training and pensions. Similarly, an effective response in the employment field has positive implications for other areas, such as health, housing and social security. Nevertheless, for ease of description, the issues are described under discrete headings.

Before turning to these issues, it is clear that any description must make some prior decision as to which age bands are being addressed. Although age discrimination is not inevitably concerned only with discrimination against older

---

[3] For training, the age range is 15–65.

people, in fact most analyses and policy formulae are concerned with older rather than younger people. The category of 'older' people itself is defined in a variety of ways. If the issue concerns early retirement, then the age band, particularly in government policy documents, tends to be 50–64. For health care and social services, the focus is generally on over sixties, but usually more specifically on over seventies or even over eighties. Similarly, the category of young persons is defined in different ways for different purposes. It is usual to consider children under 16 as a single category, allied to the age during which schooling is compulsory. Young people between 16 and 18 are again distinguished from the group between 18 and 25.

It will be argued in this paper that anti-discrimination legislation should not delineate any particular age band, so that younger people as well as older people may benefit from the protection provided. It is true that discrimination against younger people takes a different form from that against older people, and there may be a conflict of interests between younger and older people. It is true too that the major problems concern older people, making it most likely that it is this category which will constitute the major group of beneficiaries. However, age discrimination policies and legislation which deal only with older people run the risk of ignoring questions of inter-generational equity. There may nevertheless be good reasons for making specific provision for different age groups and providing specific exceptions, particularly where children are concerned.

Demographic Trends

Advances in health, nutrition and medical care have benefited humanity with greater average longevity. In 1998, life expectancy for men in the UK was 74.9 years and for women 79.8. This figure has risen steadily and continues to rise: only 14 years before, in 1984, the life expectancy of men was 71.5 years, and of women was 77.4. This has, however, meant that the UK population as a whole is ageing. Thus, in 1999, 25.4 per cent of the population were over 60, while only 20.4 per cent were under 16. The numbers of older people will continue to increase. Although the overall percentage of people over 65 is projected to remain constant for some time at around 15–16 per cent of the population, the total numbers will increase, from nine million people over 65 in 2001 to 12.4 million in 2021.[4] Probably the fastest growing section of the population are those over 75. The proportion of the population over 75 reached 7.3 per cent in 1999, up 1 per cent from 1984.[5]

Not surprisingly, given women's longer life expectancy, the gender structure of older people differs from that of the population as a whole, with women forming 64 per cent of those over 75, but only 51 per cent of people of all ages.

---

[4] *Social Trends* 29, 1999, table 1.5 and population estimates mid 1998/9.
[5] National Statistics *United Kingdom in figures* (2001 edition).

Ethnic minorities are a small but growing proportion of the older age group. Although ethnic minorities constitute over 7 per cent of the total population of Britain, they make up only 2 per cent of the over sixties.[6] However, the number of older people from black and ethnic communities increased by 168 per cent between 1981 and 1991.[7]

Labour Market Issues

Longer lifespans have, paradoxically, been associated with shorter periods in work. By the end of the twentieth century, one in three people between 50 and State pension age in Britain did not participate in paid employment.[8] This constituted a total of 2.8 million people. It is now the exception rather than the rule to remain in employment all the way to pension age. Crucially too, the vast majority of non-working people over 50 have left the labour market permanently, in that they are no longer looking for and available for work. Six out of seven non-working men aged 50–65 were classified as economically inactive rather than unemployed in 2000.

These effects are not felt uniformly across the workforce. The effects on men have been most dramatic: men's participation in paid work at age 64 has plummeted from 57 per cent in 1979 to 37 per cent in 2000. For women, the pattern is somewhat different, because of the historically low participation rate of all women in the workforce. The trend is therefore best illustrated by comparing the proportions of women aged 30 in the workforce with those approaching pension age. Whereas the younger women are 50 per cent more likely to be employed than 20 years ago, the proportion of those approaching pension age has not increased. Also important are differences based on ethnic origin. People of Indian, Pakistani or Bangladeshi ethnic origin aged between 50 and 65 fare particularly badly. Men in this age group are two thirds more likely to be out of work than whites. The result is that fewer than half of older men in this group are working. For women, the combination of age and cultural expectations militate particularly strongly against the possibility of paid work. Less than a third of older women of Indian, Pakistani or Bangladeshi origin are likely to be in work.

Nor are these trends limited to the UK. Throughout the OECD, people are leaving the labour force at progressively younger ages even though the population is ageing and individuals are living longer. According to the European Commission report on the social situation in the EU in 2001,[9] there were 60

---

[6] *Social Trends* 31, 2001, table 1.5.

[7] *National Service Framework for Older People*, March 2001.

[8] Figures in this section are taken from *Winning the Generation Game* (Report of the Performance and Innovation Unit, April 2000, ch 3).

[9] EC Commission, 'The Social Situation in the European Union 2001' available from the Office for Official Publications of the European Communities in Luxembourg.

million people aged 65 and over in the EU in 1999, compared with only 34 million in 1960, and this is set to rise to 69 million in 2010. Yet the rate of employment of workers between 55 and 64 in the EU is very low, with only 37 per cent of this age group in employment in 1999. In fact, the UK figures are better than many of our EU partners. Only Sweden and Denmark have higher rates of participation by older people in the labour market. In France, for example, the decline is dramatic: whereas over 90 per cent of men aged 50 are in the labour force, this plunges to only 40 per cent at age 60. In Belgium, France, Italy, Luxembourg and Austria, fewer than 30 per cent of people between 55 and 64 are working. In the US, by contrast, 67 per cent are still working at 60, as against 90 per cent at age 50. The shrinking workforce is causing serious concern among EU policy makers, who are urging member states to encourage the employment of older people.[10]

There are several reasons for these trends. Most importantly, labour market policies were specifically designed to manage the recessions of the early 1980s and 1990s by removing older men from the workforce.[11] An added impetus to retire early was created by the increased availability of occupational pension schemes, and the fact that many specify earlier pensionable ages than the state scheme without penalties. The European Commission in its 2001 report raises concerns about the way in which current pension systems encourage early exit from the labour market, and are frequently used by employers who wish to reduce staff levels while avoiding redundancies.[12] Equally serious have been the disincentives created by the benefit system. For example, until recently, incapacity benefit has not been tied to a requirement that the claimant be actively seeking work.[13] Incapacity benefits are often higher than the amounts a claimant might expect to earn, and therefore create a disincentive to seek paid work.

It might be expected that the end of the recession and the change in labour market policies would have solved the problem. However, the newly restructured economy has created fresh problems. The shift from manufacturing to a service economy, accompanied by dramatic changes in technology, have meant that many older workers' skills are obsolete. Older workers tend to have fewer formal qualifications than their younger counterparts, and employers are reluctant to invest money in training workers from whom they see little prospect of recouping their investment. Notably, non-working older people are less likely than average to have post-compulsory education, and the number of graduates is particularly low. Moreover, older workers do not tend to take up opportunities for education or training in later life. In addition, downsizing has meant that there are fewer options for older workers to move into less demanding

---

[10] See also, *Winning the Generation Game*, para 3.1.

[11] *Winning the Generation Game,* para 4.1.

[12] EC Commission, 'The Social Situation in the European Union 2001'.

[13] In some pilot areas, claimants must demonstrate that there are barriers to their working before they can claim incapacity benefit (www.one.gov.uk).

work. To the contrary, those that remain employed by the new leaner businesses have more work to do, so that older workers feel 'burnt out' more quickly. These trends are aggravated by the fact that some pension schemes are not portable, and do not permit flexible working.

It should be stressed that 'voluntary early retirement' is a misnomer. There is certainly a group of high earning, well educated professionals who retired voluntarily on a good occupational pension and savings, and who enjoy their increased leisure time. However, this group is a privileged minority. For those under state pension age, as many as two thirds of the early retirees would have preferred to stay in work, many for financial reasons. Many had hoped to gain further employment, but have been unsuccessful, or are reluctant to take low paid work which would jeopardise their benefit income.

The effects of recession and technological advances have not only affected older workers. A central concern in the EU as a whole is the high rate of youth unemployment. In 2001, 16.3 per cent of active young people between 15 and 24 in the EU were unemployed.[14] Research has shown that the majority of young people believe that there is age discrimination at work, and a significant minority feel they have been discriminated against at work or when looking for work on grounds of their age.

The fact that both older and younger workers are affected makes policy formulation particularly difficult. As will be seen, it is commonly argued that older workers should 'give way' to younger workers on the grounds that the former have had a fair innings. This makes it appear as if it is impossible to deal with youth unemployment and older unemployment simultaneously. However, it will be argued below that this is largely based on a simplistic representation of the labour market.

Discrimination against older and younger workers in the labour market is reinforced by statute. Thus workers over 65 or normal retirement age are specifically excluded from protection against unfair dismissal and from the right to redundancy compensation.[15] Similarly, minimum wage legislation permits a lower rate for younger workers, defined broadly to include employees under the age of 26.[16] Workers under 18 are excluded entirely, and those between 18 and 21 receive a lower minimum wage than older workers.

Material Disadvantage

Although older people who do not work have a wide range of incomes, they are on average poorer than the rest of the population. For those under pension age, early retirement can have significant effects on their financial position for the rest of their lives. It is during their fifties that people do most of their saving for

[14] EU Employment Report 2001 (see http://europea.eu.int/comm/employment_social).
[15] Employment Relations Act 1996, ss 109, 156.
[16] National Minimum Wage Act 1998, s 3.

retirement, once children have left home. Retirement at age 50 is therefore likely to lead to greater poverty in old age.[17] Nor is everyone covered by an occupational pension: as many as 57 per cent of workless people aged between 50 and 65 live in households without occupational pensions. These are nearly twice as likely than average to be in the lowest fifth of the overall income distribution. But having an occupational pension does not mean that a household is well off. In fact their income varies widely, from £326 per week to no more than £72. It is not surprising, therefore, that as many as three quarters receive some benefit income and nearly half rely on benefits for more than half their household income. The vast majority of those on benefit are on sickness and disability benefits.

For those over state pension age, poverty and disadvantage are endemic, and older pensioner households tend to have even lower income.[18] This is not surprising given the limited amounts available from the state pension. The basic pension in 2000–01 was £67.50 for a single pensioner per week, rising to £72.50 in 2001–02. Even this is only available to those who have made full contributions throughout their working lives; those who did not will get only a proportion. Inevitably, then, pensioners tend to rely on state benefits: in 1997–98, 71 per cent of pensioner households depended on state benefits for at least 50 per cent of their income (although a surprisingly high number do not claim their benefits).[19] The income support level represents a minimum income level below which a person could be considered to be living in poverty. The fact that 1.63 million people aged 60 and over in Britain received income support in August 2000 demonstrates the extent of poverty among older people. Another way of measuring poverty is to examine the proportion of expenditure on housing, fuel and food. For pensioners living alone who are mainly dependent on state pensions, nearly 50 per cent of their expenditure goes on housing, fuel and food compared with 36 per cent in other households.[20]

Many older people live in poor accommodation. As many as 10 per cent of all households where one or both members are over 60 live in homes which require essential modernisation; and this in turn signifies poor insulation and high heating bills. The ability of older owners to undertake repair and maintenance is demonstrated to be lower, partly because of income constraints but also because of mobility and other problems.[21] In terms of private renters, 149,000 older privately renting households have regulated tenancies and are often living in property in the most unsatisfactory physical condition.[22] At the poorest end of the

---

[17] *Winning the Generation Game*, para 3.3.

[18] *Pensioners' incomes series 1997/8*, DSS Analytical Services Division, 2000, s 2.

[19] *Income related benefits—estimates of take up in 1996/97 (revised) and 1997/98*, DSS, 1999, tables 1.1, 2.1 and 3.1.

[20] *Family spending: a report on the 1998–99 Family Expenditure Survey*, National Statistics, (c) Crown Copyright, 1999.

[21] English House Condition Survey, 1996.

[22] Department of the Environment, Transport and the Regions (DETR), *Quality and Choice for Older People's Housing—A Strategic Framework*, Appendix I, Housing Circumstances of Older People (http://www.housing.dtlr.gov.uk/ information/hsc/olderpeople /11.htm).

spectrum are the homeless. It is estimated that 834 older people were sleeping rough in London in 1999–2000. Nearly 40,000 others are living in inappropriate hostel accommodation or in bed and breakfast hotels. The older homeless are particularly vulnerable, but have largely remained invisible and outside public consciousness.[23] Although there is an obligation under the Housing Act 1985 to house those who are 'vulnerable because of old age', this applies only to those over 60. This is a clear example of an arbitrary age-related criterion. It excludes many homeless people who are under 60 but prematurely aged and equally vulnerable.[24]

Within the group of pensioners, women fare particularly badly. A lifetime of discrimination in the paid labour market has cumulative effects. Many women have been in the types of jobs which do not carry with them occupational pensions, a position aggravated by active discrimination in access to pension schemes for part-time workers, the vast majority of whom are women. Women's lower earning pattern also means that pensions are correspondingly low.[25] The result is that women pensioners are one of the poorest groups in society. In 1998–99, 62 per cent of single women aged 85 and over were living just on their state retirement pension and income support.

It should be stressed, however, that average figures such as these conceal a wide range of differences in material circumstances . The term 'retired population' spans an age range of 40 to 50 years and the income and lifestyles of younger pensioners (55–64) are far removed from those of older pensioners (over 75 and usually a single female). Many 'younger' pensioners are relatively affluent, with good pensions, and the health and motivation to enjoy their leisure time. This contrasts with the very old and very poor. In fact, although there has been an average increase of 62 per cent in pensioner's incomes over the past two decades, this largely reflects an improvement for the higher income groups. Thus, the income of the richest fifth of single pensioners increased by 85 per cent (£87 a week) while the poorest fifth saw no more than a 22 per cent (£10 a week) increase in the past 20 years.[26]

Social Exclusion

A serious issue which arises for all older people is the extent to which they find themselves on the margins of society. A recent survey found high levels of isolation among older people. People over 75, and older women, experience the most

---

[23] UK Coalition on Older Homelessness, Facts and figures (www.olderhomelessness.org.uk). DETR, *Quality and Choice for Older People's Housing—A Strategic Framework*, 31 January 2001 (www.housing.dtlr.gov.uk).

[24] G Kitchen and C Welch, 'Outside In: Tackling the Social Exclusion of Older Homeless People' (Help the Aged, 1998).

[25] See further, S Fredman, *Women and the Law* (OUP, 1997) ch 8.

[26] Help the Aged.

severe isolation, aggravated by low income and disability.[27] In 1996, 58 per cent of women aged 75 and over lived alone. Isolation is compounded by lack of access to transport and telephones. As Age Concern points out, a telephone is vital both as a lifeline in an emergency and as a daily contact with family and friends. Yet as many as 9 per cent of single pensioner households and 4 per cent of pensioner couple households do not have a fixed telephone, compared with an average of 5 per cent. Absence of a telephone is closely connected to poverty: high connection and line rental charges have been found to constitute a major barrier to ownership.

Similarly, many pensioners are dependent on public transport. Yet inaccessible public transport often aggravates the mobility problems associated with ageing. There are several facets to the problem. Physical inaccessibility is compounded by lack of affordability—the high cost of rail fares has been a major deterrent to travel by train, and fuel and car insurance prices have impacted negatively on the travel patterns of older people using cars and taxis. In addition, older people tend to be more fearful, choosing not to travel alone or after dark. This sense of insecurity can be aggravated by badly lit or isolated bus stops and stations, long distances between home and transport, and feelings of intimidation while on board.[28]

Departure from the labour force frequently gives the impression that individuals are no longer active contributors to society. This masks the significant amount of continuing caring work done by older people. In fact, older people, particularly older women, are deeply involved in caring activities, such as babysitting, helping family, friends or neighbours, and visiting an elderly or sick person. One in ten women between 45 and 64, who are economically inactive, are spending more than 20 hours a week caring. A quarter of older women who are not in paid work are looking after family or home. Of the 400,000 people between 50 and 65 who are looking after home or family, 85 per cent are women. This contrasts with 6 per cent of men in this group. A particularly important function is that of childcare: grandparents are the most likely people to be looking after children when the parents are absent. The caring function is even more pronounced in the over 60 age group. As many as two million of the estimated 5.7 million carers in the UK are over 60, and one fifth of these are aged 75 and over.[29] The problem here is of a different kind of social exclusion—invisibility. Approximately 20 per cent of older carers provide care for over 50 hours a week, and many have been intensively involved in caring for periods of up to 14 years, without breaks of two days or more. Older carers are one of the poorest groups in society and have little support from health and social care services. There is also express age discrimination against older carers in that invalid care allowance is only available to carers of 65 or under.

[27] Help the Aged/Mori Survey, *Isolation and Older People*.

[28] DETR, *Older People: their Transport Needs and Requirements*, 12 February 2001 (www.mobility-unit-dtlr.gov.uk).

[29] Help the Aged, 'Caring in Later Life: Reviewing the Role of Older Carers' (Executive summary).

Nevertheless, given that 80 per cent of workless people between 45 and 64 are not involved in caring, it is clear that caring and voluntary work are not replacing paid work to a significant extent. Formal volunteering activities tend to be lower among younger and older people than those in mid-life.[30] People who are not in employment are less likely to undertake voluntary activities than those who are working; in fact, even those who were involved during their working life seem to withdraw with the rise in economic inactivity.[31] Although some of this spare time is taken up in leisure activities, and many might be content and fulfilled, inactivity can in some cases lead to social exclusion through boredom, loneliness and depression.

Health Care

The vast majority of older people remain fit and healthy enough to run their own lives. The vast majority of older people still live independently in their own homes with 5 per cent estimated to be living in sheltered and very sheltered accommodation and 5 per cent living in registered care homes.[32] Nevertheless, whereas age is not necessarily correlated with failing capacity and ill health, the risks of ill health and disability rise with age. Indeed, older people form a large part of the constituency of the health service. Adult NHS and social care services are utilised by older people to a greater extent than younger people. In 1998–99, the NHS spent 40 per cent of its budget (£10bn) on people over 56, and in the same year, 50 per cent of the social services budget (£5.2bn) went on over 65 year olds. Two thirds of acute hospital beds were occupied by people over 65, and people over 75 make greater use of hospital, primary care and community health care services than other groups. Older people constitute 40 per cent of all emergency admissions.[33] Any discussion of equality must therefore have a dual emphasis. It must reveal and challenge the prejudicial nature of assumptions that old people have failing health and capability. But at the same time, those who do face ill health must be treated fairly and equitably.

To some extent, health services are inevitably responding to the changing population. However, there are two major issues which age discrimination policies need to address. The first is that failing health may be as much a product of the environment in which older people find themselves as their own physiological ageing. This is particularly true of illness and death resulting from hypothermia. Warmth is essential to the well-being of older people; but many live in 'fuel

---

[30] Home Office, 'Voluntary and Community Activities: Findings from the 2000 British Crime Survey', 4.

[31] *Winning the Generation Game*, para 3.3.

[32] DETR, *Quality and Choice for Older People's Housing—A Strategic Framework*, Appendix I, Housing Circumstances of Older People. Community Care Statistics 2000: residential personal social services for adults, England table R2.

[33] Figures are taken from the *National Service Framework for Older People*, March 2001, 7.

poverty', having insufficient income to heat their homes to the appropriate standard for health and comfort. It has been shown that in 1996, 60 per cent of single pension households suffered fuel poverty. The main causes of such poverty are low income and living in an energy inefficient home, both of which as we have seen affect older people particularly. The result is a high level of excess winter deaths. The figures for such deaths in England are well above those in other countries.

The second issue in relation to health concerns inferior or degrading treatment received by older people within the health and social services. A recent review by the King's Fund[34] suggests that age discrimination occurs across all the services provided by the NHS, at different levels and in different guises. There is evidence across a range of services that older people may be denied treatment offered to younger patients, and in some hospitals the standards of hygiene and nutrition given to older people fall below even minimum standards. In addition, older people are often negatively perceived by GPs, because of the increased workload; and there is some evidence that older people are not offered the best available treatment, partly because the effects of the treatment on older people are not properly researched. The King's Fund review concludes that while there are many examples of excellent care for older people, there is also much unfair treatment based on age, some of it being covert and implicit in decisions not to prioritise older peoples' services.

Of even more concern are the services which operate with upper age limits which are deliberately not publicised. Thus in 1991, 20 per cent of cardiac care units operated upper age limits and 40 per cent had an explicitly age-related policy for thrombolysis. According to the National Service Framework 2001, these practices have all but disappeared. However, there is evidence of age discrimination elsewhere. Older trauma victims in Scotland have been shown to be given less care than younger victims, and there is specific concern as to whether older patients are more likely to be denied cardiopulmonary resuscitation on grounds of their age.[35] A recent study co-ordinated by the RCP's Clinical Effectiveness and Evaluation Unit (CEEu) found that older patients with the same extent and types of lung cancer as younger patients are being less actively treated.[36] Quality of care has also been affected by negative staff attitudes in a number of areas and many older people and their carers have found that palliative care is not available to them.

Black and minority ethnic elders especially report negative experiences in the health system and hospitals.[37] For older members from ethnic groups, the conditions in the health system are aggravated by language barriers, insensitivity to

---

[34] See further Janice Robinson's chapter, below. King's Fund Briefing Note. (www.kingsfund.org.uk/eHealthSocialCare/assets/applets/emilie_ageism_reportPDF.pdf) pp 2–7.

[35] *National Service Framework*, para 1.6.

[36] *Royal College of Physicians News*, 11 May 2000 (http://www.rcplondon.ac.uk/news/).

[37] Help the Aged, 'Dignity on the Ward: Acting on the lessons from hospital experiences of black and minority ethnic older people'.

their religious and cultural beliefs and habits and implicit, or in certain cases, explicit racism. Ethnic elders, with the exception of older Chinese people, also seem to have more chronic diseases in comparison to white British older people of the same age. Explanations for this are poverty, poor housing and lifestyle and other factors but also include a sense of alienation and a failure to make use of statutory and voluntary services because these services are perceived as being insensitive to their needs.[38]

The problems described in this section are particularly difficult to address because their causes lie deep within the social culture. Prejudice is not simply borne from misunderstanding, or even hatred and fear of the 'other', as it is in racism or sexism. It is based in a general belief that older people's quality of life is less valuable than that of younger people; that older people have had a 'fair innings' and therefore are less deserving of limited health and social care resources.[39] This is reflected in implicit rationing of health care resources, the setting of age limits for particular types of care, whether explicit or tacitly understood, and even influences major decisions such as whether to resuscitate patients. Moreover, as the King's Fund review points out, because health problems in the older population are characterised as 'normal' aspects of ageing, expectations of what can be achieved by intervention and other services are generally low. This can be self-fulfilling, reflecting in the quality of service provided. In addition, medical research has traditionally placed less emphasis on older than younger people. This means that knowledge about the impact of treatments on older people is often poor. It also affects the esteem of those who work with older people. Work with older people is not considered to be attractive, and pay levels are often poor. The fact that the NHS is modelled on acute disease pathways means that not enough attention has been given to proper palliative care, and doctors frequently feel uncomfortable with diseases they cannot cure.[40]

Children and Adolescents[41]

The use of age as an approximation of capacity for children and young people raises different issues from those of older people, since decision-making capacity is developing. A difficult and changing balance needs to be struck between independence and participation on the one hand, and protection of the child's interests on the other.

---

[38] E Shah, 'Caring for Older People: Ethnic Elders' (1996) 313 BMJ 610–13.

[39] For evidence, see A Williams, 'Intergenerational Equity: An exploration of the "Fair Innings" Argument' (1997) *Health Economics* Vol 6 117–132.

[40] See generally above Grimley Evans ch 2, Robinson ch 5 below.

[41] I am indebted to Meghna Abraham for her contributions to this section and to Gerison Landsdowne for her very helpful advice. See further Herring ch 7 below.

The picture is particularly complex for young adults or adolescents, as they are classified legally as adults or children depending on the issue at hand. Young teenagers are not allowed to vote and are legally prohibited from drinking. Yet they are deemed adults for the purposes of criminal responsibility.[42] In 1998, legislation abolished the rebuttable presumption that a child aged 10–14 was incapable of committing an offence, unless it was proved that the child knew his or her act was seriously wrong.[43] The minimum age of criminal responsibility is now 10 years, one of the lowest in Europe.[44] The *Bulger* case highlighted many of the tensions in the criminal justice system and public perceptions about the 'appropriate' response to children and young people who commit violent crimes and what protection should be available to them through the trial and criminal process.[45]

The complex balance between protection and participation manifests itself particularly in relation to reproductive autonomy. Even though the law recognises the right of under 16s who are 'Gillick' competent to get contraception without parental consent, fear of a lack of confidentiality or of being judged or access to services may prevent a number of young people from accessing emergency contraception.[46] Children can seek to restrict the rights of parents to make decisions about them by bringing an application to the court to seek an order in respect of a particular issue. It is however rare for courts to give leave to do so, either out of a belief that such issues are trivial or better dealt with in the family[47] or because of the difficulty of children accessing courts and legal services.

Particularly worrying is the popular perception that society needs protection from children. The fear of youth crime and violence has found expression in the exclusion of children and young people from public spaces through the use of night curfews. These curfews are intended to protect the local community from the 'alarm and distress' caused by the antisocial behaviour of groups of young people and to protect children from being unaccompanied at night and against the risk of older peers encouraging them into criminal activities.[48] The Government has also recently announced the results of its consultation on the physical punishment of children, carried out between January and April 2000. Stating that 'our approach is to avoid heavy-handed intrusion into family life',

---

[42] See E Scott, 'The Legal Construction of Adolescence' (2000) 29 *Hosftra Law Review* 547.

[43] Crime and Disorder Act 1998, s 38. See No more excuses: A new approach to tackling youth crime in England and Wales (http://www.homeoffice.gov.uk/cpd/ jou/nme.htm).

[44] J Fionda, 'Crime And Disorder Act 1998: New Labour, Old Hat: Youth Justice and The Crime and Disorder Act 1998' [1999] *Crim L Rev* 36–47.

[45] See Case of *T v UK* where the ECHR held that the trial and sentencing procedure were violative of Art 6 of the Convention.

[46] 'Young Women and Emergency Contraception' (http://www.hpw.wales.gov.uk/ emergency_contraception/young_women.htm).

[47] See J Herring, 'Parents and Children' in J Herring (ed), *Family Law: Issues, Debated, Policy* (Willan, Devon, UK, 2001) 151–52.

[48] Juvenile Offenders Unit , 'Local Child Curfew Guidance' (http://www.homeoffice.gov.uk/ yousys/guidcurfew.pdf).

the Government has ruled out legal reform to stop the corporal punishment of children.[49] Both of these policies are difficult to reconcile with the rights of children and young people to physical integrity and liberty.

THE LEGAL CONTEXT

Despite complex legislation or race, gender and disability legislation, there are currently no domestic provisions in Britain relating to age discrimination. Indeed, the express preference of the Government has been for voluntary initiatives. Hence a non-statutory code of practice on age diversity in employment was launched in June 1999. Outside of the employment field, there have been a range of highly significant policy documents setting out policy and strategies for eliminating age discrimination. Thus the NHS plan has a whole chapter devoted to older people, and the National Service Framework for Older People sets out more concrete strategies. Similarly, there are strategy documents on housing and transport for older people.[50] A different approach has been adopted in Northern Ireland, where public authorities already have a duty to promote equality of opportunity on grounds, *inter alia*, of age.[51]

The impetus to bring in legally binding measures on age discrimination has come from Europe. When the new Treaty on European Union was adopted (the Amsterdam Treaty), the Community was given power for the first time to implement the equality principle, not just in the field of gender, but also on grounds of race, religion, age, disability and sexual orientation.[52] Progress since then has been swift. A directive 'implementing the principle of equal treatment between persons irrespective of racial or ethnic origin' was adopted in June 2000.[53] A second directive extending the principle of equal treatment to prevent discrimination on grounds of age, disability, religion and sexual orientation (the 'Framework Directive') was adopted five months later.[54] The Framework Directive must be implemented by December 2003, but the Government has decided to take advantage of the permission to delay implementation of age discrimination legislation until December 2006.[55]

The Framework Directive binds all persons, both public and private, and protects all age groups against age discrimination . It follows the traditional pattern of domestic discrimination legislation, defining the 'principle of equal treatment' as meaning that there should be no direct or indirect discrimination on grounds of age. (These terms are defined below). It goes somewhat further in

---

[49] http://www.londonchildrenscommissioner.org.uk/

[50] DETR, *Older People: their Transport Needs and Requirements*. DETR, *Quality and Choice for Older People's Housing—A strategic Framework* 31 January 2001 (www.housing.dtlr.gov.uk).

[51] Northern Ireland Act 1998, s 75(1)(a).

[52] Art 13 EC.

[53] Council Directive 2000/43/EC, 29 June 2000.

[54] Council Directive 2000/79/EC, 27 November 2000.

[55] Subject to a requirement of that progress is reported annually.

expressly providing that harassment is deemed to be a form of discrimination, as is an instruction to discriminate. According to the Directive, member states may set special conditions for young people and older workers 'in order to promote their vocational integration or ensure their protection'[56] and specific measures may be imposed to prevent or compensate for disadvantages linked to age.[57] But there is no obligation to impose positive duties on public bodies or employers. This sets it apart from the newly enacted UK Race Relations Amendment Act 2000 which imposes a positive duty on employers to promote racial equality and foster good race relations.

Member states are also permitted to provide that differences of treatment on grounds of age do not constitute discrimination, if 'they are objectively and reasonably justified by a legitimate aim, including legitimate employment policy, labour market and vocational training objectives, and if the means of achieving that aim are appropriate and necessary.'[58] Ages for admission to or entitlement to retirement or invalidity benefits may be specifically excluded, provided this does not result in discrimination on grounds of sex. The Directive is 'without prejudice to measures laid down by national law which, in a democratic society, are necessary for public security, for the maintenance of public order, for the protection of health and for the protection of the rights and freedoms of others.'[59] So far as enforcement is concerned, member states must ensure that organisations with a legitimate interest in ensuring that the provisions of the Directive are complied with, may engage in any enforcement procedures on behalf of or in support of the complainant.[60] But whereas the race directive creates an obligation to establish a commission, there is no similar obligation in the Framework Directive.

The Framework Directive is limited to discrimination within employment, vocational training and membership of organisations of workers or employers. Social security is excluded.[61] The narrow scope of the Directive contrasts with the much wider race directive, which extends more broadly than the labour market, to include 'social protection, including social security and healthcare; social advantages; education; and access to and supply of goods and services which are available to the public, including housing.'[62] The Directive is also narrower than existing discrimination legislation. Race and gender legislation outlaws discrimination in education, employment and the provision of services, while the Disability Discrimination Act covers employment, the provision of goods, facilities and services, premises, education and transport. Most advanced is the recent Race Relations Amendment Act 2000. Crucially, this is not confined

---

[56] Art 6(1)(a).
[57] Art 7.
[58] Art 6.
[59] Art 2(5).
[60] Art 9.
[61] Council Directive 2000/79/EC, Art 3(3).
[62] Council Directive 2000/43/EC, Art 3.

to employment, education and services, but applies to all functions of specified public authorities. Law enforcement, whether by the police, local authorities or tax inspectors, is for the first time to be subject to anti-discrimination laws, as are the core functions of the prison and probation service, the implementation of the Government's economic and social policies, certain public appointments, and the activities of immigration and nationality staff when they exceed what is expressly authorised by statute or Ministers.

The limitation of the directive to employment and vocational training means that many areas of age discrimination will be untouched if domestic legislation goes no further than the Directive. However, it is argued here that legislation on age discrimination would be defective if it was confined to employment. Even if the aim were solely to address age discrimination in employment, legislation would not be effective unless it extended to other areas, such as health care, life-long education, and social security and pensions. Absence of relevant training, and disincentives in pensions and social security, are just as serious barriers to older people in the workforce as explicit prejudice in the form of age limits. In any event, as will be seen, there are many issues in the health service, education and elsewhere which need to be addressed if measures against age discrimination are to make a real impact. The narrow scope of the directive also makes it tempting to deal with the issues by means of an individual litigation model. This model leaves it to individual litigants to provide the impetus for change; while courts and tribunals must formulate the legal response based on the facts of individual disputes, rather than the whole picture. Equally problematically, it puts the main burden of change onto the employer, rather than requiring the state and other bodies to take active measures to deal with the causes of the problem.

THE CONCEPT OF EQUALITY

Introduction

Equality in the context of age raises particularly complex issues. Much anti-discrimination legislation has been aimed at redressing prejudice against 'discrete and insular minorities' with little access to political or economic power. This was the impetus behind the race discrimination legislation in the US. Similarly, the pervasive legal and social barriers faced by women through the centuries has provided the impetus for policies and legislation to achieve gender equality. However, age does not define a fixed delineated group. Moreover, not all distinctions are discriminatory. The crucial challenge is therefore to demarcate valid from invalid distinctions.

What role then can equality play? This requires a clearer and more focused understanding of the meaning of equality itself and of its aims and objectives.[63]

---

[63] See further S Fredman, *Discrimination Law* (Clarendon Law Series, OUP, 2002).

Closer examination reveals that equality is not a unitary concept, but can be defined differently depending on what aims and objectives are identified. A familiar aim of equality is to achieve consistency: likes should be treated alike. This is closely related to the 'merit' principle, that is that individuals should be treated according to their merit, and not according to irrelevant characteristics. Merit may be appropriate to the job market. But in the health service it gives way to a different conception of equality, namely that individuals should be treated according to their need. A less individualistic approach characterises the purpose of equality in terms of distributive justice. It will be argued here that all these approaches, while not wholly useless, are flawed. Instead, the aims of equality should be seen as the facilitation of choice or autonomy, the protection of dignity and the enhancement of participative democracy or social inclusion. A legislative model should be shaped to achieve these objectives.

Before elaborating on these points, it is necessary to deal with one sort of argument, which holds that there is in fact no real inequality on the grounds of age. On this view, an individual needs to be considered in terms of her whole lifespan, so that, provided we all bear equal burdens at similar stages in our lives, there is no inequality. One defence of mandatory retirement ages is phrased in these terms. Since we all will be subject to mandatory retirement ages at 65, the argument goes, there is no breach of the equality principle.[64] This argument is, however, fallacious. Two life-spans cannot genuinely be compared, not just because there are too many variables, but because a change in policy at some point in time might affect those who happen to be of the appropriate age, but would not have affected those older than them. In addition, the same event might affect two people of different generations quite differently, even if it occurs to both at the same age, because of the deep cultural differences between generations. It is therefore argued here that the use of age as a criterion for distinction between two individuals at any one point in their lives can be a manifestation of age discrimination, regardless of how the same individuals might be treated in the future or in the past.

Equality as Consistency: Treat Likes Alike

The most basic concept of equality is the Aristotelean notion that likes should be treated alike. This is an intuitively powerful concept and is reflected in the legal concept of direct discrimination (see further below). However, it immediately comes up against the question: are two people of different ages 'alike' in the relevant sense? And if they are, should they always be treated alike? Uniform treatment in some situations merely exacerbates disadvantage. The principle of equality as consistency does not assist us in distinguishing invidious discrimina-

---

[64] See the discussion by D McKerlie, 'Equality between Age-Groups' (1992) 21 *Philosophy and Public Affairs* 275–96.

tion from appropriate differentiation. Moreover, it is a blunt tool. Only 'likes' qualify for equal treatment; there is no requirement that people be treated appropriately according to their difference

Equality as consistency is also limited by the fact that it is merely a relative principle. It requires only that two similarly situated individuals be treated alike. There is no substantive underpinning. This means that there is no difference in principle between treating two such people equally badly, and treating them equally well. For example, flexible retirement could be make a useful contribution to extending the working life of older people. However, if the employer refuses to allow workers of any age group to work in this way , an older person could not claim that a refusal to permit flexible working breaches the principle that likes should be treated alike. The principle of equality as consistency does not give a right to flexible working; it only requires an employer to treat employees consistently regardless of their age.

Even more problematically, the absence of substantive underpinning means that a claim of equal treatment can just as easily be met by removing a benefit from the relatively privileged group, and equalising the two parties at the lower point (levelling down), as by extending the benefit to the relatively underprivileged individual , and equalising the parties at a high point (levelling up). This would mean, in the health service for example, that inequality in allocating particular resources could be dealt with by withdrawing that resource from everyone.[65] All would then be treated equally, but equally badly. Similarly, when older men complained they were being treated less favourably than older women because the state pension age was 65 for men and 60 for women, the response was simply to raise women's pension age to 65. This achieved equality but only by removing a benefit from older women without improving the position of older men.

Individual Merit

The flaws in the bare notion of equality as consistency point us towards the merit principle. The hallmark of prejudice and inequality has always been detrimental treatment based on a person's race, gender or other irrelevant characteristic. It is therefore a fundamental aim of equality to ensure that an individual is treated according to her merit, free of stereotypical assumptions. The merit principle has been a central plank of business and government promotion of age equality. Employers who exclude workers on the basis of stereotypical views about their capacity, it is argued, are thereby precluding themselves from benefiting from a pool of potentially talented workers.[66]

---

[65] J Harris, 'The rationing debate' (1997) *British Medical Journal* 314:669.
[66] See *Code of Practice on Age Diversity in Employment*.

Central to this discussion is the complex relationship between age and capability. So far as older people are concerned, there is convincing evidence that age is not a good proxy for capability. For young people, the relationship between age and capacity is more complicated. On the one hand, it is recognised that children and young people are not always in a position to look after themselves or to make the best decision in their own interests. On the other hand, age should not be mechanically related to decision-making capacity or maturity, thereby denying equal rights to make decisions to those who are in fact able to do so. A vital aim of equality legislation is therefore to prevent stereotypical assumptions about an individual's capability based on her age. The argument that individualised assessment is too costly does not prevent an equality claim from arising. It may of course be raised as a potential limit on equality; but then its legitimacy must be judged according to the strength of its claim to displace equality.

However, sole reliance on merit yields a principle of equality which is too limited. Most importantly, neither capability nor merit are scientific, objective criteria. Instead, they are measured against a particular norm, that of the able bodied, prime age adult. Uniform treatment of all age groups, based on this norm, will in practice disadvantage those who do not conform, among whom there will be a disproportionate number of older and younger people. For example, mobility is relative to the accessibility of means of transport. Because transport is structured and run in such a way as to cater for the needs of the healthy able-bodied adult, those who do not conform to this norm are relatively immobile. Similarly, because training is structured according to the cultural expectations of the current generation of 'prime age' workers, older people seem to be less 'capable' of being trained. Nor is 'merit' a fixed quantity. Instead, it is largely a result of social input, which can itself be distorted by prejudice. For example, older workers are often rejected because they are not qualified for a job. Yet the absence of qualification is partly due to the fact that employers are reluctant to invest money in training older workers. Moreover, a focus on 'merit' assumes that the individual should fit the job, rather than that the job should be adjusted to fit the worker. Yet it may well be possible to accommodate the needs of an older worker without undermining the requirements of the enterprise. This can already be seen in moves towards flexible retirement ages. The EU Part-Time Workers Directive, for example, advocates part-time work in part to encourage employers to facilitate gradual retirement of older workers.

Finally, while the merit principle benefits those whose capacity is unaffected by age, it is of course of little use to those who find that they have age-related limitations. Within the employment context, if the aim is to find more workers with the relevant talents, workers without these 'merits' will continue to be excluded. The merit principle is particularly invidious in respect of health care or other social services. In this context, it could easily translate into a principle that the criteria for allocating health care resources are calculated according to whether an individual 'merits' the resources, that is whether she will continue to have a full or productive life. This approach is in fact reflected in decisions which judge the suitability of the patient on the basis of their capacity to benefit. [67]

To Each According to Her Need

A better analysis is to declare openly that the health service responds to need rather than merit, stressing that age is irrelevant to need. This is encapsulated in the policy statement of the National Service Framework for Older People,[68] where it states:

> Denying access to services on the basis of age alone is not acceptable. Decisions about treatment and health care should be made on the basis of health needs and ability to benefit rather than a patient's age . . . That is not to say that everyone needs the same health or social care, nor that these needs should be met the same way. As well as health needs, the overall health status of the individual, their assessed social care need and their own wishes and aspirations and those of their carers, should shape the package of health and social care.

A similar formulation is appropriate for all aspects of public services, including social services, housing and transport.

The use of need as a criterion is intuitively appropriate. However, care must be taken to ensure that the definition of need does not in itself incorporate age-based presumptions. It is notable that the formula above includes both health needs and ability to benefit. As Harris argues: 'To define need . . . in terms of capacity to benefit and then to argue that the greater number of life years deliverable by health care, the greater the need for treatment . . . is just to beg the crucial question of how to characterise need or benefit.' Instead, he argues, the principal of the NHS should be to offer beneficial health care on the basis of individual need, 'so that each has an equal chance of flourishing to the extent that their personal health status permits.'[69]

Fair Distribution

A less individualist objective of equality is to correct inequities in the distribution of social benefits, monetary or otherwise. More particularly, as the Canadian Supreme Court has articulated it, the aim of equality is to prevent the imposition of particular burdens on grounds of group membership. This approach is specifically asymmetric, in that it only challenges classifications which burden group members; leaving the legitimacy of beneficial classifications unquestioned.

---

[67] See below Robinson ch 5 and above Grimley Evans ch 2.
[68] Para 1.7.
[69] J Harris, 'The rationing debate' (1997) *British Medical Journal* 314:669.

The distributive aim recognises that equality of treatment can perpetuate disadvantage. For example, equality of treatment of all in the health service would substantially disadvantage the elderly. Unequal treatment, in this sense, aims to achieve greater equality of results. A rich concept of equality therefore requires more than just uniform treatment. It is also asymmetric. This means that discrimination is prohibited if it imposes burdens on group members. Actions which lead to fairer distribution will be permissible, even if they involve some differentiation on the prohibited ground.

The distributive aim is, however, a difficult one to apply in practice. Why should we insist that social goods such as jobs, representation in Parliament, and other positions of power be distributed proportionally among different age groups? One explanation is that given by proponents of 'age diversity', which has been central both to the Government's promotional campaign in support of the voluntary code of practice, and to employers' organisations. Age diversity has been promoted on the grounds that a range of ages within employment is good for business because it combines the benefits of the experience of older workers with the flexibility and enthusiasm of younger ones. Older workers can maintain the 'corporate memory' and older customers might prefer to deal with older salespeople or financial advisors. Formulated in this way, it is obvious that this approach runs counter to the merit principle, in that it is based on an assumption that people of different ages bring different characteristics to the job simply due to their age. It is true that this draws on positive stereotypes associated with different age groups, rather than negative ones. However, it still falls into the trap, which has been recognised in feminist literature, of 'essentialising' age, that is assuming that any particular age is invariably associated with a fixed set of characteristics. In addition, a strategy based on age diversity alone can legitimate the exclusion of some people because of their age. If there are already sufficient representatives of a particular age, the age diversity argument requires that any new recruits of that age be excluded. Moreover, on closer inspection it can be seen to be grounded, not so much in genuine redistribution, but in business strategy.

Within the health service and other social services, the distributive aim is even more complex. Equality of representation in the health service is not appropriate: we have already seen that older people take up more of the resources of the health service than other groups. A different version of the distributive aim concentrates on inter-generational equity, and constitutes a variant of the 'fair innings' argument. On this view, the aim is to equalise the lifetime experience of health of all people in society. Alternatively, it is argued that the objective should be to improve the health of the nation as a whole as much as possible. This means that priority should be given to those who will benefit most from the resources available.[70] Both of these explicitly outcomes-based views, however,

---

[70] A Williams, 'The rationing debate: Rationing health care by age: the case for' (1997) *British Medical Journal* 3114:20 (15 March) .

have the effect of legitimating a lower allocation of health care resources to older people. The first version leads to the conclusion that those who have had a 'fair innings' should not expect to have as much spent on health improvement as would be spent on someone who has not yet attained or may never attain that level of health.[71] The approach based on improving the aggregate health of the nation as a whole has the effect that, for treatments which yield benefits which last for the rest of a person's life, resources should be allocated to younger rather than older people. Williams expressly recognises, and indeed endorses the conclusion, that improving the health of the nation as a whole is likely in some circumstances to lead to indirect discrimination against older people.[72] Similarly, he concludes, 'the notion of intergenerational equity requires greater discrimination against the elderly than would be dictated simply by efficiency objectives'.[73]

This discussion shows that a notion of fair distribution based primarily on results can be problematic; indeed, it may even legitimate a lesser allocation to older people. It is argued here that an emphasis on results is important in high-lighting the limitations of an approach based on identical treatment. However, the distributive aim must be allied to a strong notion of individual rights to avoid collapsing into utilitarianism. Thus, the emphasis on results should imply a right to an equivalent quality of life so far as possible; without having to trade off one individual's rights against those of another. I therefore turn to more individual rights-based arguments.

Choice or Autonomy

An aim of equality is to give all people, regardless of their sex, race, or age, an equal set of alternatives from which to choose and thereby to pursue their own version of a good life. Equal treatment is not sufficient if obstacles exist on the basis of a prohibited characteristic to the genuine exercise of choice. However, provided the choices exist, there is no reason to expect that everyone will make the same decision. Thus, while this formulation of the aims of equality requires more than equality of treatment, it does not go so far as to require equality of outcome. Difference in outcome, on this view, is not attributable to discrimination but to difference in the exercise of individual choice.

This objective (often allied with the principle of equality of opportunities) holds much promise in the field of age discrimination. One of its most important implications is the removal of age barriers in a variety of contexts, whether in employment, health care, social services or training. The removal of a series

---

[71] A Williams, 'Intergenerational Equity: An explorations of the "Fair Innings" Argument' (1997) *Health Economics* Vol 6 117–132.

[72] 'The Rationing debate'.

[73] 'Intergenerational Equity', 117.

of age-related criteria opens up a range of choices for individuals. However, it has long been recognised that the formal existence of choice does not necessarily mean that people are genuinely in a position to make use of the opportunities thereby presented. We have already seen that although many people retired early under what were nominally 'voluntary' early retirement schemes, in fact, given a real choice, two thirds would have remained in employment. Similarly, women over 70 are not offered breast cancer screening automatically, but may choose to have it. In fact, there is a widespread lack of awareness among older women of the availability of screening, and the overall rate of self-referrals is very low. Indeed, as the King's Fund research concludes, the very existence of an age limit may give a discriminatory message, indicating that older people are considered to be less valuable, or that risks of contracting breast cancer are lower.[74]

If equality of opportunities is limited to the provision of nominal choices such as these, it is unlikely to make a significant impact. However, a more substantive sense of equality of opportunity would require measures to be taken to ensure that people of all ages have real choices, and are genuinely able to pursue those choices. This is a potentially radical approach, which requires active measures such as the provision of training, the adjustment of pension schemes, the introduction of flexible working and the appropriate allocation of health care resources and information. It could go even further and require a greater adaptation of the built environment to accommodate the needs of older people. For example, better public transport would increase the range of options provided, particularly for those who have failing eyesight and can no longer drive. For older people, the choice to continue to live at home may only be a genuine one if there is assistance in modernising or adapting housing. As has been shown above, many older people live in houses which are poorly insulated and dilapidated. The debilitation caused by cold, hunger and financial anxieties in themselves significantly limit older people's ability to make meaningful choices. Age Concern goes on to argue that older people's choices of housing should be widened to include appropriate, accessible two-bedroom accommodation, with part-ownership options for older people who do not have sufficient capital to make a full purchase. Real choice also entails giving the older people the right to choose to relax and enjoy leisure activities. It can be seen from this that employers can only be expected to deliver a small aspect of equality of opportunity; many of the more far-reaching measures need to be taken by the state.

Dignity

Also a potential aim of equality is to ensure that everyone is treated with equal dignity and concern. As the Canadian Supreme Court has declared: 'Equality

---

[74] King's Fund Briefing Note, 'Age discrimination in health and social care'.

means that our society cannot tolerate legislative distinctions that treat certain people as second-class citizens, that demean them, that treat them as less capable for no good reason, or that otherwise offend fundamental human dignity.'[75] Dignity is also central to the new South African constitution and the German Basic Law. Most importantly, the newly proclaimed EU Charter of Fundamental Human Rights specifically grounds the equality rights of the elderly in the dignity principle. Thus, Article 25 proclaims the right of the elderly 'to lead a life of dignity and independence'. Dignity as a value has also been recognised in the domestic context. The National Health Service Plan commits the Government to providing for the 'dignity, security and independence in old age.'[76] Finally, the Framework Directive itself bases the right to protection against age-related harassment on the dignity of the person.

Dignity is an irreducible minimum. It has the important effect of underpinning equality, making it impossible to argue that a 'levelling down' solution is as good as one that that 'levels up'. Equality based on dignity must enhance rather than diminish the status of individuals. It also means that equality need not be based on a demonstration of equal merit or capability. A person must be treated with respect regardless of his or her merits or capabilities. Dignity is also given an important substantive boost by allying it with a right to independence. The right of the elderly to lead a life of independence requires a positive response, action on the part of both public and private actors to facilitate the right. This has been expressly recognised in the NHS Plan.

Dignity is of course frequently an opaque concept, subjective and difficult to measure. It is also malleable, can be used for varying purposes. For example, many have argued that the elimination of mandatory retirement ages undermines the dignity of individuals, since senior workers will be subjected to degrading personal appraisal instead of the less intrusive mechanism of automatic retirement. However, it is also an affront to the dignity of the individual to assume that he or she automatically shares the characteristics of everyone else in his or her age group. Personal appraisal is now a part of the working life of most individuals of whatever age: it is only degrading if actual diminishing of capability due to age is considered stigmatic. Far better to respect each individual regardless of her capability, but also to avoid attaching stereotypical views of capability to certain age groups.

Participative Democracy

The final substantive value underlying equality is that of participative democracy. Thus, Young argues that social equality, while referring in part to the distribution of social goods, primarily refers to the full participation and inclusion

---

[75] *Egan v Canada* (1995) 29 CRR (2d) 79 at 104–5.
[76] HMSO, The NHS Plan, July 2000.

of everyone in major social institutions.[77] A rich idea of equality sees equality as participation and inclusion of all groups.[78] This goes beyond participation in elections. It extends to participation in all aspects of social life. This ideal is strongly reflected in recent EU policy documents, which refer not just to the need to augment the workforce with older workers, but to the more general principle of combating social exclusion. Notably, Article 25 of the EU Charter of Fundamental Rights includes not just the right of the elderly to lead a life of dignity and independence but also to 'participate in social and cultural life'.

Participative democracy also entails full involvement in decision-making which affects older or younger people. This is recognised in the National Service Plan for Older People, which stresses the need for representation of older people across every organisation, both in decision-making and in setting and monitoring standards. However, the representative aspect of participative democracy is not uncomplicated. There is an assumption that an older person, simply by being in the appropriate age range, will 'represent' older people's interests. No attempt is therefore made to specify how such representatives will be chosen and how their representativity and accountability will be maintained. However, as we have seen, older people do not constitute a homogeneous group. More attention clearly needs to be paid to who such representatives will be if participation in decision-making of older people is to be meaningful.

It is argued here that the central aim of equality should be to facilitate equal participation of all in society, based on equal concern and respect for the dignity of each individual. This aim requires a complex amalgam of strategies, some of which might involve treating different age groups differently. It also requires positive measures to facilitate participation.

This formulation of equality suggests that the aims of equality might be different for younger people and children. It is noteworthy that the rights of children are formulated quite differently in the EU Charter. This stresses the rights of children, on the one hand to 'such protection and care as is necessary for their well-being' and, on the other, to express their views freely, and to have 'their views taken into account on such matters that concern them in accordance with their age and maturity'.[79] This combination of parentalism and respect for their views provides a useful benchmark against which to assess the meaning of equality in relation to children.

LIMITS ON EQUALITY

As with many social rights, the right to age equality is not unlimited. Whatever decision is taken as to the aims and objectives of age equality, it is still necessary

---

[77] I Young, *The Politics of Difference* (Princeton University Press, 1990), 173.
[78] Young, ibid, 158.
[79] Art 24.

to consider whether and in what circumstances, other, non-equality based values should trump equality concerns. There are two aspects to the question. First, which interests are permitted to displace equality? Secondly, what weight should be given to those interests? Is it enough for the conflicting aim to be convenient or strategic, or must it be demonstrably necessary to achieve the stated objective?

The 'Fair Innings' Argument

There are several ways in which the limits to equality have been framed. The first is the 'fair innings' argument. We have seen that discrimination against older people in the health service has been defended on the grounds that older people have had a 'fair innings' and therefore are less deserving of limited health and social care resources. Similarly, employers have argued that older workers have had a fair innings and should give way to younger workers. This was the argument which was used to justify the policy of early retirement in the recessionary period at the end of the twentieth century. It is still used to justify policies of mandatory retirement. Underlying these arguments is the view that it is wrong to consider a particular stage of life in isolation. The opportunities available to an individual throughout his or her lifespan should be considered cumulatively, and once a person has had those opportunities, she or he should not expect any more. Indeed, it has distributive overtones: because older people have once arguably been treated to all the benefits of society, they should now let others have their share.

This argument, is, however, fundamentally unsound. In particular, the notion that older workers should give way to younger ones is based on flawed assumptions. It assumes that there is a fixed number of jobs which can simply be handed from one worker to another. This might in some circumstances be true at the level of the individual firm, But at the macro level, driving people out of the labour market at 50 does not create jobs for young unemployed people. Conversely, keeping older people in work does not 'use up' jobs which could be reallocated to younger people. Known as the 'lump of labour' fallacy, this approach ignores the fact that jobs can create further jobs, so that the size of the labour market is determined by the scale of demand for jobs, not the supply of jobs. In fact, it has been demonstrated that countries with a high level of employment of older people also have high levels of employment of younger people, not the opposite as might be expected. Population growth does not itself lead to higher unemployment, particularly if the economy is buoyant.[80]

The fair innings argument is also flawed in its application to health resources. It might be argued that health care differs fundamentally from the labour market,

---

[80] *Winning the Generation Game* and see N Campbell, 'The Decline of Employment among Older People in Britain' (CASE paper 19, Jan 1999).

since health care resources are finite. Therefore, the use of resources on older people inevitably 'uses up' resources that could otherwise be spent on younger people. However, as in the case of jobs, the use of health care resources is not a 'zero sum game'. Health care that facilitates independence or improves health can actually pay for itself. As Sir John Grimley Evans demonstrates, the resources spent on interventions such as hip replacements for older people improve their quality of life dramatically, as well as decreasing the need for other resource input. In addition, a healthier older person might care for others. In fact, the fair innings argument only really applies to life threatening illness. Health care resources which are withheld from an older person with a chronic illness or disability will be displaced to the social services budget, or be financed from private family income (unless, that is, we are prepared as society to countenance older people living in degradation and pain).Others go so far as to argue that the apparent limitation on health care resources is not an absolute fact, but is an outcome of socially determined forces, which can themselves be manipulated.[81] The duty to promote equality should provide an impetus to manipulate those forces in the direction of age equality, rather than permitting the mere assertion of a limitation on resources to justify inequality.

Costs of Equality: Business Interests and Public Spending

The cost to business of age equality is frequently put forward as a justification for limiting age equality. It is sometimes argued that this is because equality infringes on the liberty of individual employers. More often, it is based on the argument that the good of the individual business will further the good of all, even if it subordinates particular equality rights. On this argument, if a business is required to retain unproductive workers, or to bear too great a portion of social costs, the business might no longer be viable, causing unemployment and dislocation. This is a complex argument which needs to be dissected into several different issues.

The first is to determine the extent to which age equality is indeed a cost to business. As has been seen above, there are many ways in which age equality is good for business. It opens up a wide pool of talent from which employers can draw, and yields a diverse workforce with a range of skills and experiences. There is evidence that older people stay longer and reduce turnover costs, and leading companies such as Tesco, B & Q and Sainsbury's report that employing older workers (over 50) contributes to high quality of customer service, increased sales and customer satisfaction, less absenteeism and less shrinkage than other stores. We have also seen that older workers respond well to appropriate training and there is no evidence of decreased flexibility in older workers.

---

[81] G D Smith, S Franke and S Ebrahim, 'Rationing for Health Equity: Is it necessary?' (2000) *Health Economics* 9: 575–79.

One way of rebutting the cost argument is to demonstrate that, in practice, the employer is not bearing the costs. Instead, the employer is simply repaying the worker in the later, less productive years of his or her life for the 'super-productive' mid-life period. American commentators have argued that one of the justifications for age discrimination legislation is based on the 'life-cycle model'. On this model, the employer benefits from the employee's prime productivity during the middle stages of his or her career, paying less than marginal productivity. This is compensated for by paying a wage premium during the training stages of employment and again at the end stages of the employee's career. However, the employer is tempted to take advantage of the intermediate period of super-productivity and then to discharge the employee without honouring the implied obligation to pay more than his or her productivity in the end stages of his or her career.[82] Legislation, on this view, is necessary to prevent this from occurring.[83]

At the macro-economic level, a similar line of argument is followed. Age equality, particularly in the health service, will constitute too great a drain on public resources, it is argued. However, the costs here too need to be carefully examined. There are many ways in which age equality can save public money. The money spent, for example, in giving greater educational opportunities to older people ultimately saves money by opening up opportunities for older people to continue in paid work, to participate in unpaid caring or voluntary work and to take more care of their own health and finances. The money spent in health care aimed at greater independence and autonomy of older people saves costs to the social services as a whole and to individual carers. Moreover, older people in work are less likely to suffer from a range of illnesses, particularly mental illness such as depression, and poverty related illnesses.

This is not to deny that there may be net costs associated with age equality. The next step, however, is to be clear as to what these costs are and who should bear them. It is often forgotten that there is also a cost to age inequality, but because this cost is borne privately by individuals and their families, it appears invisible. As Humphries and Rubery show, 'many costs and benefits associated with economic well-being are not captured in the accounting framework adopted by single organisations; even at the national level, the tendency has been to sum up the estimated costs to individual employers without reference to the effects on other areas of economic and social life.'[84] This is particularly true in respect of health and social services. Resources saved to the public purse do not necessarily mean that there is no cost at all. As Robinson argues, such costs

---

[82] D Neumark, 'Age discrimination Legislation in the US' in Z Hornstein (ed), *Outlawing age discrimination* (London, Policy Press, 2001) 55 and see EP Lazear, 'Why is there mandatory retirement?' (1979) vol 87 no 6 *Journal of Political Economy* 1261–84.

[83] The life-cycle model is limited by the fact that it is based on the paradigm of a worker who remains in the same employment all his or her life.

[84] J Humphries and J Rubery, *The Economics of Equal Opportunities* (Equal Opportunities Commission, 1995) 399.

are currently borne by older people themselves and their families, especially female relatives, who take on responsibilities of caring for older relatives who are ill or disabled.[85]

The real question then becomes, not what is the cost of age equality, but how should the cost be equitably distributed? The three main possible cost-bearers are the employer, the state and the individual or her family. This too is a complex matter. Some costs, such as the costs of training, may be better borne by the state than the individual employer. Even where costs are better borne by the employer, it is clear that not all firms face the same level of costs and benefits. Many factors influence this, including the position of the individual firm in the product and labour market, the kinds of skills they need, whether these are firm-specific and the expense of in-firm training.[86]

These issues have been analysed in some detail in respect of gender discrimination. Although a similar analysis remains to be conducted in respect of age, it is clear from the earlier work on gender that all these issues show that if change is left to the voluntary initiative of the employer, it will not take place at any optimal pace. 'There is a disjuncture between what is rational for some individual enterprises . . . and what would collectively benefit employers in their need for a highly-productive workforce.'[87] Competitive pressures can then prevent firms from making the necessary short-term investment to reap the longer-term benefits of age equality. This points strongly in favour of a legislative rather than voluntary solution. It also demonstrates that the employer should not bear the whole cost.

Ultimately, the movement towards age equality rests on the ethical arguments identified above. Certainly, the more evidence that such equality also furthers business and macro-economic interests, the better. Where there is a real cost, however, the solution must be addressed holistically, moving in favour of a fair distribution of costs between individual, employer and state, rather than assuming that shifting the cost away from the employer is the only dimension of justification needed.

How then should the fairness of the distribution be determined? Certainly the primary decision should be for elected and expert policy-makers, rather than courts. The role of legal principle should, nevertheless, be to structure decision-making in such a way as to ensure that the relevant interests are properly considered. This entails transparent decision-making and a duty to give due consideration to the effects on age of particular decisions.

It also requires proof that the reasons given for age discrimination are strong enough to displace the value of equality. But how weighty should those reasons be? This requires a proportionality analysis, requiring proof that the restriction on equality is pursuing a legitimate aim, and that the restriction (the means

---

[85] Robinson, ch 5 below.
[86] Humphries and Rubery, *The Economics of Equal Opportunities*, 15.
[87] Breugel and Perrons in Humphries and Rubery above n 86, 168.

chosen) are proportionate to that aim. But proportionality is an elastic concept. It can be applied relatively loosely, requiring only that the state or employer demonstrate that it is reasonable to override equality in order to achieve the aim in question (a rationality test). At the other end of the spectrum is the necessity test, which insists on proof that the restriction is necessary to achieve that end, in the sense that there is no non-discriminatory alternative to achieve the same end (a necessity test).

A necessity test has been preferred in the gender discrimination field in the UK and the EU[88] and in the race discrimination field in the US.[89] But the age discrimination cases in Canada have accepted the rationality test. For example, in a recent Canadian case, it was held that a rule was discriminatory on grounds of age, but this was justifiable because it involved the distribution of limited resources among competing groups, and the legislature was entitled to decide to allocate the benefit on efficiency grounds.[90] Similarly, several cases have upheld mandatory retirement ages, on the ground that a rational relationship can be established between this and the ends sought.

I argue that the rational relationship test is not stringent enough. Instead, a strict justification test is warranted, requiring proof that there is no viable non-discriminatory alternative. For example, it has been argued that age limits in screening programmes can be justified if there are no overall benefits to women in older age groups. The application of such an approach can be seen by considering two examples from the NHS: cervical cancer screening, and breast cancer screening. Women are not routinely screened for cervical cancer over the age of 64; whereas women between 20 and 64 are called up for screening every five years. Age limits for cervical cancer screening are justified by the very low risk of women over 65 developing cervical cancer if they have had a negative smear history before exiting the programme. However, a different picture emerges in respect of breast cancer screening. Women are only called up for breast screening between 50 and 64. Women over this age will not be offered the same service automatically, but will need to refer themselves. An extension to age 70 is planned by 2004. However, it is difficult to justify even the age limit of 70 in view of evidence that 1,500 lives could be saved annually if the programme were extended to all women over 70.[91]

Rights and Interests of Others

Perhaps even more difficult is the need to balance the equality interests of some groups against those of others. Should older people be given priority within the

---

[88] *Bilka Kaufhaus.* C–170/84 [1986] ECR 1607.

[89] *Griggs v Duke Power.* 401 US 424 (1971).

[90] *Sutherland v Canada* 208 NR 1; 123 FTR 80 (1997) Federal Court of Canada, Appeal Division per Isaac CJ.

[91] Age Concern England, *Older women unaware of breast cancer risk*, ACE 11 October 2000.

workforce at the expense of the progression of younger people? Or of people from other marginalised groups such as women, ethnic minorities or disabled people?

Here again the potential conflict needs to be closely scrutinised. In fact, as we have seen, older women are among the most disadvantaged groups in society. Similarly, older members of ethnic minorities suffer from cumulative disadvantage and there is a higher proportion of disabled older people than younger people. It is therefore not always correct to see age discrimination as conflicting with other sorts of discrimination.

Age discrimination legislation in the US is often perceived to privilege older and more affluent white men at the expense of others. While it is true that the vast bulk of litigants in court are white men in well paid jobs, this reflects the costs and risks of litigation rather than the effect of the law as a whole. Not only is the litigation process extremely expensive, it is also hostile. Very few litigants are successful. Therefore only those with much to gain will attempt it. But this is not to say that age equality necessarily benefits these groups. It is very important to ensure that age discrimination legislation is fashioned in such a way as to further equality among disadvantaged groups and not at their expense.

This can be achieved by reverting to first principles. The aim of age equality is to enhance dignity, choice and participation . Where a measure distinguishes on the basis of age, in order to achieve greater equality for one age group, it does not necessarily discriminate against another age group. Thus in a major recent Canadian case,[92] a 30-year-old woman claimed that she had been discriminated against on grounds of her age because survivors' pensions were not available to childless spouses under the age of 45. The Canadian court stressed that the aim of equality law was not to prohibit all age differentiation. It only prohibits differential treatment which reflects the stereotypical application of presumed group characteristics, or perpetuates the view that the individual is less capable or worthy of recognition or value as a human being. Was a 30-year-old widow part of a group which had been consistently and routinely subjected to the sorts of discrimination faced by some of Canada's discrete and insular minorities? Clearly not. Therefore no unlawful discrimination had been established.

Perhaps a more straightforward limit is for health and safety. When capability is genuinely impaired due to age, then jobs such as airline pilots in which lives are at stake may be subject to age limits. However, like other limits, this must be objectively justified and proportional. Testing must be individualised and clear evidence of loss of capacity must be produced. Proportionality also means that the solution is not necessarily total exclusion from the job. Other interim options might achieve the appropriate health and safety protections. For example, instead of automatically retiring airline pilots at 55, it could be sufficient to test them twice a year up to age 60 or 65.

---

[92] *Law v Canada (Minister of Employment and Immigration* [1999] 1 SCR 497.

LEGISLATING FOR EQUALITY

Having set out the principles behind any legislation, I now attempt to translate these into legislative form. As we have seen, the Framework Directive follows well established contours, applying only to discrimination within employment and vocational training and relying on the traditional definition of direct and indirect discrimination . Enforcement is conceived of as an individual right to apply to a court. Although positive action is permitted, it is not required; and the Directive does not require the establishment of a Commission. It is evident from the above discussion that this approach is too limited. It will be argued below that the legislation should extend beyond employment to cover all public functions and the provision of goods and services. It should also extend the frontiers beyond the negative prohibition on direct and indirect discrimination and set out a series of positive duties to promote equality.

In addition, sole reliance on individual litigation is too limited. Such an individualistic model, which has been mainstay of US age discrimination in employment legislation, leads to an adversarial and defensive attitude among respondents. It also favours individual complainants who can afford to bring proceedings and for whom the major incentive is compensation rather than structural change. Instead, I argue for a 'mainstreaming' approach, a positive duty to take steps to promote equality, such as is found in more recent equality legislation in the UK. Nor are these ideas wholly radical. Important steps have been taken in this direction already. The Race Relations Amendment Act 2000 already places a positive duty to promote equality on all public bodies when carrying out their functions. The National Service Framework on Health in Older People, and the policy documents on housing and transport already constitute positive measures to promote equality, as does the Code of Practice on Age Diversity in Employment. Similarly, the European Commission Report *The Social Situation in the EU 2001* emphasises that the responsibility lies on government to develop policies to enable workers to remain in the labour force for as long as possible .

Formulating the questions in these terms also makes it clear that it is not appropriate to use secondary legislation under the European Communities Act 1972 to bring in new measures. It is argued strongly that there should be primary legislation, giving a proper opportunity for full debate. Regulations are inevitably limited to the requirements of the Directive and no more.

Legislation on age discrimination has been delayed until 2006, on the grounds that age discrimination raises 'new, wide-ranging and complex issues'.[93] However, the Government's response has been disappointing and unimaginative in respect of the other new strands (religion and sexual orientation) on which legislation is required by 2003. Coverage is limited to employment and

---

[93] 'Equality and Diversity: The Way Ahead' (DTI, 2002), para 91.

training, the central concepts of direct and indirect discrimination are not substantially modified, and, pending decisions on a possible Single Equality Body, it is not proposed to give powers to any of the existing commissions to deal with the new strands. Possibly the only new development is in the provisions on positive action. However, these do not impose a positive duty on employers to take measures to promote equality. Instead, specified positive action is permitted, in the form of training or encouragement focused on specific groups, where this prevents or compensates for disadvantage.[94]

In the extended period before concrete proposals emerge for age discrimination, there is still plenty of scope for arguing for change. In the following section, I examine how the principles argued for in this chapter could be translated into legislation. I examine the scope and coverage of legislation, the definitions of discrimination and the nature of positive duties, before turning to questions of enforcement.

Scope and Coverage

As suggested earlier, legislation should aim to achieve a concept of equality which enhances individual choice and autonomy, protects individual dignity and facilitates social inclusion. This requires more than a prohibition on discrimination in employment and vocational training. As we have seen, the problem of age discrimination extends beyond employment, to include a wide range of public services. Even if the aim were only to achieve equality in employment, this could not be achieved without legislating in a far wider range. This is because many aspects of age discrimination interact and reinforce one another. Better health care enhances employability, and employment enhances health. Better housing and transport for older people make it more likely that they will be able to participate actively in society, whether as volunteers or paid workers. Rigid tax rules prevent flexible retirement, incentives within the pension system encourage early retirement and a dearth of training inhibits re-employment of older workers. Legislation focusing on employment will be ineffective unless it addresses these wider issues.

To restrict legislation to employment also puts a burden on employers which they cannot necessarily discharge. The ability of employers to bring about change by removing stereotypical assumptions is necessarily limited. In order to be properly effective, and to avoid distortions, government and other public bodies need to be actively harnessed to the cause. For example, tax and pension rules need to be changed before employers can be expected to introduce flexible retirement ages. . Training of older workers needs to be a state responsibility, and not left to employers. Also essential to effecting real change are promotional and educational measures to help dispel the image of older people as dependent

---

[94] See for example, The Employment Equality (Sexual Orientation) Regulations, reg 30.

or inferior. Thus, age discrimination legislation should follow the example of the Race Relations Amendment Act 2000, which broke new ground by applying to all public services.

It is also important to determine who should fall within the scope of legislation. There is no doubt that different problems confront younger and older workers, and these interests might even conflict. However, age discrimination policies and legislation which deal only with older people run the risk of ignoring questions of inter-generational equity. Indeed, one of the major criticisms of the US legislation has been that it has permitted older people to capture a disproportionate share of social benefits.[95] Arguably, this is because of the focus in the US legislation on older people to the exclusion of younger people.

Thus, legislation should apply to all ages, while permitting or requiring provisions aimed particularly at benefiting a particular age group, where this is necessary for the promotion of their interest. This reflects the approach in the Directive, which permits exceptions for special treatment to promote a group which has previously been disadvantaged.

The Definition of Discrimination

The Directive defines discrimination according to the traditional distinction between direct and indirect discrimination.

Direct Discrimination

Direct discrimination is defined in the Framework Directive as occurring 'where one person is treated less favourably than another is has been or would be treated in a comparable situation on [grounds of age].'[96] Direct discrimination clearly has an important role to play in respect of age. As we have seen, many of the problems arise from explicit or blatant prejudice, including age limits.

Direct discrimination is grounded in the principle, discussed above, that likes should be treated alike, or that basic fairness requires consistent treatment. Consequently, it shares the weaknesses of the consistency principle (see above). First, it is merely a relative principle. There is no substantive standard: as long as the complainant is treated the same as a similarly situated comparator, there is no direct discrimination regardless of whether they are treated equally badly or equally well. Secondly, a comparator must be found. Inconsistent treatment can only be demonstrated by finding a similarly situated person who has been treated more favourably than the complainant. In the area of age discrimination, this is particularly problematic since age is a process rather than a fixed quality. How much of an age difference is necessary? Must it be a person much

---

[95] S Issacharoff and E Worth Harris, 'Is Age discrimination Really Age discrimination?' [1997] 72 *New York University Law Review* 780–840.

[96] Art 2(2).

younger or older, or will any age difference suffice?[97] Thirdly, direct discrimination is an all-or-nothing concept. If two people are considered different, then the equality principle is simply not triggered. Detrimental treatment is permitted even if it is disproportionate to the degree of difference. Similarly, if two people are considered alike, the principle is fully satisfied by equal treatment. This means, first, that differential impact goes unremedied, and second, that differential treatment will always be illegitimate, even if the treatment aims to promote a previously disadvantage group. This symmetry of direct discrimination rules out positive action *ab initio*.

These problems are not, however, insurmountable. They can be dealt with by moving away from a comparative approach. Instead, legislation should provide simply that it is discriminatory to subject a person to a detriment because of her age. This approach makes it unnecessary to identify a specific comparator who has been more favourably treated, following the trend set in relation to pregnancy[98] and disability[99] discrimination . It also makes it impossible to argue that equality can be achieved by subjecting others to the same detriment. In this way, direct discrimination is interpreted consistently with the dignity aim identified above. Finally, the definition is expressly asymmetrical, identifying detrimental treatment as the mischief to be addressed by the law and therefore by implication permitting positive treatment. It is therefore suggested that instead of using the direct discrimination definition in the Directive, legislation should simply make it unlawful to subject a person to a detriment on the grounds of her age.

Less easily resolved is the question of what limits should be placed on the prohibition against direct discrimination. As we have seen, there may be good reason to subject a person to a detriment on grounds of age. A minimum voting age is a good example. There are two possible legislative techniques to create such limits. The first is to permit any justification on a ground unrelated to age, leaving it to the court to decide if the proposed justification is sufficient. The second is to set out specific exceptions, for example, for positive action, or where age is a 'genuine occupational qualification'. Both techniques depend heavily on the standard of justification demanded by the court. If employers are permitted simply to assert that the age criterion is a business requirement, or the state could simply assert a public policy reason, the basic value of equal treatment could be undermined. On the other hand, if the court requires a high standard of proof, including a demonstration that there is no non-discriminatory alternative, this approach could form a useful means of distinguishing legitimate from illegitimate discrimination.

---

[97] In a recent case in the US, it was argued that the relevant comparator had to be under 40. The US Supreme Court rejected this argument, holding that as long as there was a significant age difference, discrimination could be proved by showing that the complainant had been treated less favourably than a person within the protected group.

[98] Case C–177/88 *Dekker* [1990] ECR I–394; Case C–32/93 *Webb* [1994] I–3567 (after the end of maternity leave, however, the comparative approach reasserts itself); *Brookes v Canada Safeway Ltd* (1989) 1 SCR 1219.

[99] *Clark v Novacold* [1999] 2 All ER 977 (CA).

The importance of the court's role in preventing such a risk from materialising can be seen from the experience of the US legislation, which permits age discrimination 'where age is a bona fide occupational qualification [BFOQ] reasonably necessary to the normal operation of the particular business.' In a recent case, the US Supreme Court rejected an employer's argument that compulsory retirement at age 60 of flight engineers was 'reasonably necessary' to the safe operation of the airline. The airline company argued that the requirement was a bona fide occupational qualification, 'reasonably necessary' to the safe operation of the airline on the grounds that the physiological and psychological capabilities of persons over age 60 could suddenly undergo a precipitous decline which could not be detected in time by medical science. Conflicting expert evidence on this question was presented by the parties. The Supreme Court emphasised that the standard of justification was a high one, of reasonable necessity, not reasonableness. Justice Stevens held that to establish a bona fide occupational qualification defence, an employer had to show more than that it was rational to believe that identification of unqualified persons cannot occur in an individualised basis. Instead, in order to establish that age is a legitimate proxy for safety-related job qualifications, an employer must prove it is impossible or highly impractical to deal with older employees on an individualised basis. Even in cases involving public safety, the Act did not permit the court to give complete deference to the employer's decision.[100]

Existing race and sex discrimination legislation does not provide for any justification for direct discrimination, whereas the equal pay and disability legislation permits such a defence. Limited exceptions are, however, provided in the form of a genuine occupational qualification. In the Directive, it is specifically stated that differences of treatment on grounds of age can be justified (Article 6). The contentious issue of mandatory retirement ages is dealt with in detail in subsequent chapters.[101] In respect of the more general principle, the standard of justification is set reasonably high: a derogation is only permitted if it is objectively and reasonably justified by a legitimate aim, and the means of achieving that aim are appropriate and necessary.[102] The Directive gives three examples of justifiable differences of treatment. The first caters for the need for affirmative action. Secondly, it may be justifiable to require workers to be over a given age, experience or seniority before they are given access to employment or advantages linked to employment. Thirdly, a maximum age for recruitment may be set if it is based on the training requirements of the employer, or the need for a reasonable period of employment before retirement. This last exception is particularly worrying, since both training and retirement age are in the hands of the employer.[103]

---

[100] *Western Airlines v Criswell* No 83–1545.
[101] Hepple ch 4, Friedman ch 8, below.
[102] Framework Directive, Art 6(1).
[103] For different ways of implementing the justification defence, see O'Cinneide, ch 9 below.

Indirect Discrimination

The principle of indirect discrimination performs an important complementary function to direct discrimination, capturing instances of apparently equal treatment which impact more heavily on people of a particular age. For example, a stress on formal qualifications might exclude a disproportionately large number of older people, who, as we have seen, tend to have fewer such qualifications. Such a set of criteria or practices would be indirectly discriminatory, unless it can be shown that formal qualifications are necessary for the position.

Despite its potential, existing indirect discrimination provisions in the sex and race discrimination legislation have proved difficult to operate, largely because of the complexity involved in measuring and assessing differential impact. Much litigation has been generated simply in respect of the comparison, since the figures can vary substantially depending on which groups are chosen. Should the comparison be between two age groups in the population as a whole or in the relevant workforce? Or should it between two age groups all of whom are qualified for the job? Once this has been settled, it is still necessary to decide whether a small difference in impact is sufficient, or whether the difference must be considerable.[104]

Some attempt has been made to resolve these issues in the Framework Directive, which defines indirect discrimination as having occurred where 'an apparently neutral provision, criterion or practice would put persons having . . . a particular age . . . at a particular disadvantage compared with other persons.'[105] It is notable that the Directive simply refers to the need to compare persons of 'a particular age' with 'other persons'. This seems to indicate that a comparison between persons of a particular group with any other person should suffice, and a particular disadvantage can be established if any detriment is proven. This would avoid much unnecessary litigation on the threshold question. The respondent then has the opportunity in the justification defence to show that the differential treatment was justifiable. However, the standard of justification is high. It is not enough for it to be convenient, appropriate or desirable. As the Directive provides, disparate impact is discriminatory unless it is 'objectively justified by a legitimate aim and the means of achieving that aim are appropriate and necessary . . .'.

Fears have been expressed that indirect discrimination could have absurd effects, since almost any criterion or practice can be potentially indirectly discriminatory. Can older people challenge a literacy requirement for a job on the grounds that older people are significantly more likely than younger people to be illiterate? The key, however, is job-relatedness. Indirect discrimination does not outlaw criteria which are job related. If a practice or condition can be shown

---

[104] *R v Secretary of State ex p Seymour Smith and Perez* (No.1) [1994] IRLR 448 (DC); [1995] IRLR 464 (CA); [1997] IRLR 315 (HL); [1999] IRLR 253 (ECJ); (No.2) [2000] IRLR 263 (HL).
[105] Art 2(b).

to be necessary for the job then it passes muster. There are in fact advantages to both business and the state to show that the criterion is necessary for the business or to further public policy aims. The threat of an indirect discrimination claim might have the positive effect of requiring employers to revisit their criteria for selection or promotion to be sure that they in fact produce the best person for the job. A requirement of formal qualifications might exclude those with relevant experience and thereby preclude the employer from finding the best person for the job. For example, a degree in media studies might be a criterion for eligibility for a job as a journalist, excluding older workers who were educated before such degrees were available. It could well be shown that such a degree is not a necessary requirement for a job as a journalist.

Thus, indirect discrimination should be defined simply so that a prima facie case is established if an apparently neutral practice has a particularly detrimental effect on an individual. The case can be rebutted by clear evidence of job relatedness.

Proportionality

While most statutory discrimination statutes rely on the concepts of direct or indirect discrimination, constitutional and human rights documents tend to use more open-ended notions of equality. This requires the courts to create principles for distinguishing legitimate from illegitimate instance of unequal treatment. To do this, many courts have developed a proportionality analysis. This approach acknowledges that not all distinctions are discriminatory, even if based on a prohibited ground. Instead, the aim is to provide a mechanism to distinguish between invidious discrimination and appropriate differentiation. This is done by a means—end test. The respondent must first show that it has instituted differential treatment for a legitimate purpose, and second, that the differentiation is appropriate to achieve that purpose.

This approach is well developed in the case law of both the US and Canada, and most relevantly for our purposes, by the European Court of Human Rights (ECHR) in interpreting Article 14 ECHR, the equality guarantee. This has been formulated by the Court of Human Rights as follows:

> A difference in treatment is discriminatory if it has no reasonable justification: that is if it does not pursue a legitimate aim, or there is not a reasonable relationship of proportionality between the means employed and the aim sought to be realised.[106]

Proportionality can in some respects be a weaker test than the one above, as even direct discrimination can be justified. But it also has some important strengths. Instead of being an 'all-or-nothing' approach, proportionality permits treatment to differ according to the degree of difference in the subjects.

---

[106] *Belgian Linguistice Case* (No. 2) Series A No 6 (1968) 1 EHRR 252 at para 10, *Marckx v Belgium* Series A No 31 (1979) 2 EHRR 330 at para 33.

Thus, while it may be appropriate to treat two people differently according to their age, the differential treatment must not create a burden which is disproportionately large. In addition, it is asymmetric. To treat a group in a disadvantageous way could be disproportionate, while to give them extra benefits might be appropriate in order to redress past discrimination or to achieve legitimate government objectives.

Proportionality is particularly appropriate in respect of age, where distinctions are not necessarily invidious. As Mr Justice La Forest of the Canadian Supreme Court put it: 'The truth is that, while we must guard against laws having an unnecessary deleterious impact on the aged, based on inaccurate assumptions about the effects of age on ability, there are often solid grounds for imparting benefits to one age group over another in the development of broad social schemes and in allocating benefits.'[107] For example, in a recent case,[108] the Canadian Federal Court of Appeal rejected a claim of age discrimination arising from a rule limiting eligibility for credit from a 'goods and service' tax (equivalent to VAT) to those aged 19 and over. The adoption of the age of 19 as a proxy for dependency had a sufficiently rational relationship with the legitimate state aim, that of protecting those on lower income against regressive taxation. In short, held the court, this legislative provision created a distinction which was not discriminatory.[109]

However, as noted above, proportionality is an elastic concept, and its intensity depends on whether restricting equality will only be acceptable if it is necessary, in the sense that there is no other alternative, or whether a rational explanation will be good enough. In the field of age discrimination, the courts have in practice been more deferent to policy-makers than in other areas, such as race discrimination. The danger then is that courts will be too ready to accept a proffered justification.

The ease with which the constraints of equality can be diluted is demonstrated by contrasting the reasoning of the majority and the minority of the Canadian Supreme Court in the important case *McKinney v University of Guelph*.[110] In this case, the applicants challenged, first, the mandatory retirement age set by the university and second, the provision in the Human Rights Code excluding people over 65 from protection against age discrimination in employment. The majority held that although both these measures were prima facie discriminatory because they distinguished between people on grounds of their age, they were justified. Applying a rationality standard, the majority concluded that the universities had a reasonable basis for concluding that manda-

---

[107] *McKinney v University of Guelph* [1990] 3 SCR 229 at 297.
[108] *Lister v Her Majesty the Queen* [1995] 1 FC 130.
[109] Contrast *R v M* (1995) 30 CRR (2d) 112 an age of consent of 18 for anal intercourse conducted between two consenting persons in private was discriminatory on ground of age when the age of consent of other sexual activity in Canada was 14 years.
[110] [1990] 3 SCR 229.

tory retirement was appropriate to achieve their objectives, namely academic excellence. Staff renewal was a vital means to achieve academic excellence, ensuring as it did an infusion of new people and new ideas and a better mix of young and old.

This can be contrasted with the dissent. Ginsburg J expressly considered whether an element of human dignity was at issue. Were academics being required to retire at age 65 on the unarticulated premise that with age comes increasing incompetence and decreasing intellectual capacity? The answer was clearly yes. The measures were therefore prima facie discriminatory. Nor did they constitute a justifiable limit on equality. Applying a necessity standard, Ginsburg J emphasised that it was not sufficient to argue that there were limited resources. In a period of economic restraint, competition over scarce resources will almost always be a factor in the government distribution of benefits. Moreover, she stressed, recognition of the constitutional rights and freedoms of some will in such circumstances almost inevitably carry a price which must be borne by others. To treat such price as a justification for denying the constitutional rights of the appellants would completely vitiate the purpose of entrenching rights and freedoms. Although she acknowledged that in some circumstances the court should defer to legislative distribution of resources, this was not one. Young academics were not the kind of 'vulnerable' group contemplated in those cases applying a relaxed standard of minimal impairment. By denying protection to older workers, she concluded, the Code has the effect of reinforcing the stereotype that older employees are no longer useful members of the labour force and their services may therefore be freely and arbitrarily dispensed with.

Given the resource implications and the need for judicial deference to State policy, the proportionality analysis may well be appropriate for challenging state policy outside of employment. However, the justification should be based on a necessity test rather than one of mere rationality. This is not to argue that decisions on resource allocation should be shifted from governments to courts. Instead, governments should be required to take into account the rights of people of all ages in coming to decisions on resource allocation. Any decision which unduly burdens a particular age group needs to be justified to a high standard. That is, the burden is only justifiable if it serves a legitimate government interest and there are no alternatives with a lower burden.

Positive Duties

The anti-discrimination model used in the directive is based on a traditional model, which sees the discrimination as a set of individual acts of prejudice, and the role of the law as being to establish who is at fault and to require compensation to be paid to the victim. Experience of sex and race discrimination has shown that this model is of limited utility, in that it is only responds to ad hoc individual complaints and cannot bring about more far-reaching change. In the race relations field this has now been complemented by a a positive duty to promote equality, rather than just to refrain from discriminating.

Recognising that societal discrimination extends well beyond individual acts of prejudice, the duty goes beyond compensating identified victims and aims at restructuring institutions. Correspondingly, the duty-bearer is not the person 'at fault' or responsible for creating the problem. Instead, the duty-bearer is identified as the body in the best position to perform this duty. Nor is it left to the victim to initiate action. Instead, duty bearers are responsible both for identifying the problem (eg by monitoring) and for participating in its eradication. Public bodies are often in the best position to carry this responsibility, but suitably framed, it is possible too to impose positive duties on private employers. This approach means too that a wider definition of inequality can be used than that in the traditional direct-indirect discrimination formula. Positive duties need not be triggered only by proof of acts of individual prejudice, nor of unjustifiable disparate impact as a result of a practice or condition. Instead, they arise from evidence of structural inequality, such as chronic under-representation of people in a particular age group in particular types of work or positions of power. Social exclusion of older people, for example, might trigger a duty on the state to implement policies to remedy it.

A particularly important dimension of positive duties is their potential to encourage participation by affected groups in the decision-making process itself. Because the duty is prospective, and can be fashioned to fit the problem at hand, it is not a static duty, but requires a continuing process of diagnosing the problem, working out possible responses, monitoring the effectiveness of strategies, and modifying those strategies as required. If participation is built in as a central aspect of such duties, not only is it likely that strategies will be more successful, but the very process of achieving equality becomes a democratic one. Thus, positive duties further the aim of participatory democracy identified above.

Positive duties to promote equality are being actively developed in several jurisdictions. At EU level, this has taken the form of 'mainstreaming' of gender equality, so that gender is one of the factors taken into account in every policy and executive decision.[111] In Northern Ireland, legislation introduced in 1989 imposed a positive duty on employers to take measures to achieve fair participation of Protestant and Catholic employees in their workforces.[112] The Northern Ireland Act 1998 mainstreams equality by providing that public authorities must have 'due regard to the need to promote equality of opportun-

---

[111] *Incorporating Equal Opportunities for Women and Men into all Community Policies and Activities* Commission Communication COM(96) final; see generally T Rees, *Mainstreaming Equality in the European Union: Education, Training and Labour Market Policies* (London, Routledge, 1998).

[112] Fair Employment Act 1989, now contained in Fair Employment and Treatment (Northern Ireland) Order (FETO) 1998, Part VII; C McCrudden, 'Mainstreaming Equality in the Governance of Northern Ireland' (1999) 22:4 *Fordham International Law Journal* 1696.

ity' in carrying out all their functions.[113] Most recently the Race Relations Amendment Act 2000 (RRAA 2000), which came into force in April 2001, imposes a general statutory duty on a wide range of public authorities not just to eliminate unlawful racial discrimination, but to 'promote equality of opportunity and good relations between persons of different racial groups'.[114] As well as the general duty, the Home Secretary is given the power to impose specific duties on listed public authorities 'for the purpose of ensuring the better performance of the general duty'.[115] These specific duties can be tailor-made to meet the requirements of the particular public authority.

It is submitted that positive duties are the most appropriate way for public authorities to advance age equality. We have seen that there are many interrelated institutional factors which entrench age discrimination, including such wide-ranging factors as the structure of incentives in benefit and pensions systems, the image of older people portrayed in the media and in advertising, the absence of formal qualifications and the lack of appropriate lifelong education, and the strategic priorities of the NHS. If the aims of enhancing individual choice, protecting dignity and facilitating social inclusion are to be met, public bodies must play a role in actively promoting equality. Such a duty need not necessarily take the same form as that in the RRAA 2000. In particular, a focus on increasing representation in a workforce or elsewhere would not, as argued above, be appropriate for age discrimination, where the problems are different. Instead, a positive duty would need to be fashioned to meet the identified causes of disadvantage due to age according to the principles of enhancing individual choice, protecting dignity and facilitating social inclusion.

Positive duties are particularly well suited to the promotion of social inclusion, as part of the overall goal of achieving the equal right of all, regardless of age, to participate as full and valued members of society. Barriers to social inclusion include inadequate transport facilities and lack of access to telephones. Positive duties need to pinpoint such barriers and work towards dismantling them. More accessible, cheaper and more flexible modes of public transport, for example, would go far towards relieving social exclusion. Proactive measures on health are also vital to achieving this aim. Winter deaths of older people as a result of fuel poverty is a paradigm example of an aspect of ill health which could easily be avoided. Positive duties could also facilitate the care already generously given by the family and friends of older people. Many older people are looked after by their adult children, usually their daughters who have family and work commitments of their own. The introduction of family leave for carers of older people would greatly assist their efforts, as would the financial

---

[113] Northern Ireland Act 1998, s 75; and see C McCrudden, 'The Equal Opportunity Duty in the Northern Ireland Act 1998: An Analysis' in *Equal Rights and Human Rights—Their Role in Peace Building* (Committee on the Administration of Justice (Northern Ireland), 1999), 11–23.

[114] Race Relations Act 1976, s 71(1) (as amended).

[115] Race Relations Amendment Act 2000, s 71(2)–(3).

assistance provided by the recent introduction of vouchers with which the older person can purchase assistance, giving the carer a break.

It is therefore proposed that any legislation on age discrimination should include a positive duty on public bodies to promote equality. In order to avoid a proliferation of definitions of a 'public body', the definition in the RRAA 2000, which lays down a list of public bodies, which can be expanded by the Home Secretary, should be followed. In particular, the public body should remain responsible for complying with the general duty even if it has contracted out some of its functions to private or voluntary organisations. Crucial too is that the positive duty should place the onus of identifying the discrimination or inequality on the public body itself. This requires an authority to consider the impact of policies on people of different age groups, and actively devise programmes, such as education, public promotions, primary health care and retirement policies, which promote the interests, particularly of older people. As in the RRAA 2000, this duty should include the duty to prepare an Equality Scheme setting out these aims and objectives. The inclusion of affected people in decision-making is also of major importance.

In the private sector, there are equally good arguments for instituting proactive duties, although again, the nature of the duty would need to be fashioned to meet the identified problems. Positive duties could in fact be seen as providing benefits for business. Instead of waiting for individual litigation, employers are better served by taking proactive action. The removal of age limits and other express criteria on age would not only forestall damaging and expensive litigation, but would open up the whole range of talents to employers. Pre-emptive action is even more important in respect of indirect discrimination. As we have seen, indirect discrimination only prohibits criteria which are not strictly job related. Employers who have screened their job descriptions and promotion and training policy to ensure that they are age related would then be relatively insulated from litigation. More importantly, they will ensure that they are not excluding talented workers from jobs or training by criteria or practices which are not necessary for the job. The positive duty could also go further than simply pre-empting challenges based on direct or indirect discrimination. It could require employers to positively accommodate older or younger people, for example by instituting flexible retirement ages. This is similar to the duty to make reasonable accommodation, already found in the Disability Discrimination Act. For all these positive duties, detailed guidance, both in the form of a Code of Practice, and active promotion by the relevant government department, is essential to institute the deep-seated change in culture required.

Positive duties in the private sector should not be limited to employers. They should apply equally to private contractors providing public services. For example, extensive privatisation of transport services has meant that the only means of promoting change within the transport sector is to ensure that private providers are under a duty to promote age equality. The Department of the Environment, Transport and the Regions has recognised this in its report on older people's transport needs, which recommends the incorporation of transport operators into the total transport strategy. This would include the provision of more accessible buses (already required under the Disability Discrimination Act 1995) and staff training. Nor are these simply recommendations for good practice. The report suggests that local authorities should monitor customer service performance on contracted services and implement penalties on operators that fail to meet the agreed minimum standard.[116]

Nor are these proposals as radical as they might at first seem. Most of these points are already made in the Code of Practice on Age Discrimination in Employment. In the introduction to the Code it is stressed that employment decisions based on age 'are both short-sighted and unfair. Unfair because they can prevent talented individuals from being full players in the labour market. Short-sighted because they can restrict a company's growth and potential.'[117] In many respects, it is an excellent example of 'mainstreaming', encouraging employers to avoid using age limits in job adverts, to think strategically about where advertisements are placed, to use a mixed age interviewing panel and ensure interviewers are trained to avoid prejudices and stereotypes. Age should not be a barrier to training; and different learning styles and needs are addressed. In redundancy, it is stressed that age should not be the sole criterion for redundancy, and flexible options such as part-time working should be considered. Similarly, retirement schemes should be based on business needs and phased retirement should be used, where possible to allow employees to alter the balance of their working and personal lives and prepare for full retirement.

Other examples of positive duties are also in place. The 2001 EU Employment report stresses that every young person should be offered a new start within six months of unemployment and every older person within a year. Within the UK, this has been put into practice through the establishment of various 'New Deal' schemes, offering targeted training, personal advice and help with job-seeking, as well as a small cash grant to make up for loss of benefits, and in-working training grants.. Notably such schemes specifically differentiate between age categories, offering different packages to workers over 50, from those available to workers between 18 and 24, and again those over 25. Thus there is a New Deal 50 Plus, a New Deal for Young Workers, a New Deal 25 plus, and a New Deal for Disabled People. This is a good example of a case in which express differentiation is an appropriate way of achieving substantive equality of opportunity.

An even stronger example of a positive strategy to promote equality is the NHS Plan, published in July 2000 and the corresponding National Service Framework for Older People, published in March 2001. The NHS plan has a chapter devoted specifically to older people. As well as making available additional funding for older people, the plan specifically commits the Government

---

[116] DETR, *Older People: their Transport Needs and Requirements*.
[117] Code of Practice on Age Diversity in Employment, para 6.

to take positive steps to eliminate ageism and promote the autonomy, dignity, security and independence of older people. These objectives are taken forward in detail in the National Service Framework (NSF). The NSF contains some of the crucial components of a successful positive action strategy. First, it encourages participation. Thus it requires every NHS council and council with social services responsibilities to ensure that older people are properly represented in decision-making.[118] Secondly, it requires transparency of decision-making through the implementation of local resuscitation policies. Thirdly, the plan goes beyond the removal of discrimination to the positive promotion of equality. This includes extending access to services, notably by involving older people in agreeing their own personal care plan. It also provides extra resources to promote independence through intermediate care, noting that this could save other resources by freeing up beds in acute wards.

The substance of these plans is of course potentially controversial. For example, in the commitment to remove arbitrary policies based on age alone, there is no express definition of what is arbitrary. This raises the question of the distinction between rational and arbitrary policies, demonstrating the importance of explicating the aims and meaning of equality, discussed above. In addition, the question of whether the policies proposed will in fact improve older people's position remains controversial. The answers to these are beyond the scope of this chapter. What is important is that the commitment to positive duties already exists. However, what remains unresolved is the question of compliance. It is to compliance therefore that the final part of this chapter is devoted.

ENFORCEMENT

There has been a general reluctance to translate the commitment to removing age discrimination into legally enforceable duties. It is for this reason that the Labour Government in its early years opposed a legislative solution and opted instead for the non-enforceable Code of Practice on Age Diversity in Employment. The NHS Plan and the National Service Framework for Older People give little attention to compliance, relying primarily on transparency measures and monitoring. [119] Opponents to enforceability argue that much time and money will be wasted, by individuals bringing unmeritorious claims and forcing a defensive attitude in respondents. What is needed is a cultural change, rather than a set of individual remedies, and this, it is argued, is better achieved through a promotional approach based on information and encouragement. So far as health, education and social services are concerned, opposition has been

---

[118] *National Service Framework*, 15.

[119] For example, the NHS plan requires NHS organisations to include in their clinical audit programme compliance with resuscitation policies, while progress should be assessed by the Commission for Health Improvement.

based on the reluctance to allow courts to second guess policy-makers' decisions on the allocation of resources.

However, the promotional approach has not proved effective. A recent survey of 800 companies indicated that only 1 per cent had introduced change as a direct result of the Code of Practice on Age Diversity in Employment, and only 4 per cent thought that future change was likely. The main reason given was the belief that company policy or practice already met government guidelines. By contrast, a study of British residents over 50 found that a large majority believed that employers discriminated against older workers.[120] This contrasts strikingly with research showing that almost nine out of ten firms have developed or revised their employment policies as a direct result of the Disability Discrimination Act 1995.[121] This debate has now been overtaken, in the employment sphere, by the Directive, which requires enforceable legislation on age by 2006.[122] There is also a strong case for enforceability outside of the employment field: it has been clearly demonstrated that, while it is important to harness the positive goodwill and energy of major actors, some enforcement mechanism must be available to keep all actors in line.[123]

What sort of enforcement is therefore appropriate? It is argued here that compliance measures need to draw on the strengths of the promotional approach, aiming to facilitate cultural change through cooperation, participation of all affected parties, and proactive measures. However, these requirements must not be a matter of goodwill alone, but be backed up by appropriate sanctions. This suggests that sole reliance on individual litigation is inappropriate. Not only does this created a heavy burden on the individual litigant, it also prompts a defensive attitude in respondents, and leaves the courts to elaborate principles in a fragmentary and ad hoc manner. The problems of sole reliance on individual litigation can be seen in the experience of the US. Much of the criticism of the operation of the ADEA has focused on the fact that litigation has largely benefited well-off white men. This, it is argued, undermines the rationale of anti-discrimination legislation, which is to redress disadvantage in society.[124] However, on closer inspection, it can be seen that this is largely due to the model of enforcement. ADEA claims centre almost entirely on individual litigation, with a jury trial and the prospect of high damages awards. In practice, therefore the claim is only available to those who have the financial and emotional resources to pursue the claim in the first place. The individual litigation model is also unsuitable as a sole compliance mechanism in other areas such as the

---

[120] (2000) 93 Equal Opportunities Review 8.

[121] Ibid.

[122] Legislation should be in place by 2003, but the Government may apply to extend the deadline to December 2006 subject to a reporting requirement.

[123] B Hepple, M Coussey and T Choudhury, *Equality: A New Framework Report of the Independent Review of the Enforcement of UK Anti-Discrimination Legislation* (Oxford, Hart, 2000) para 3.3; Rees, above n 110, 36.

[124] S Issacharoff and E Worth Harris, 'Is Age discrimination Really Age discrimination?' [1997] 72 *New York University Law Review* 780–840.

delivery of public services, particularly because it involves courts in complex distributive questions which they are not necessarily equipped to resolve. This is particularly true for positive duties, because of their proactive and policy-oriented nature.

The aim then is to secure compliance through cooperation, by building mainstreaming into existing decision-making procedures. Proper monitoring and progress reports function both as a discipline on decision-making and a means to ensure transparency. However, voluntary cooperation is not sufficient. A specific responsibility for auditing progress on age equality needs to be established, initially in existing audit mechanisms, such as the Commission for Health Improvement, or the DTI, and ultimately, in an independent commission.[125] As a very last resort power, the commission should be able to issue an enforcement notice, and if necessary apply to a tribunal for an order requiring compliance.[126] Compliance mechanisms provided to enforce the new duty on public authorities introduced by the RRAA 2000 reflect this approach. The Commission for Racial Equality (CRE) is empowered to issue a compliance notice to any public authority that fails to fulfil a specific duty to promote race equality which has been imposed by order under the statute. The notice may require the authority to comply with the duty and provide information to the CRE of steps taken to do so. If the commission considers that a person has not complied with any requirement of the notice within three months it may apply to a designated county for an order requiring the person to comply with the requirement of the notice. The Audit Commission is already required to mainstream the Act into its inspections of local authorities and from April 2003 will do so systematically. It would also be subject to the duty to promote race equality.

It can be seen from this that a proactive duty cannot be operated without a commission. The Framework Directive does not require member states to establish a commission, by contrast with the race directive, which does. The Department for Work and Pensions has taken active steps to promote age diversity, and has undertaken various monitoring exercises. It is possible to argue that this function should be retained within government. However, it is clear on closer inspection that an independent body, with clear powers, would be more effective.

There is currently a vigorous debate on the question of whether there should be a Single Equality Commission and what powers it should have.[127] For the present, the Government has stated that it has no plans to create separate commissions for religion, sexual orientation or age, or to give powers to existing commissions. It is crucial that whatever institutional machinery is chosen includes powers in respect of age discrimination. There should be at least three

---

[125] Hepple, Coussey and Choudhury, above n 122, para 3.4.
[126] Ibid, paras 3.21–3.22.
[127] C O'Cinneide, *A Single Equality Body: Lessons from abroad* (Manchester: EOC Working Papers Series no 4, 2002); Cabinet Office, *Towards Equality and Diversity: Implementing the Employment and Race Directives* (Consultation document) (London 2001).

functions associated with age. First, it should have the power to support indi-vidual in litigation where appropriate. Secondly, it should be responsible for promoting equality by bringing about a change in culture through education and promotion. This is allied to the third function, which is to assist public bod-ies and employers to promote equality within their institutions or establish-ments. The Commission should have a duty to produce relevant codes of practice, based on close consultation with responsible bodies. Compliance mechanisms should, at the first stage, consist of non-adversarial advice and assistance from the Commission with a corresponding duty on the respondent to cooperate. The Commission should be able to intervene of its own initiative, thus inviting a strategic approach instead of an ad hoc series of actions. Particularly important is the fact that power is specifically directed at a practice of discrimination rather than a particular discriminatory act against an individ-ual. The intervention should be an interactive process, during which the Commission aims to secure a change in discriminatory practices through dis-cussion, negotiation and conciliation. The aim is to secure change through cooperation. For example, age discrimination in the NHS might prompt inter-vention by the Commission, rather than an individual challenge. This would mean that the Commission could enter into detailed discussion with all the rele-vant actors, to gain a fully rounded picture in a non-adversarial setting, and attempt to work through alternative strategies rather than the 'win-or-lose' response in individual litigation. As a last resort, and after a set period of time, the Commission should be able to issue a compliance notice and eventually apply to court for an order, in a parallel set of procedures to that under the RRAA 2000.

CONCLUSION

I have argued that the function of equality is to enhance the dignity, autonomy and participation of all age groups. The impetus from Europe offers a unique opportunity to produce 'state of the art' legislation, drawing on the experience of existing discrimination law and extending its frontiers. It is to be hoped that legislators and policy-makers will have the vision and the political courage to use the opportunity. The third age could indeed be a golden age.

4

Age Discrimination in Employment: Implementing the Framework Directive 2000/78/EC

BOB HEPPLE QC

WHY LEGISLATION AGAINST AGE DISCRIMINATION IN EMPLOYMENT IS NEEDED

THERE IS A danger that legislation against age discrimination in employment will be seen as simply another burden imposed by the EU. It is therefore important to reiterate two points. First, action against age discrimination is an appropriate and necessary aspect of UK employment policy. Secondly, such action cannot rely solely on a voluntary code and other promotional measures, but must be supported by an effective, efficient and equitable regulatory framework . This framework should be aimed at encouraging personal responsibility and self-generating efforts to promote age equality at work.

In this chapter, I explore the reasons why age discrimination legislation would contribute to the Government's employment policy objectives as well as protecting the dignity of individuals. I consider the respective roles of voluntary measures and of legislation in delivering equality in training and employment and ask whether the terms of the EU directive are fit for purpose, demonstrating a number of ways in which it is defective. Finally, I consider the way in which UK legislation needs to be drafted and enforced, including provisions on compulsory retirement and unfair dismissal, if it is to be effective.

Employment Policy

Increasing the Participation of People aged over 50 in the Labour Force

One of the key objectives of government policy is to increase employment opportunities for older workers. This is considered to be essential in order to meet the challenge of longer life spans, longer retirement, and the decline in pension provision by some employers.[1] The good news is that while there is an ageing population, senescence (the process of deterioration with age) is being retarded by developments in medicine, diet and lifestyle.[2] We are generally able to work longer, and so to contribute to the economic growth which will be necessary in order to sustain the costs of supporting ourselves and others in 'old age',[3] itself a moveable concept with enormous variations between individuals.

For a greater number of older people to be in employment, however, the tendency towards early retirement will have to be reversed and there will have to be improved opportunities for older people to work beyond current retirement ages. Widespread early withdrawal from the labour market as a result of restructuring in the 1980s and early 1990s exacerbated the problem of pensioner poverty. In 1979 84 per cent of men between 50 and the state pension age were employed; by 1993, this had fallen to 64 per cent.[4] Since 1993 there has been some improvement in the employment rates of men aged 50–64, but absolute employment rates remain 20 per cent lower for men in this group than for those aged 25–49, a far larger gap than in 1979.

There is some evidence that the processes leading to increased labour market withdrawal among older men are abating: from 1993–2001, the employment rate for men 50 plus increased by 6.1 percentage points, significantly higher than the rate for men aged 25–49. This may be due to factors such as the shift from manufacturing employment, the move towards defined contribution pension schemes, a run down of pension surpluses which were used to fund early retirement schemes, changes in public policy aimed at increasing labour market participation (such as the New Deal for over-50s), and a tighter labour market making it difficult to sustain discriminatory practices.[5]

Men are, however, still entering the labour market *later* and leaving *earlier* than in previous generations, thus reducing their pension entitlements. While women will continue to have *longer* working lives than before, so enhancing their capacity to accumulate pension entitlements in their own right, this is likely to be offset by the concentration of women in low-paid, part-time and temporary jobs without adequate occupational pensions.[6] The result is that at least a significant minority of older men and women will not have accumulated adequate resources across their working lives. On present trends, there is likely to be increasing polarisation among the elderly, with growing inequalities

---

[1] *Simplicity, security and choice: working and saving for retirement*, Department for Work and Pensions, December 2002, Cm 5677 [Pensions Green Paper], esp ch 6 .

[2] See Sir John Grimley Evans, above ch 2.

[3] Cf Phil Mullan, *The Imaginary Time Bomb* (London, Palgrave Macmillan, 2002), who argues that economic growth will be more than sufficient to provide support for an ageing population.

[4] For further details see R Brooks, S Regan and P Robinson, *A New Contract for Retirement* (London, IPPR, 2002) 6–9; *Winning the Generation Game* (Report of the Performance and Innovation Unit, April 2000), ch 3; and Sandra Fredman, above, ch 3.

[5] Brooks et al (above n 4).

[6] See Green Paper on Pensions, ch 7.

between those with full 40-year work histories, who have acquired pension rights and housing wealth, and those who have not.[7]

'Two nations in retirement' (in Richard Titmuss' phrase) will impose costs that are socially and economically unacceptable. First, there will have to be a substantial inter-generational transfer to support those without adequate resources; secondly, if that kind of transfer is not provided through public or private financial institutions, the state will have to provide a substantial social security safety net. The UK—like other developed countries—needs to act now to avoid severe social and economic disruption.[8] This aim is reflected in Recital (8) of the Framework Employment Directive 2000/78/EC which identifies the need 'to pay particular attention to supporting older workers, in order to increase their participation in the labour force'.

Reducing Youth Unemployment

At the other end of the job market are those young people who are unemployed. In 2001, 16.3 per cent of young people aged between 15 and 24 in the EU were not in work . For this generation, unemployment is both an individual and social tragedy. For individuals, when there is no work or career after leaving school, there can be demoralisation, dependence on welfare and antisocial behaviour. The absence of work reduces the opportunities for young people to gain the skills and experience required for secure careers and also their capacity to accumulate resources for later life. From society's viewpoint, this imposes heavy economic costs and social disorder. For this reason, action against youth unemployment is a key feature of European employment strategy under the Employment Title inserted in the EC Treaty by the Treaty of Amsterdam.

Promoting a Skilled, Trained and Adaptable Labour Force

This aim of UK employment policy is reflected in Recital (7) of the Directive. At the level of the individual enterprise it is known as the Business Case for Age Diversity. This case is made in the Introduction to the Code on *Age Diversity in Employment* (1999). In the Preface the Minister states that 'to base employment decisions on pre-conceived ideas about age, rather than on skills and abilities is to waste the talents of a large part of the population.' There is now a mass of evidence from employers that by removing unnecessary age-related criteria, they have a wider choice of applicants with experience and expertise. They are able to minimise staff turnover because older people stay longer, to increase

---

[7] Mara Evandrou and Jane Falkingham, 'Looking back to look forward: lessons from four cohorts for ageing in the 21st century', *Population Trends* 99 (Spring 2000) 27–36.

[8] Mrs M Hodge, the Minister, told the House of Commons Select Committee on Education and Employment that 'the economy will not survive without using the talents and experience of older workers': Seventh Report, Session 2000–2001, para 12.

productivity by building a multi-skilled workforce, and to improve customer satisfaction and the organisation's image.[9]

However, older people can only contribute in this way if they have opportunities both for re-skilling and for lifelong learning. Older people are less likely than younger ones to have formal qualifications and more likely to have poor numeracy and literacy skills. They tend to have been in their last job for a long time and may have very specific job experience and obsolete skills; are less likely to participate in training schemes for the unemployed (although this has recently increased); and the kind of training they receive is not always well-adapted to their needs.[10] Employers are reluctant to invest in training employees whose working lives will be too short for them to recoup their investment. If the employment of older people is not to be confined to unskilled and semi-skilled jobs, active state-led training policies are essential in order to help people make transitions in the labour market.

Age Discrimination

Discrimination related to age seriously undermines these objectives of employment policy. There has until recently been a lack of robust evidence as to the extent of this discrimination. A starting point is the pattern that emerges from statistics of labour force participation. From this it may be possible to discern causes of detachment from the labour market. We have already seen that these statistics indicate the low participation rates of older men in the labour market (above). Stephen Fothergill has shown that there are principally two groups of older men detached from the labour market. The slightly smaller group is typified by middle class men with access to pensions who have left work largely through choice. The majority is characterised by men who have been subjected to compulsory redundancy.[11] Restructuring in the face of two major recessions involved a substantial fall-out of older craft and manual workers from declining manufacturing sectors. During the early 1980s and early 1990s downsizing was achieved by encouraging early retirement often funded by occupational pension schemes. Workers took such opportunities, sometimes reluctantly, and then found that they could not get another job. Older manual workers who used to move down to less strenuous jobs in the same or another organisation found themselves not working at all. They are also reluctant to take low-paid work where it exists because this would jeopardise their benefits or increase their tax liabilities. At the other end of the age scale, youth unemployment rates in the UK

---

[9] See eg Third Age Employment Network Briefing, 'Key Facts on Age Diversity and Employment' (October 2001), and *Equal Opportuinities Review*, No 100 (November/December 2001), 27–35.

[10] *Winning the Generation Game*, 37–39.

[11] Annex 1 to the Seventh Report of the House of Commons Select Committee on Employment (above n 8).

in the period 1995–2000 have remained significantly higher than overall unemployment rates, indicating structural problems relating to the integration of young persons into the labour market.[12]

The statistics also indicate that the rise in female participation in the labour force has not benefited older women to the same extent as younger ones. Women aged 30 are nearly 50 per cent more likely to be employed than 20 years ago. For women aged 50 the growth has been more modest and for those approaching pension age participation has remained stable. Moreover, women are less likely than men to return to a job after a period out of work because of lack of opportunities combined with greater family responsibilities than men.[13]

The conclusion to be drawn is that loss of traditional job opportunities for men in former industrial sectors, the inadequacy of post-school training and work experience for young people, and the absence of opportunities for older women seeking 'family-friendly' working patterns is a substantial cause of detachment from the labour force. This lack of opportunity is in part due to the disappearance of traditional jobs and the lack of flexible working arrangements for older people.

Another substantial reason for detachment from the labour force is age discrimination. There is now no shortage of surveys of age-discriminatory employment practices. Most of these relate to older people and are based on subjective accounts of the extent to which they believe that they have experienced age discrimination, or accounts by managers. Among the findings are: 55 per cent of managers said that they used age as a criterion for recruitment, and 60 per cent said that they focused on older workers when restructuring.[14] One in four people aged between 50 and 69 claimed to have experienced age discrimination at some point in their lives;[15] 23 out of 25 older persons looking for a job gave up after 12 months because of the lack of opportunities;[16] up to 41 per cent of job adverts had age limits;[17] the likelihood of receiving employer-based training peaks in a worker's thirties and forties and then declines;[18] and less than 10 per cent of all training costs is spent on the older one-third of people of working age.[19] Many young people also believe that they have been the victims of age discrimination, although managers frequently claim that it is the lack of training

---

[12] *Employment in Europe 2001: Recent Trends and Prospects*, European Commission, Employment and Social Affairs (July 2001) 26.

[13] *Winning the Generation Game*, at 16.

[14] Institute of Management Survey, reported in *Labour Market Trends*, 1996, 195; see generally, M Sargent, *Age Discrimination in Employment* (Institute of Employment Rights, 1999) ch 2.

[15] National Opinion Polls: Social and Political; an earlier survey by Austin Knight found that 33% of a sample of 1,000 had experienced age discrimination; *Characteristics of Older Workers*, DfEE Research Report RR45 (1998) found that 7.2% of those between 50 and 54 believed they had been discriminated against because of age.

[16] Sheffield Hallam University study.

[17] Carnegie Third Age Programme.

[18] *Characteristics of Older Workers*, DfEE Research Report RR45 (1998) 68.

[19] Carnegie Third Age Programme.

and experience of young persons which is the principal reason for not employing more of them.

There are many reasons for age discrimination against older people. First, there is widespread reluctance (especially among younger managers) to appoint older employees because of negative stereotypes of them as being hard to train, lacking creativity, over-cautious, unable to adapt to new technology and inflexible.[20] In fact, chronological age is not a good predictor of performance.[21] Variations in productivity within a given age group have been found to be wider than variations between one age group and another.[22] Secondly, it often suits both management and trade unions to achieve downsizing by 'buying off' older workers with redundancy packages, while preserving the jobs of younger workers. This is partly due to the widely held belief that those who have had a 'fair innings' should make way for others,[23] and partly because these packages favour older workers on the basis of age and seniority. Thirdly, managers have in the past tended to believe that it is in the interests of their organisations to formalise internal labour markets by using age and seniority-based remuneration and promotion systems; systems which are now being replaced by performance-based reviews which rely heavily on subjective judgments. While removing overt age discrimination, these reviews are open to prejudice and manipulation. Finally, there is the fact that age discrimination—unlike race, gender and disability discrimination—is not unlawful (and, indeed, is built into the institutions of the labour market and pension schemes). This encourages the perception that it is legitimate and fair.

Voluntary Measures and the Role of Legislation

In recent years a range of important government measures has been put in place to promote increased participation of older workers. These include steps to remove incentives in pension and social security schemes which encourage early retirement; the movement towards flexible pension ages; and, in some pilot areas, the reduction in the state incapacity benefit system of disincentives to work. New Deal 50 plus started nationally in April 2000. It is open to the over-50s on any kind of benefit, but it is not compulsory. It includes advice, a training allowance and an 'employment credit' to help people move from benefits to jobs without being worse off. This helped 86,000 people aged 50 plus to move from benefits back in to work between April 2000 and October 2002. Of these, one third were people with disabilities, and almost one third women.[24] In-work training grants help to increase skill, as do Third Age apprenticeships. Financial

---

[20] Philip E Taylor and Alan Walker, 'The ageing workforce: employers' attitudes to older people' *Work, Employment and Society,* vol 8 (1994), 569.

[21] S Scrutton 'Ageism: the Foundation of Age Discrimination' in E McEwen (ed), *Age: the unrecognised discrimination* (Age Concern, 1990).

[22] M Maguire, *Demographic ageing—consequences for social policy* (OECD, 1988).

[23] See Sandra Fredman, above, ch 3.

[24] Pensions Green Paper, 95.

incentives, such as employment credits (working-tax credit from April 2003), have helped to keep beneficiaries in work.[25]

Increased participation by young workers has been helped by the New Deal for Young People (open to 18–24 year olds who have been claiming jobseekers' allowance for six months or more). A quarter of a million young people have found work through this scheme. It has reduced unemployment and it has enhanced literacy and numeracy.[26]

A number of other government programmes for employment, enterprise and adult learning should help both older and younger workers. The amalgamation of the Employment Service and Benefits Agency as the Working Age Agency is particularly important for those aged 50 or more who are on benefits. The Regional Development Agencies, to promote growth in English regions, should be involved in increasing participation. Action Teams for Jobs in 63 areas of Britain are helping people back to work, with 50 plus persons one of the priority groups. The Learning and Skills Councils (replacing the former TECs), responsible for all post-16 education, are specifically charged with ensuring equal opportunities. The Department for Education and Skills has designated people aged 50–65 as a special group for targeting by Information, Advice and Guidance Partnerships (which bring together careers and other organisations). The Learning and Skills Councils also have responsibility for improving basic skills and learning opportunities.[27]

In respect of age discrimination, a voluntary Code of Practice on Age Diversity in Employment was published in 1999.[28] The purpose of the Code is to help employers, employees and applicants by setting a standard of good practice in recruitment, selection, promotion, training and development, redundancy and retirement. The Code has no statutory basis or legal effect. Case studies conducted for the Cambridge Independent Review of the Enforcement of UK Anti-Discrimination Legislation, indicated that human resources managers generally believed that without legislative support the Code would be ineffective.[29] Although an evaluation commissioned by the Government indicated that the proportion of employers expressly using age as a recruitment criterion had halved from 25 per cent to 13 per cent,[30] other surveys indicate that only between 25 per cent and 50 per cent of employers are aware of the Code, and less than one in ten is actually using it.[31] The Government did not rule out legislation at a later

---

[25] Ibid.

[26] House of Commons Select Committee on Education and Employment, Session 2000–2001, 8th Special Report, Annex Response from the Department for Education and Employment.

[27] See generally, *Training Older People* (April 2001).

[28] This followed *Advantage*, Consultation on a Code of Practice on Age Diversity in Employment (DfEE,1998); and *Action on Age,* Report of the Consultation on Age Discrimination in Employment (DfEE,1998).

[29] B Hepple, M Coussey, T Choudhury, *Equality: a New Framework* (2000), 120.

[30] *Evaluation of the Code of Practice on Age Diversity* (December 2001).

[31] The DfEE survey, *Age Diversity Summary of Research Findings,* indicated one-third in the period March 1999 to October 2000; the Employers' Forum on Age survey 25% and a CBI survey, 50%, but the latter also found only 9% were using it.

date, and it has now recognised that the Code has not been sufficiently effective in combating age discrimination. This was put forward as a justification for accepting the EC Framework Directive in December 2000.[32]

A crucial point, which is made in the Report of the Independent Review,[33] is that a voluntary approach may work in influencing the behaviour of some organisations (eg a leading edge company whose market is among older people will readily accept age diversity), but not others which for economic or social reasons are resistant to change. This led to our proposals for an enforcement pyramid. At the base, regulators assume voluntary compliance and promise co-operation. When this fails the regulators climb up the pyramid with progressively more deterrent penalties until there is compliance. In order to work, there must be gradual escalation and, at the top of the pyramid sufficiently strong sanctions to deter even the most persistent offender. It is the knowledge that non-compliance can ultimately be costly, that makes voluntary methods work. Merely enacting legislation against age discrimination will not change employment practices unless the regulatory mechanisms are effective, efficient and equitable.

In summary, legislation can help to change cultural attitudes to age and it can strengthen the commitment by employers not to rely on age in an arbitrary way. But its capacity to change employment practices will depend on the way in which it is framed in its national context. Above all legislation can work only if it is seen as an aspect of a broader employment strategy in conjunction with other measures to increase the participation of older and younger workers and to develop a skilled and adaptable labour force.

IS THE EU FRAMEWORK DIRECTIVE ON AGE FIT FOR PURPOSE?

There is now a consensus that action must be taken to tackle unfair age discrimination in employment. There is also widespread acceptance of the Cabinet Office Performance and Innovation Unit's conclusion that 'age discrimination legislation would have a positive effect on British culture and would build—as other discrimination Acts have—on a growing sense of public interest and concern about this issue.'[34]

However, if the legislation is to go beyond a merely symbolic declaration of public policy, it has to be constructed in a way which not only promises the ideal of facilitating equal participation of all in society, based on equal concern and respect for the dignity of each individual, but also is capable of making a significant impact on employment practices. Unfortunately the Framework Directive is rooted in an out-dated approach to anti-discrimination law. If it is simply

---

[32] House of Commons Select Committee, Seventh Report (above n 8) para 21.
[33] Hepple et al (above n 29), paras 3.4–3.5, 57–58.
[34] *Winning the Generation Game*, 60.

transposed into UK law without elaboration it may at best have limited effect, and at worst have some quite negative consequences.

The first defect of the Directive is that it is limited to a miscellaneous set of grounds of unfair discrimination, namely religion or belief, disability, age or sexual orientation. There remain a separate set of directives on sex discrimination, and one on discrimination on grounds of race or ethnic origin. The Council missed the opportunity provided by Article 13 of the EC Treaty to adopt a comprehensive approach to equality, by adopting a single unified Directive. Article 13, inserted by the Treaty of Amsterdam, for the first time granted the Council the power to take action against discrimination, not only on grounds of sex (as allowed since 1957) but also on all the other grounds.

By adopting three separate sets of instruments, the Council seems to be replicating one of the major defects of the current UK legislative framework. The Independent Review highlighted the many inconsistencies, gaps and anomalies between more than 30 Acts, 38 statutory instruments, 11 Codes of Practice and 12 EC Directives and recommendations which make up the body of UK anti-discrimination law. Notwithstanding the similarities between the new directives, there are several inconsistencies and gaps. We concluded that 'the first overriding consideration is to reduce the weight of anti-discrimination law and to render it more comprehensible to those affected by it, so as to encourage the active promotion of equality, rather than dependence on the external enforcement of a mass of detailed rules.'[35] We proposed a Single Equality Act, supplemented by regulations and regularly up-dated codes of practice. This is the model in several countries, such as Australia, Canada, Ireland, South Africa and New Zealand.

The starting point of all equality legislation is the right of individuals to autonomy, dignity and participation. The fact that there are different justifications for the various grounds of discrimination does not affect the basic principle. The specific justifications for age discrimination can be set out (see below) within a broad framework of the principle of equal treatment. The CBI has rightly castigated the Directive for lacking the clarity which employers require;[36] the implementing legislation will be incomprehensible unless firmly based on principle with clear and specific exceptions where age discrimination is justified.

A model Single Equality Bill, based on our proposals, was introduced in the House of Lords by Lord Lester of Herne Hill QC in January 2003. However, instead of proceeding in this way, the Government seems to be intent on dealing with each strand of discrimination separately. Consultation papers,[37] and draft regulations published in October 2002, compound the existing complexity of

---

[35] Hepple et al (above n 29) 22.

[36] CBI Evidence to the House of Commons Select Committee on Employment (2000).

[37] *Equality and Diversity: the way ahead,* and *Equality and Diversity: making it happen* (October 2002); these follow the earlier *Towards Equality and Diversity: Implementing the Employment and Race Directives* (December 2001).

UK anti-discrimination law. There are separate instruments relating to discrimination on grounds of race, religion or belief, sexual orientation, sex, sexual orientation and disability. There is to be separate legislation on age discrimination by December 2006. The use of subordinate legislation under the European Communities Act, rather than primary legislation, means that Parliament cannot amend the draft orders, and that these instruments cannot go beyond the provisions of the Directive. It is symptomatic of the Government's fragmented approach that no less than five departments are involved.[38]

The second defect of the Directive, discussed by Sandra Fredman in chapter three, is that it is limited to 'employment and occupation' (Article 1).[39] By contrast, the EC Race Directive 2000/43/EC covers, in addition, social protection, including social security and health care, social advantages, education and access to and supply of goods and services which are available to the public including housing. This is in line with the coverage of the British Race Relations Act, as amended in 2000. The Sex Discrimination and Disability Discrimination Acts also have extended coverage of most of these areas. Fredman argues persuasively that even if the aim were only to achieve equality in employment this could not be achieved without legislating on a far wider range because many aspects of age discrimination interact and reinforce one another (eg better health care enhances employability, employability enhances health, and better transport encourages participation in work). Moreover, to legislate only in respect of employment places burdens on employers which they cannot be expected to discharge unless corresponding duties are placed on public providers of education, health care and transport.

A third defect is that the Directive is based only on negative prohibitions against direct and indirect discrimination, rather than a positive duty to promote equality. This is similar to the now outdated British Sex Discrimination Act 1975 and Race Relations Act 1976, which have been characterised as 'third-generation' anti-discrimination legislation.[40] The UK, however, is moving to a fourth generation in which positive duties are an essential feature. For example, the Disability Discrimination Act 1995, in addition to outlawing direct discrimination (subject to a defence of justification) also prescribes a positive duty to make reasonable adjustments for disabled persons. The Fair Employment and Treatment Order 1998 in Northern Ireland (updating the Fair Employment Act 1989) shifted the emphasis from the elimination of unlawful discrimination on grounds of religion and political opinion to the reduction of structural inequal-

[38] The Office of the Deputy Prime Minister, the Home Office, the Women and Equality Unit, the Department for Work and Pensions, and the Department for Trade and Industry.

[39] This includes both public and private sectors in relation to (a) conditions of access to employment, to self-employment or to occupation, including selection criteria and recruitment conditions, and promotion; (b) access to all kinds of vocational guidance, vocational training and practical work experience; (c) employment and working conditions including dismissals and pay; and (d) membership and involvement in workers and employers' and professional organisations.

[40] The first generation was the Race Relations Act 1965 (limited to discrimination in public places); the second, the Race Relations Act 1968.

ity in the labour market, whether caused by discrimination or not. The Northern Ireland Act 1998 established a positive duty on public authorities to have due regard to the need to promote equality of opportunity, not only in respect of the Protestant and Roman Catholic communities, but also between persons, *inter alia*, of different age. The Race Relations (Amendment) Act 2000 in Britain has imposed similar positive duties on public authorities in respect of race.

The case for positive duties in general is discussed by Sandra Fredman in chapter three. The finding of the independent review[41] was that at present the main initiatives being taken by employers tend to be passive and separate from each other. While equal opportunities policies stimulated by codes of practice setting broad standards have been important for changing corporate behaviour, most organisations still do not have a sustained and coordinated strategy to improve diversity in the workforce. What is needed is an approach which recognises that equality of opportunity increasingly depends not simply on avoiding negative discrimination, but on training and improving skills, and encouraging adaptability. The content of this positive duty in the case of age discrimination will be discussed below (The Principle of Equal Treatment).

A fourth defect of the Directive—related to the absence of positive duties—is that it adopts a top-down rule making approach which concentrates on individual fault-finding and depends on retrospective investigation of an act alleged to be motivated by unlawful age discrimination. This adds credence to the CBI's fear that it will increase the regulatory burden and cost on employers, particularly by exposing them to high levels of costly and potentially spurious individual litigation.[42] This kind of fear will encourage negative and defensive attitudes rather than positive steps to promote diversity.

These are all serious defects. They can be remedied only by a comprehensive Single Equality Act, covering all areas of discrimination, and providing for positive duties to promote equality in addition to negative prohibitions on direct and indirect discrimination.

THE PRINCIPLE OF EQUAL TREATMENT

The basic principle to be implemented is that of 'equal treatment' which means that there must be no direct or indirect discrimination on grounds, *inter alia*, of age (Article 2.1). There is also a prohibition on harassment on grounds of age (Article 2.3). Although not mentioned in the Directive, it would be desirable to add a positive duty on public bodies to promote equality for the reasons given above.

---

[41] Hepple et al (above n 29) esp 19, 33 and Annex 1.
[42] CBI Evidence to the House of Commons Select Committee on Employment (above n 36).

Direct Discrimination

This is taken to occur 'when one person is treated less favourably than another is, or would be treated in a comparable situation' (Article 2.2(a)). Sandra Fredman has explained in her chapter why a comparative approach is not appropriate to questions of age discrimination. In particular age is a process and not an immutable characteristic like gender or race, so it may be arbitrary to choose a particular comparator: must a person be much younger or older or will any age difference suffice? I agree with Fredman that the solution to this problem is to provide that it is direct discrimination to subject a person to a detriment on grounds of his or her age. This avoids the need to find a different-age comparator.

This approach also helps to resolve what has been called the 'age-proxy' problem. This refers to a method of proof that permits a finding of age discrimination to be based on an employer's reliance on an age-related factor. The basis of this theory is that the age-related factor is a proxy for age itself. The solution adopted in the US by the Supreme Court is that a 'disparate treatment' claim cannot succeed unless the employee's age actually played a role and had a determinative influence on the outcome.[43] This means that if the substantial reason for an employment decision is not age but some other lawful factor, there is no direct discrimination. For example, linking salary to seniority or selecting an employee for lay-off because of his or her high salary is not direct age discrimination. Although these factors may have a greater impact on older workers they are said to be analytically distinct from age, because a younger worker may have worked for longer for the employer than an older but recently joined employee. So too, it has been held that termination of employment close to the vesting age for retirement benefits in order to save costs to the employer is not age discrimination. Nor is it age discrimination to dismiss an employee because he or she is perceived to be over-qualified, or 'has been around too long', unless the reason for that belief is the age of the employee.[44]

Similar conclusions could be reached by UK tribunals applying a 'but for' (causal) theory of direct discrimination.[45] The burden of proof will be on the claimant to prove facts from which it may be presumed that age was the determinative cause, but it would then be open to the respondent to show some other credible reason.[46] The question is whether but for his or her age the claimant would have been differently treated.

---

[43] *Hazen Paper Co v Biggins* 507 US 604 (1993).

[44] Eg, *Sperling v Hoffmann La Roche Inc* 924 F Supp 1396 (1996) (US District Court).

[45] As laid down by the House of Lords in *James v Eastleigh BC* [1990] 2 AC 751 in respect of sex discrimination, and in *Nagarajan v London Regional Transport* [1999] Industrial Cases Reports 942 in respect of race discrimination.

[46] Directive, Art 10.1.

Indirect Discrimination

The Directive makes it possible to bring claims where a practice, policy or criterion has a disparate impact on a particular age *group*. For example, a criterion of high physical fitness (expected in jobs such as airline pilots, divers and offshore riggers) may have a disparate impact on older people. However, it will then be open to the respondent to prove that this criterion is objectively justified (ie is job-related) and is appropriate and necessary. The justification could include cost factors, such as the actuarial factors which will affect the employer's liability for insurance and health and safety requirements. Cost factors may also be relied upon in defending seniority-based pay systems, terminations linked to retirement status and the like, so long as these can be shown to be proportionate .

While the intent is clear, the wording of the Directive (Article 2.2(b)), is, however, ambiguous. It says that indirect discrimination is taken to occur,

> . . . where an apparently neutral provision, criterion or practice would put persons having . . . a particular age . . . at a particular disadvantage compared with other persons unless—
>
> (i) that provision, criterion or practice is objectively justified by a legitimate aim and the means of achieving that aim are appropriate and necessary; . . .

Literally interpreted, there will be indirect discrimination if two or more persons of a 'particular age' suffer a 'particular disadvantage', even without evidence that the age *group* (eg all persons over 60) as such suffers from that disadvantage. This interpretation would assimilate the concepts of direct and indirect discrimination because, as already explained, the former occurs where the effect of the respondent's action is to put an individual at a disadvantage on grounds of age, even without any conscious motivation on the part of the discriminator. If the distinction between direct discrimination (disparate treatment) and indirect discrimination (disparate impact) is to be maintained, then the latter should be confined to cases where it is possible to make a comparison between persons of the claimant's age *group* and all other persons.[47] The choice of the appropriate pools could, however, be difficult, and this would limit the application of the concept of indirect discrimination. It is to be noted that in the US, the Supreme Court has left open the question whether the disparate impact theory, regularly applied under Title VII of the Civil Rights Act in cases of gender and race, has any application to the Age Discrimination in Employment Act.[48] Lower courts have been reluctant to utilise disparate impact theory in cases such as firing older workers because of their high salaries.[49]

---

[47] See further C Barnard and B Hepple, 'Substantive Equality' (2000) *Cambridge Law Journal* 562 at 568–9.

[48] *Hazen Paper* case (above n 43).

[49] David Neumark in *Outlawing Age Discrimination: Foreign lessons, UK choices* (ed Z Hornstein) (2001) 51.

The solution to this problem proposed by our Single Equality Bill is to provide that a person ('P') indirectly discriminates against another person ('B'):

Where B is of any given age and P applies to B a provision, criterion or practice which he applies or would apply equally to other persons without regard to their age but which—

(a) puts or would put, persons of B's age (or of a similar age), at a particular disadvantage when compared with other persons; and

(c) puts B at a disadvantage.

This definition retains the group character of indirect discrimination, defines the pool on terms of persons of a similar age, and requires the complainant to be a victim of the indirect discrimination. The latter requirement does not mean that only an individual can complain. The proposed Equality Commission, independent trade unions and other public interest bodies should be able to institute proceedings on behalf of the victim.

The Directive allows justifications of differences of treatment on grounds of age and these too will reduce the risk of abuse of the principle of equal treatment (see below).

Positive Duty to Promote Equality

The Independent Review proposed two kinds of positive duty. The first is one on public bodies to have regard to the need to eliminate unlawful discrimination, and to promote equality of opportunity. The second is a duty on employers (in both public and private sectors) to conduct workforce reviews and to implement employment equity plans. In the Single Equality Bill, the former applies to all prohibited grounds including age, but the latter applies only to race, sex and disability.

Why the distinction? It is apparent that the content of the positive duty in respect of age discrimination could not be identical to that for gender and race equality and disability. Age does affect individuals differently, and may be a relevant factor in some situations, while gender and race are always irrelevant to employment decisions, with very limited exceptions. Under-represented groups can be identified for purposes of gender and racial equality and disability, or in Northern Ireland community affiliation. But in the case of age it would be difficult and arbitrary to treat people in particular age bands as 'groups' who must be fairly represented. Older workers, unlike women and ethnic minorities, are not segregated into particular job categories. Their pay is depressed not simply because of age but because of job evaluations based on factors such as training, effort, skill and responsibility. There is no expectation that firms should have a particular age structure which exists in other firms or in the labour market generally.

Accordingly, when one speaks of positive duties in relation to age, what should be envisaged is action—in the words of the Code of Practice on Age

Diversity in Employment—'as part of a wider personnel and equal opportunities strategy to create a flexible and motivated workforce. An effective strategy will begin by reviewing the current position to clarify what needs to be done and to monitor progress.' The duty would be to take reasonably practicable steps to ensure that the provisions of the Code are being observed in the organisation.

It is to be noted that the Northern Ireland Act imposes a positive duty on public authorities to have due regard to the need to promote equality of opportunity, *inter alia*, 'between persons of different ages'. This appears to refer only to inter-generational equality, and for this reason seems to be inadequate in the context of employment by public authorities, to whom the same positive duty as proposed above should apply. The Single Equality Bill refers, instead, to promoting equal opportunities for 'persons generally without regard to their age'.

When it comes to employment equity plans, these are in effect limited by the Single Equality Bill to removing the under-representation of black people, women and disabled persons. As argued earlier, it is inappropriate to apply the concept of under-representation to particular age groups. There are also pragmatic reasons for introducing such a duty cautiously because of the opposition of employers to new duties which are perceived as leading to increased bureaucratic burdens. However, the aims of removing barriers for older (and younger) people, and promoting their special needs should be undertaken as voluntary positive action, as is now encouraged by the Government's Age Positive campaign (see further below).[50]

JUSTIFICATIONS FOR DISCRIMINATION

A General Defence?

The Directive provides a number of ambiguously worded justifications for age discrimination. The first issue to be considered is whether UK implementing legislation should allow a general defence of justification (subject to the limits set in the Directive) to direct discrimination, as is the case with disability discrimination. In respect of race and gender discrimination only a few specific justifications are allowed. In the consultation process for the Independent Review,[51] only two individuals favoured a general defence on the ground that this would provide a 'safety valve' in extreme cases and make it easier to raise considerations not covered by the specific defences. Everyone else who was consulted thought that a general defence would create uncertainty and confusion, and would undermine the general principle of equal treatment. In the case of disability discrimination, unlike race and gender, disability can make a legitimate difference to the way in which a person is treated. But even in that case, Brian

---

[50] Pensions Green Paper, 97.
[51] Hepple et al (above n 29) 35–37.

Doyle[52] has suggested that the general defence should be replaced by a reference to rational grounds for discrimination such as a genuine occupational qualification (GOQ).

Age can be a rational criterion for employment decisions in some situations. The Directive (Article 6) provides that member states may provide that differences of treatment on grounds of age shall not constitute discrimination if, within the context of national law certain requirements are met. These are (1) they must be objectively and reasonably justified by a legitimate aim, including legitimate employment policy, labour market and vocational training objectives; and (2) the means of achieving that aim are appropriate and necessary. Three groups of examples are then given relating to (a) positive action; (b) minimum conditions of age etc. for access to employment or certain advantages of employment; and (c) a maximum age for training. There would be greater certainty and more guidance for employers and other decision-makers if in place of these ambiguous exceptions, there was a non-exhaustive list of specific exceptions.

Genuine Occupational Qualifications (GOQs)

The Directive (Article 4.1) permits age to be used as a basis for differential treatment 'where by reason of the nature of the particular occupational activities concerned or of the context in which they are carried out, such a characteristic constitutes a genuine and determining occupational requirement, provided that the objective is legitimate and the requirement is proportionate.' Two obvious examples, found in Australian states, are dramatic performances or other entertainments where a person of a particular age or age group is required for reasons of authenticity, or where the job-holder provides welfare services which can most effectively be provided by persons of a particular age or age group.[53] In the US, age discrimination is permitted 'where age is a bona fide occupational qualification reasonably necessary to the normal operation of the particular business.' In a case involving the compulsory retirement of flight engineers on alleged safety grounds at age 60, the Supreme Court recently held that the employer must establish that age is a legitimate proxy for safety-related job qualifications in that it is impossible or highly impracticable to deal with older employees on an individualised basis.[54]

The best approach for the UK would be to provide an exception from the principle of equal treatment where the employer can show that the essential nature of the activities to be carried out by the person, or the context in which the activities are to be carried out, requires that they be carried out by a person of a particular age or age group. The age requirement would have to be shown

---

[52] Independent Review, Working paper no.4 (1999) 4.
[53] Sol Encel in *Outlawing Age Discrimination* (above n 49) 18.
[54] *Western Airlines v Cresswell*, discussed by Fredman, above ch 3.

to be a genuine and determining requirement that is proportionate to a legitimate objective. This could be amplified by examples such as those mentioned above, either in the statute or in a code of practice.

Minimum Conditions of Age for Employment or Benefits

The Directive gives as an example of legitimate justifications the fixing of minimum conditions of age, professional experience or seniority in service for access to employment or certain advantages linked to employment (Article 6.1(b)).

This raises the question of the age coverage of the law. By way of comparison the US law covers only those over 40, and the Irish Employment Equality Act covers those from 18–65 for employment and 15–65 for training. In the UK, there is special legislation for the protection of children (under the compulsory school-leaving age), and of young persons (over compulsory school-leaving age but under age 18). The most important of these implement the Young Persons Directive 94/33/EC.[55] These can be justified as protective measures under Article 6.1(a) of the Directive, and also as legitimate minimum conditions under Article 6.1(b). It would, therefore, be appropriate to limit the coverage of UK age discrimination law in respect of employment and occupation, including training, to those over compulsory school-leaving age, and to maintain the special measures relating to children and young persons. A specific exception may be needed in respect of the national minimum wage (see below). Where these specific exceptions do not apply, employers who specify minimum ages for employment or benefits of employment will have to provide objective justification for the discrimination, showing that the age requirement is genuine and determining and one that is proportionate to a legitimate objective.

The issue of 'advantages linked to employment' is more complex. As already indicated, pay and other benefit schemes linked to professional experience or seniority are unlikely to amount to direct discrimination if the definition advocated above is adopted. However, they may constitute prima facie indirect discrimination unless justified. It is a matter for consideration whether in order to provide clear guidance for employers and tribunals, it should be declared that pay and other terms of employment based on seniority in service or professional experience are justifications for differential treatment. In the Irish Employment Equality Act a three-year period was prescribed for phasing out age-related pay, and the Act states that it is not age discrimination to provide different rates of remuneration or different terms of employment based on seniority or length of service in a particular post or employment. A similar approach could be taken in the UK.

---

[55] See esp the Children (Protection at Work) Regulations 1998, SI 1998 No 276, and the Children (Protection at Work) Regulations SI 2000 No 1333 and SI Scot 2000 No 149.

Length of Service Requirements for Training

The Directive (Article 6.1(c)) recognises that the fixing of a maximum age for recruitment which is based on the training requirements of the post in question or the need for a reasonable period of employment before retirement may be legitimate and appropriate. The Irish Employment Equality Act contains a specific exception along these lines. It is dubious whether a specific provision is required in UK legislation, since this might weaken the strictly defined genuine occupational qualification (above).

Significantly Increased Costs

The Irish Employment Equality Act provides that discrimination on grounds of age is not unlawful where it is shown that there is clear actuarial or other evidence that significantly increased costs would result if the discrimination were not permitted in those circumstances. This is not specifically mentioned in the Directive (save in relation to admission to occupational pension schemes and entitlement to retirement or invalidity benefits).[56] The Irish clause should not simply be copied in the UK because it does not make it clear that it is subject to the general requirement of proportionality in Article 6.1 of the Directive (above). The increase in costs must be balanced against the extent of the discrimination involved.

Positive Action

The Directive (Article 6.1(a)) gives as an example of permitted age discrimination 'the setting of special conditions on access to employment and vocational training, employment and occupation, including dismissal and remuneration conditions for young people, older workers and persons with caring responsibilities in order to promote their vocational integration or ensure their protection.' The Irish Act provides a model in relation to age-related benefits to an employee in respect of family members, change in marital status or to assist with caring responsibilities. The Irish Act could also be followed in relation to positive action in order to facilitate the integration into employment either generally or in particular areas or a particular workplace, of persons who have attained the age of 50 years. Moreover, it may be necessary to exempt the provision by or on behalf of the state or other providers of training or work experience for younger or older workers. The Irish Act requires in such cases a certification by the Minister that in the absence of the provision in question the disadvantged group is unlikely to receive similar training or work experience. The Single

[56] Art 6.2.

Equality Bill proposes a wide definition of positive action including any steps providing specific advantages to persons identifieds by reference to a particular age group in order to compensate them for any disadvantage.

RETIREMENT

Should Mandatory Retirement Ages be Abolished?

The Directive applies to dismissals (Article 3.1(b)) and so would prohibit mandatory retirement on grounds of age. However, recital 14 states that 'the Directive shall be without prejudice to national provisions laying down retirement ages.' The UK has no national age for retirement from employment, although it has a fixed age for eligibility for a state retirement pension. Many employers have mandatory retirement ages, typically 60 or 65, but some are earlier (eg 50 for police constables, 55 for airline pilots) and some later (eg judges at 70). The earliest at which an occupational pension can be received is 50. The Government has proposed a number of measures to encourage people to work over normal retiring age, for example by raising the age at which an occupational pension can be drawn to 55 by 2010, and raising the age to 65 from the present 60 for new entrants to public sector pension schemes.[57] The Directive (Article 6.2) in fact totally exempts admission to occupational pension schemes, and entitlement to retirement and invalidity benefits. However, mandatory retirement from employment will have to be justified (under Article 6.1, see above) as being in pursuance of a legitimate aim and 'appropriate and necessary'.

The first option open to the UK would be to ban mandatory retirement ages altogether. This has been done in several countries, including the US, Australia and New Zealand. This reflects the view that the right to age equality is as fundamental as that to gender and race equality; and that mandatory retirement stigmatises 'age' in an arbitrary way without reference to individual circumstances.

The second option would be expressly to permit mandatory retirement without qualification, as is the case in Ireland where the Employment Equality Act does not apply to those aged 65 or over and it is lawful to fix different ages of retirement, whether compulsory or voluntary, for different employees or classes of employees. This reflects the view that age is a process which affects everyone, and that mandatory retirement provides an impersonal criterion that enables individuals to leave the labour market without the stigma of incapability, lack of adaptability, or 'slowing down', on which employers would have to rely in the absence of the proxy of age.

---

[57] Pensions Green Paper, 93.

A third option would be to permit mandatory retirement only if certain conditions are met. This is closest to the position in Canada, where the Supreme Court upheld mandatory retirement as a contractual arrangement that could be shown to preserve the integrity of pension plans and to foster the prospects of younger workers . This was held to be rationally connected to the fixed age and to impose minimal impairments on the equality rights of older workers.[58]

The key question is which of these three options is the most effective way of achieving the legitimate aims of maintaining the dignity and increasing the participation of older and younger workers in the labour market and promoting their adaptability. It has been suggested that international comparisons show that abolishing mandatory retirement is unlikely to improve significantly the job prospects for older (or younger) workers.[59] One must, however, be extremely cautious about drawing direct lessons from other jurisdictions.[60] The outcomes of age discrimination legislation have been relatively little researched, even in the US, where the Age Discrimination in Employment Act has been in force for over 30 years, and much of the data precedes the abolition of the mandatory retirement age in 1986. Foreign laws have to be studied and understood in their overall national and cultural context. For example, the age of withdrawal from the labour market in the US continued to decline after the abolition of mandatory retirement, the median dropping below 62 and only recently has this by one measure risen slightly.

This can only be understood in the context of the Older Workers Benefit Protection Act 1990 which legitimated retirement packages in which the worker waives any claim of age discrimination in return for improved pension or medical benefits. Early retirement had great attractions for middle class workers in the 1990s because of the extraordinary performance of the US stock market and high real estate values. The other important ingredient in the US story is high numbers of immigrants performing both low paid and certain skilled jobs. US researchers have highlighted the shift in wealth to older white male professionals who are seeking to hold on to jobs they already have rather than Congress' intended beneficiary of the greying workseeker refused a job.[61] This may be a specific consequence of the litigation-driven, contingency-fee based US model of anti-discrimination legislation which in effect has become a functional equivalent of UK unfair dismissal legislation, but with much higher awards for plaintiffs.

We must consider some of the stronger arguments for allowing mandatory retirement. The first of these is that it can open up job and promotion opportunities for younger workers. One must beware the 'lump of labour' fallacy, that

---

[58] *McKinney v University of Guelph* (1990) 76 Dominion Law Report (4th) 545.

[59] CBI Evidence to House of Commons Select Committee on Employment (2000).

[60] See the extremely useful study by Zmira Hornstein, Sol Encel, Morley Gunderson and David Neumark, *Outlawing Age Discrimination: foreign lessons, UK choices* (Policy Press, 2001).

[61] S Issacharoff and E Eorth Harris, 'Is Age Discrimination Really Age Discrimination: the ADEA's Unnatural Solution' (1997) 72 New York University LR 780–840.

there is a fixed number of jobs in the economy and every job occupied by an older person precludes a job available for a younger person. But it is true that in individual undertakings there may be a limited number of senior positions, and it is vital to the success of the organisation for new ideas and outside experience to be brought in by removing older workers in a way which preserves their dignity. This suggests that while prohibiting all mandatory retirements is too blunt an instrument, mandatory retirements from certain positions may be justifiable.[62]

A second argument in favour of mandatory retirement is that it can facilitate planning on the part of employer and employee. A related role for mandatory retirement is that it facilitates deferred or backdated compensation systems, in which workers are 'underpaid' relative to their productivity when younger in return for being 'overpaid' relative to their productivity in later career.[63] Mandatory retirement promotes deferred wage profiles.[64] Here Japan provides a salutary lesson. Mandatory retirement is allowed at the age of 60 (raised from 55 in 1994), but not before. Japanese firms have traditionally adopted mandatory retirement as a device for removing workers from the system of lifetime job security. This enables employers to reduce labour costs through redeployment based upon the criterion of age. The 'psychological contract', so important in Japanese culture, is that in exchange for the employee's loyalty the enterprise undertakes the care of the employee whatever the economic circumstances, with wages and promotion based on seniority without regard to performance and with a full retirement pension at the age of 60.

Employers reacted to the recession and to the raising of the mandatory retirement age through measures which had a deep impact on this psychological contract, such as 'in-house unemployment' of older employees, in-house transfers of workers close to retirement, replacing traditional wage seniority systems with pay for performance, and freezing salary scales at age 55. Complicating this was the raising of the pension age from 60 to 65 (in stages from 2001 to 2013), with workers being expected to receive partial pensions or to accept re-employment or employment extension as non-regular workers from age 60–64. This has produced a pensions crisis, leading some Japanese scholars to advocate the abolition of mandatory retirement and instead the enactment of an age discrimination law to promote the employment of older persons. This would bring Japan closer to the American solution of leaving older workers to their own devices when subjected to lay-offs, under strong incentives to recycle themselves, but with the important safety net of an age discrimination law. However, the Employment Measures Law (which came into operation on 1 October 2001)

---

[62] Compare *Winning the Generation Game*, at 40, with Sol Encel in *Outlawing Age Discrimination*, 35–36.

[63] So-called 'Lazear contracts' after EP Lazear, 'Why is there mandatory retirement?' (1979) 87 *Journal of Political Economy* 1261–84.

[64] In relation to the US in this respect see D Neumark and WA Stock, 'Age Discrimination laws and labour market efficiency' (1999) 107 *Journal of Political Economy*, 1081–1125.

simply 'requests' employers not to discriminate on age grounds in recruitment and hiring. With unemployment at a record 5.4 per cent at the end of 2001, it was considered that it would do more harm than good to allow mandatory retirement before the age of 60.[65] A lesson one may draw from the Japanese experience is that simply raising the mandatory retirement age may have negative consequences unless this is closely linked to the age at which full occupational and state pensions are available.

Before 1989 it was UK policy to use state retirement pensions to discourage workers from remaining in the labour force.[66] Receipt of a state pension was subject to a stringent retirement condition and the 'earnings rule' effectively penalised those pensioners who remained in employment after they became eligible to receive a pension. However, in 1989 the retirement condition and earnings rule were abolished making it possible for pensioners to retain their employment without losing entitlement to benefit. Now that the policy is to encourage participation of older workers, there seems to be no justification for linking mandatory retirement to the state pension age. However, different considerations may apply to the integrity of occupational pension schemes to which the employer has contributed. Where the age of mandatory retirement is the same as that at which the employee is entitled to an occupational pension, and is based on contractual arrangements between employer and employee, the mandatory retirement may be said to further the legitimate aim of encouraging planning of retirement as a form of deferred compensation, and the means (a contractual arrangement) are proportionate.

Some safeguards may be necessary. First, in order to reduce inducements to early retirement the minimum age at which an occupational pension can be drawn (other than on grounds of illness or disability) should be raised, as the Government now proposes, to 55, with strong financial incentives to work longer. In order to avoid the US phenomenon, waivers below this age should not be permitted. This would be consistent with the policy of improving participation. It would not produce any great shocks given the decline in pension fund surpluses as a means of funding voluntary redundancies. Secondly, the occupational pension scheme should be one approved under pensions legislation, and the employee must have given informed consent after taking independent advice, either at the time of taking the job or by subsequent agreed variation. Thirdly, any commission with powers to enforce age discrimination legislation (see below) should be able to conduct a formal investigation into contractual arrangements of this kind where the Commission has reason to believe that the arrangements in relation to the age of retirement are oppressive or unfair.

This third way—between outright prohibition and outright permission—appears to be wholly compatible with the Directive. It allows for a contractual

---

[65] I am grateful to Professor Takashi Araki for this information; see further *Japan Labor Bulletin*, vol 40, No 11 (November 2001) 4.

[66] The growth of mandatory retirement—a post-War phenomenon—is described by Pat Thane, *Old Age in English History* (Oxford, Oxford University Press, 2000) ch 20.

break at a defined age.[67] It would mean that where there is no contractual arrangement to retire at a certain age (at 55 or over) in return for an approved occupational pension, the employer will have to justify a practice of mandatory retirement on a case by case basis. This may be on a 'lump of labour' argument affecting the individual undertaking or as a proportionate means of fulfilling some other legitimate aim. It would be no bad thing if this encouraged employers to have contractual arrangements for retirement linked to occupational pension schemes. One might add that the need to justify where there is no contractual scheme is unlikely to be a significant problem given the growing coverage of occupational schemes. It may lead to a reduction in the current pattern of one in three workers leaving prematurely.

Unfair Dismissal and Redundancy Compensation

The right not to be unfairly dismissed currently does not apply to an employee who has attained the 'normal retiring age' in the undertaking, (whether that is above or below the age of 65), or, where there is no normal retiring age, the age of 65.[68] So if there is a normal retiring age of 60, but the employee is kept on and is then unfairly dismissed for any reason or no reason there is no remedy.[69] There is also no right to a redundancy payment if the employee has attained the age of 65, or the normal retiring age if that is *lower*.[70]

An attempt has recently been made in the *Rutherford* and *Bentley* cases[71] to challenge these provisions as being indirectly discriminatory on grounds of sex and therefore unlawful. The Employment Appeal Tribunal remitted the case to an employment tribunal for reconsideration, and gave guidance on the use of statistics to prove disparate impact and on the defence of objective justification. The statistics originally provided were considered unsatisfactory because they referred to all people over the age of 65 and not only those who are employees and might be affected by unfair dismissal legislation; they also covered retired persons who might no longer wish to work. In relation to objective justification,

---

[67] The possibility exists of offering a further fixed-term contract after the retiring age, but this would have to be in conformity with the Fixed-Term Employees (Prevention of Less Favourable) Treatment Regulations 2002, in particular a maximum period of four years, including the initial period, unless there is objective justification for a longer period.

[68] Employment Rights Act 1996, s109, as interpreted in *Nothman v Barnet LBC* [1979] ICR 111 (HL).

[69] There are exceptions protecting a post-retiring age employee against dismissals related to leave for family reasons, health and safety, shop and betting workers refusing Sunday work, working time, trustees of pension funds, employee representatives, trade union membership and participation, protected disclosures, and asserting statutory rights, and race, sex or disability discrimination.

[70] Employment Rights Act 1996, s 156(1); the employee over these ages is also not entitled to the basic award for unfair dismissal: s 119(4)–(5).

[71] *Harvest Town Circle Ltd v Rutherford* [2001] *IRLR* 591, EAT; on rehearing joined with *Bentley v Secretary of State for Trade* (2002) *Equal Opportunities Review* No 111 (November 2002) 25 (ET).

the EAT wanted the tribunal to consider whether every person over 65 who remains in work excludes some younger (unpensioned) person from the job. When the case was reheard, the tribunal took as the appropriate pool those working, seeking work or wanting to work. Over a period of years labour force statistics showed a consistently higher percentage of males in the age group 65–74 within the labour force, than the percentage of females. The tribunal went on to hold that the Secretary of State had failed to provide objective justification for this. This decision is under appeal, and it is by no means certain that it will be upheld.[72]

The more promising development will be the introduction of age discrimination legislation. This will necessitate the repeal of these provisions unless they can be objectively justified under Article 6 of the Directive (above). The EAT's guidance in *Rutherford* suggests one argument which may be raised in relation to unfair dismissal, namely that there are a fixed number of jobs in the economy—a 'lump of labour'—and it is therefore 'fair' to dismiss an employee over the retiring age. Another justification for upper age limits in respect of unfair dismissal and redundancy has been said to be that those of pensionable age should not be entitled to employment rights. It has been argued above that these two considerations may be relevant to a mandatory retirement age. However, the present exemptions in respect of unfair dismissal and redundancy are plainly disproportionate to these possibly legitimate aims. First, although the contractual retiring age is in principle the 'normal age', it has been held that this may be displaced by evidence that the employer regularly departs from this in practice.[73] This means that the safeguard of informed consent is lacking. Secondly, the age of 65 is arbitrarily being linked to the age for state retirement pensions which, as pointed out above, are no longer dependent upon giving up paid employment. In principle, there seems to be no reason why older workers should not be protected against unfair dismissal. These provisions should be repealed.

REMOVING DISCRIMINATION IN LEGISLATION, ADMINISTRATIVE PROVISIONS AND COLLECTIVE AGREEMENTS

The Directive requires member states to ensure that any laws, regulations and administrative provisions contrary to the principle of equal treatment are abolished (Article 16(a)). While most employment and discrimination legislation applies to workers of any age,[74] there are some cases where older and younger workers are excluded. The following are the main examples.

---

[72] See the critical comments by M Rubenstein , *Equal Opportunities Review*, No 111 (November, 2002) 25–27.

[73] *Waite v GCHQ* [1983] *ICR* 653 (HL).

[74] Eg the Sex Discrimination Act 1975, s 5(2) applies to women and men of any age; the Disability Discrimination Act 1995, applies to disabled persons without any mention of age.

Unfair Dismissal and Redundancy Payments

See above, Unfair dismissal and redundancy compensation.

National Minimum Wage Act 1998 (NMWA)

Regulations under the NMWA directly discriminate against certain young persons by excluding from the national minimum wage all workers under the age of 18, apprentices under the age of 19, and apprentices under the age of 26 during the first year of their apprenticeship. They indirectly discriminate against young persons by excluding certain trainees employed on trial periods for less than three weeks; and *au pairs*, family workers, and certain workers receiving training at a higher education institution. Those aged 18 or over but less than 22 receive the minimum wage at a lower initial rate, as do workers aged 22 or over who are in the first six months of their employment with a new employer, and who have agreed to take part in an accredited training course for at least 26 weeks during that six-month period. There can be little doubt that the Government—which has regard to the advice of the Low Pay Commission— would seek to justify the exclusions and the lower rates for young workers and trainees (under Article 6 of the Directive) as being appropriate and necessary in order to maintain levels of employment for young people while at the same time providing them with decent remuneration.

The Working Time Regulations 1998

These regulations provide more favourable treatment to 'young workers' (defined as those over compulsory school age and under 18) than to others, eg not to have to work between 10 pm and 6 am, and to be allowed a 12-hour rest period every 24 hours, a rest period of not less than 48 hours in each seven-day period, and a 30-minute rest break if working for more than 4½ hours. These provisions reflect the requirements of the Young Persons' Directive 94/33/EC, and are plainly justifiable under Article 6(1)(a) of the Directive since they are aimed at 'ensuring [the] protection' of young workers.

Restrictions on the Employment of Children and Young Persons

See above, Minimum Conditions of Age for Employment or Benefits.

Collective Agreements, Professional Rules etc

The Directive requires discriminatory provisions in collective agreements, contracts, internal rules of undertakings and those of professional and occupational organisations to be declared null and void. Employment tribunals should be given jurisdiction for this purpose.

ENFORCEMENT

The question of enforcement, was extensively researched by the Independent Review,[75] whose conclusions are applicable to the specific issue of age discrimination. In summary, the main points of relevance are the following.

1. There should be a single Equality Act covering all grounds of unlawful discrimination, including age.

2. There should be a Human Rights Commission for Britain, the functions of which would include the review and scrutiny of legislation, giving advice and assistance to individuals, conducting investigations and inquiries, giving guidance to public authorities and generally promoting human rights including the right to age equality.

3. There should be a separate single Equality Commission for Britain, covering all grounds of unlawful discrimination, whose functions would include the strategic enforcement of age discrimination legislation, formal investigations of discriminatory practices, and advising and assisting individuals with complaints of age discrimination.

4. The duty on public authorities to have due regard to the promotion of equal opportunities should include age equality, and effect should be given to this, in accordance with a code of practice, through the normal system of best value reviews, audit and inspection.

5. The time limit for bringing claims of unlawful discrimination in employment tribunals should be six months from the date of the alleged act of discrimination.

6. Tribunals should make awards of aggravated damages where appropriate, and tribunals should have power to award reinstatement or re-employment and to recommend other specific action by the employer in all discrimination cases.

7. There should be improved arrangements for conciliation and mediation in discrimination cases.

---

[75] Hepple et al (above n 29), esp chs 3 and 4.

5

Age Equality in Health and Social Care

JANICE ROBINSON

INTRODUCTION

THERE IS A substantial body of evidence indicating that older people experience age discrimination in health care. Such discrimination is regarded as unacceptable by the current Labour Government, whose National Service Framework for Older People requires health and social care agencies 'to root out age discrimination'. The Government's recent recognition that age discrimination takes place in health and social care, and their determination to put an end to it, can be seen as a major step forward in tackling inequalities in public services.

Scrutinising health and social care services in order to identify age discrimination is a complex and contentious process. Age-based differences in the organisation and delivery of care are not necessarily discriminatory, but it can be difficult to distinguish between those policies and practices that disadvantage older people and those that do not. Arguments can be put forward to justify age-based approaches to care as fair or legitimate on other grounds. However, it is not always easy to judge the merits of those arguments, nor to reach agreement with others on the judgments or action necessary to eliminate age discrimination.

For any real progress to be made in eliminating age discrimination, people involved in scrutinising services will need a good understanding of what age equality in health and social care means. All the indications are that, at the moment, there is considerable uncertainty and confusion among service staff who are held responsible for ensuring that their services do not discriminate against older people. This chapter aims to shed light on the meaning of age discrimination and equality in the context of health care for older people, and to show how this understanding should shape policies to counter age discrimination in health and social care. I conclude that while the National Service Framework for Older People is an important step forward, it lacks both a sufficiently clear definition of the meaning of age discrimination, and a sufficiently incisive enforcement mechanism. Legislation on age equality is crucial if real change is to be effected.

A problem for older people or all age groups?

In this chapter, discussions about age equality in health care focus mainly on the experience of older people, rather than younger age groups. This emphasis on older people—who can be loosely defined in this context as people aged 60 and over—springs from the fact that health care decisions based on age criteria more commonly disadvantage older age groups rather than younger ones. It is nevertheless recognised that younger people—particularly children and adolescents—can also be disadvantaged by restricted access and availability of health services. Reference to the shared experience and consequences of age discrimination at both ends of the age spectrum will therefore be made where appropriate.

An issue for health and social care?

While this chapter's primary focus is on health care, reference is made frequently to 'health and social care'. Health care entails preventative interventions (such as screening or immunisation), as well as treatment, care and support provided for people with diagnosed conditions that are life threatening or disabling. Treatment may involve medication, surgery, or a range of therapies designed to cure the condition or to minimise or delay its impact.

However, a good deal of the care and support provided for people with chronic ill health and long-term disability has become categorised as 'social care', even though interventions are designed to maintain or enhance the health and well-being of individuals. These interventions encompass the personal care required by people who are unable to feed, wash or use the toilet unaided; equipment and building adaptations that assist mobility, communication and the everyday tasks of daily living; and the social and psychological support that facilitates recovery and a return to independent living following illness or injury.

In this respect, it is often difficult to distinguish between health and social care. I will therefore refer to both health and social care when referring to the care of individuals with chronic ill health and disabilities. I will nevertheless distinguish between the NHS and local authorities, which have shared and separate responsibilities for organising and delivering care services.

AGE DISCRIMINATION IN HEALTH AND SOCIAL CARE

A matter of growing public concern?

The current discourse about age discrimination in health care is taking place at a time of growing criticism about the availability and quality of services for older people. That concern is not new but, historically, criticism has tended to focus on the provision of long-term care in hospitals and care homes. Ever since the establishment of the National Health Service more than 50 years ago, care for frail older people, including those with dementia, has often been associated with 'Cinderella' services. This long-established concern about care services for older people with chronic ill health and long-term physical or mental disability now extends to concern about restricted access to a wide range of health care, including acute care provided in general hospitals and the preventative or rehabilitative care provided by community health and social care staff.

The claim that age discrimination is at the root of the problems afflicting health and social care for older people has been voiced throughout the last decade. Successive reforms of the NHS and of community care have raised questions about the best way of providing and financing care for an ageing population. Researchers have looked at the implications of changes in the funding and organisation of care and have questioned practices affecting older people and their carers that have gone virtually unchallenged for many years. Lay and professional groups, concerned about civil rights, have spoken out against practices seen to be denying older people equal opportunities and equal access. Voluntary organisations, such as Age Concern and Help the Aged, have mounted successful campaigns drawing public attention to older people being subjected to demeaning conditions in hospital wards and denied treatment altogether on grounds of age. Both organisations have called for action to stop age discrimination.

By the late 1990s, when the Labour Government produced the NHS Plan announcing its intention to improve health services for older people,[1] it was compelled to acknowledge that systematic age discrimination was taking place in the health service, and to promise action to remove that barrier to service improvement. The result was evident in the National Service Framework for Older People,[2] where the first of eight standards focused on 'rooting out age discrimination' and ensuring that older people 'are never unfairly discriminated against in accessing NHS or social care services as a result of their age.'

For the first time, NHS bodies and local authorities were required to put in place a number of measures to champion older people's interests, to scrutinise

---

[1] Secretary of State for Health, *The NHS Plan—A Plan for Investment, A Plan for Reform* (The Stationery Office, London, 2000).

[2] Department of Health, National Service Framework for Older People, 2001.

all age-related policies in health and social care, and to report on action taken to end any unfair discrimination identified.

What is the evidence that age discrimination exists?

At first sight, it is not obvious that age discrimination takes place in either health or social care. Older people are major consumers of care, exhibiting apparently low levels of dissatisfaction or complaint with the care received. Although people aged 65 and over constitute around 16 per cent of the general population, they occupy two-thirds of acute hospital beds[3] and account for 25–30 per cent of NHS expenditure on drugs and 45 per cent of all items prescribed.[4] People over 75 make greater use of hospital, primary and community health services (apart from dentistry) than younger people.[5] Most residential, domiciliary and day social services are provided for older people, notably those aged 75 and over and those living alone. User surveys consistently find that older people are more satisfied with health services than younger users, and there are very few complaints alleging discrimination of any kind (race, sex or age) regarding hospital and community health services.[6]

However, a King's Fund review of the evidence indicates that age discrimination has been taking place throughout the health and social care system throughout the last decade.[7] That discrimination takes two forms, one direct and the other indirect. Direct age discrimination occurs when a person is treated less favourably than another because of their age, for example, when a 70-year-old who has had a stroke is not helped by the local stroke care team who restrict their services to people aged 65 years old and under. Indirect age discrimination takes place when care is offered in such a way that particular age groups are disadvantaged because they are disproportionately affected. For example, policies to shorten lengths of stay in hospital and to maximise throughput in hospital beds can have adverse consequences for older patients, who take longer than average to recover from surgery or illness. Where no intermediate care is available to aid recuperation and rehabilitation outside the hospital, older patients—especially those living alone—can be at risk.

While age discrimination is usually defined in negative terms as acting to the detriment of older people, some policies and practices may be regarded as 'positive discrimination'. For example, people over 60 are entitled to free prescriptions and eyesight tests. Such positive discrimination is undertaken to address (or redress) health inequalities—older people are more likely to need medication

---

[3] Department of Health, Shaping the Future NHS (National Beds Inquiry) 2000.
[4] National Pharmaceutical Society, *Medication for Older People*, 1997.
[5] A Tinker, *Older People in Modern Society* (London, Longman, 1997).
[6] Department of Health, *Handling Complaints* 2000.
[7] E Roberts, *Age Discrimination in Health and Social care—a briefing note* (King's Fund, London, 2000).

and to be on low incomes and unable to pay for their prescriptions. Measures like this nevertheless constitute age discrimination, since they exclude younger age people who may also have high health needs and low incomes. Where there are no alternative measures to meet the needs of those individuals, the 'positive discrimination' benefiting older people inevitably discriminates against younger people in similar circumstances.

The King's Fund review of evidence found examples of both direct and indirect forms of discrimination against older people.

Access to Health and Social Care

The most visible forms of age-related policies and practices occur when upper or lower age limits have been set to restrict access to care. This is evident in:

1. **Preventative health care.** Examples include free screening for both breast and cervical cancer, which has been restricted to women aged under 65. A decision was recently made to extend breast cancer screening to all women up to the age of 70 by 2004. Annual general health checks are offered to all patients aged 75 and over who are registered with a GP.

2. **A range of surgical and medical interventions.** In one study,[8] GPs claimed to be aware of upper age limits restricting access to heart by-pass operations (34 per cent), knee replacements (12 per cent) and kidney dialysis (35 per cent). Other studies[9] have shown that 20 per cent of cardiac care units operate upper age limits and 40 per cent had an explicit age-related policy for thrombolysis. Upper age limits have been fairly common in cardiac rehabilitation programmes[10] and in high or intensive care units following surgery.[11] There are many more examples where older people are known to experience restricted access to health care, even though no explicit age cut-offs have been set. For instance, older people are less likely than younger age groups to be offered health promotion advice by GPs and other primary care staff;[12] to have their mental health problems recognised and treated; and to be referred by GPs to hospital services because of their age.[13] They have also been shown to be treated less favourably than younger people in some accident and emergency departments,[14] where they were less likely to receive

[8] Age Concern, *New survey of GPs confirms Ageism in the NHS* (Age Concern England Press Release, 17 May 2000).

[9] N Dudley and E Burns, 'The influence of age on policies for admission and thrombolysis in coronary care in the UK' (1992) *Age and Ageing* 21, 95–8.

[10] J Whelan, *Equal Access to cardiac rehabilitation* (Age Concern England, 1998).

[11] National Confidential Inquiry into Preoperative Deaths, *Extremes of Age* (NCEPOD, 1999).

[12] P Little, 'Who is targeted for life style advice? A Cross-sectional Study in two General Practices' (1999) *British Journal of General Practice* 49, 806–10.

[13] 'The influence of age on policies for admission and thrombolysis in coronary care in the UK' (n 9 above).

[14] P Grant et al, 'The Management of Elderly Blunt Trauma Victims in Scotland—Evidence of Ageism' (2000) *Inquiry* 31: 519–29.

appropriate treatment for their injuries and more likely to die (even when taking into account differences in co-morbidity and frailty).

Older people are less likely to be accepted for treatment for end-stage renal failure;[15] and to be offered the best treatment for cancer.[16] They are also likely to have to wait longer for some forms of heart surgery.[17] Older people living in nursing and residential care homes are more likely to experience difficulties in accessing GP services.

In social care, many local authority social service departments set lower ceilings on the costs of care packages that they will make available for older people who have long-term care needs than on those for younger service users.

Older people's access to free care has also been reduced as care that was previously provided free of charge by the NHS has been progressively redefined as social care, and made subject to means testing by local authorities. This applies to all kinds of social care provision, including care homes (where the value of residents' own homes is taken into account in means testing). Policies that require older people to contribute financially to their personal care are a good example of indirect age discrimination, as the policy applies to people with chronic ill health and long-term disability—and older people make up the majority of people affected.

As social service departments have sought to address the needs of populations with greater levels of severe and complex disabilities within fixed budgets, they have tended to restrict services to those clients perceived to be in greatest need. This has meant that older people with 'low level' needs tend to have restricted access to state-supported care until they reach crisis point.[18] When charging for social care services, one-third of local authorities have been found to levy charges that leave service users living below the poverty level; this practice is thought to deter people from taking up services.[19]

Quality of Care

The quality of care is reflected in both the attitudes and behaviour of staff delivering care and in the standards of care provided. There is a good deal of evidence indicating that some staff working in acute hospital care have very negative attitudes towards older people. This can be evident in their reluctance to work with

---

[15] B New and N Mays, 'Age, Renal Replacement Therapy and Rationing' in A Harrison (ed), *Health Care UK 1996/7* (King's Fund, London, 1997) 205–33.

[16] N Turner et al, 'Cancer in Old Age—Is it Inadequately Investigated and Treated?' [1999] *British Medical Journal* 319, 309–12.

[17] D Hughes and L Griffiths, 'But if you look at the coronary anatomy . . . risk and rationing in cardiac surgery' (1996) *Sociology of Health and Illness* 18: 172–97.

[18] S Baldwin, 'Charging users for community care' in M May et al (eds), *Social Policy Review 9* (Social Policy Association, London, 1997).

[19] Audit Commission, *Charging with Care*, 2000.

older people, in patronising ways of communicating with them,[20] and in the extent to which they fail to meet even basic standards of nutrition and personal hygiene for older patients under their care.[21] Negative attitudes have also been identified among staff working in residential and nursing homes and providing care in people's own homes.[22] At worst, this puts older people at risk of various forms of abuse,[23] particularly those suffering from dementia.[24]

When care services are commissioned at a strategic level, commissioners have been found to have lower expectations of provision for older people compared with those for younger people.[25] Furthermore, those low expectations do not appear to reflect the aspirations of older people themselves for independence, dignity, and a chance to live as normal a life as possible.[26]

Older people from black and ethnic minority communities may experience 'double discrimination' through staff attitudes towards age and ethnicity. For instance, doctors have been found to act less favourably towards Asian patients who differ from white patients in the way they describe their symptoms or comply with health advice.[27]

Why Does Age Discrimination Occur?

The King's Fund research offers a number of reasons why older people are treated differently. Factors include:

1. **Low value placed on older people's lives.** For example, younger people have been found to value older people's quality of life less than older people themselves do. When young, relatively inexperienced junior doctors hold these views they may decide not to resuscitate older patients, having consulted neither patients nor their families.

2. **Lower social and economic merits of care.** A range of arguments have been put forward to justify age-related care, including the concept of older people having had a 'fair innings', and being less likely to benefit from particular kinds of care. These justifications are considered in more detail later in this chapter.

[20] S Lookinland and K Anson, 'Perpetuation of Ageist Attitudes among Present and Future Health Care Personnel: Implications for Elder Care' (1995) *Journal of Advanced Nursing* 21, 47–56.

[21] Health Advisory Service 2000, *Not because they are old* (An independent inquiry into the care of older people on acute wards in general hospitals HAS 2000, 1998).

[22] S Farrell, J Robinson and P Fletcher, *A New Era for Community Care? What people want from health, housing and social care services* (King's Fund, London, 1999).

[23] K Sone, 'What would you do for a quiet life?' [1997] *Community Care* 16, 18–19.

[24] R Means and J Langan, 'Charging and quasi-markets in community care: implications for elderly people with dementia' [1996] *Social Policy and Administration* 30: 244–62.

[25] C Gazder, *That's the way the money goes: Inspection of Commissioning Arrangements for Community Care Services Social Services Inspectorate* (The Stationery Office, 1999).

[26] *A New Era for Community Care?* (n 22 above).

[27] W Ahmad et al, 'General practitioners' Perceptions of Asian and non-Asian Patients' (1991) *Family Practice* 8: 52–6.

3. **Social distance.** Sociological studies of medical consultations suggest that professionals modify the information, advice and interventions they provide according to the 'social distance that exists between themselves and their patients or clients'. Under this theory, older people and other social groups (black, poor, and so on) may be treated less favourably.

4. **Perception of dependence.** Studies have shown that older people are frequently viewed as passive, dependent and a burden on society. In our society, achievement and contribution to society is often measured by economic activity, and this can lead to younger people, who are actively engaged in the workforce, being given higher priority for treatment.

5. **Cultural differences.** Traditionally, older people have been rather less demanding than younger people in their relationship with health and social care professionals. Studies have shown that they tend to be more acquiescent and less willing to speak out when dissatisfied. This may be changing now, but these generational differences would account for professionals responding more quickly to those who are more assertive (or aggressive).

What Does the Evidence Mean?

Five principle conclusions can be drawn from the King's Fund review of age discrimination in health and social care:

1. **Current relevance.** It cannot be assumed that all of the evidence of age discrimination identified still applies to modern day services. Some of the evidence may now be out of date. Although the review focused on recent research undertaken after 1990, changes may have taken place during that period, resulting in the scrapping of formal age-related policies. It is worth noting, by way of example, that the National Service Framework referred to research undertaken in 1991 revealing explicit upper age limits for cardiac care units but claimed that policies restricting access to such units are 'now almost unknown'.

2. **Incidence.** The evidence does not indicate that age discrimination is universally and comprehensively applied by all health and social organisations and practitioners. The incidence varies considerably from place to place and according to different types of care. Indeed, a number of studies have identified excellent care that can be promoted as best practice alongside examples of appalling neglect and prejudiced behaviour.

3. **Visibility.** While it is clear that age discrimination takes place, we do not really know how widespread it is and therefore, how serious a problem. Even with the more visible age based policies that limit access to health and social care, members of health boards and social service committees who are ultimately accountable for services may not be aware of them—although most

senior managers and practitioners can be expected to know of their existence. It is even more difficult to identify and quantify discriminatory practice resulting from individual judgments and decisions made by thousands of health and social care staff. This can only be determined by identifying and comparing patterns of referral, treatment, care and support relating to people of different age groups. Unfortunately, very little of the information that is routinely collected to measure performance in health and social care can be used for that purpose. More research is therefore needed to clarify the extent to which older people are being disadvantaged (or not) by this kind of hidden discrimination. Even then, it will be important to disentangle age discrimination from other issues around gender, poverty, ethnicity, and chronic ill health and disability.

4. **Controversy.** Fierce debates can surround the evidence on age discrimination, as research findings do not always provide conclusive proof that age discrimination is actually taking place. A closer look reveals that this is frequently because there are widely differing ideas as to what constitutes discrimination itself. Some argue that practices appearing to disadvantage older people are not discriminatory, because they are legitimately based on the capacity to benefit. It is only because older people tend to have a lower capacity to benefit that the disadvantage appears to be concentrated among older people. For example, New and Mays[28] have contested whether restricting access of older people to treatment for end-stage renal failure constitutes age discrimination, arguing that age is statistically associated with the clinical ability to benefit. Grimley Evans[29] takes a different view, arguing that it is discriminatory and unfair to deny treatment to individual older people on the basis of the likely benefits to the 'average' older person. As will be seen below, this disagreement depends in part on different notions of what constitutes discrimination. Even if there is agreement on whether the practice is discriminatory, further controversy arises as to when discrimination can be justified. In particular, can cost-effectiveness be used to justify discriminatory policies and practices? Even then, there will still be arguments as to whether particular policies are necessary and proportional.

5. **Rationing relevance.** Much—though not all—of the age discrimination identified is the result of explicit or tacit decisions to ration scarce resources using age criteria. However, age related rationing is rarely acknowledged officially to be taking place. When rationing is questioned, professionals and others may defend it using either 'fair innings' arguments[30] or cost-effectiveness justifications.

These are key issues that will have to be addressed when scrutinising health and social care services in order to identify age discrimination taking place and to decide on the action required to eliminate it.

---

[28] 'Age, Renal Replacement Therapy and Rationing' (n 15 above).
[29] JG Evans, *Age discrimination: implications for the ageing process*, above, ch 2.
[30] A William, 'Inter-generational equity: an exploration of the "fair innings" argument' (1997) *Health Economics* 6: 117–32.

JUSTIFYING AGE-RELATED APPROACHES TO HEALTH AND SOCIAL CARE

The National Service Framework for Older People requires the NHS and local authorities to review all age-related policies and 'to examine the justification for an age-based approach, explore alternative ways of managing access to the service and propose changes necessary.' The Framework, and subsequent guidance issued to assist with the policy reviews, made it clear that, in the Government's view, some age-related distinctions can be regarded as legitimate. The objective of the reviews is therefore to distinguish between those policies that can be regarded as fair or justified on other grounds, and those that cannot.

Judging whether age-related policies are legitimate is by no means simple and straightforward. As the survey conducted by the King's Fund in 2001 showed,[31] many senior managers in health and social services were not clear how to judge whether age-related approaches to care constituted age discrimination, nor how to decide whether such approaches are unfair and therefore 'unacceptable'.

As efforts are made to 'root out age discrimination' in health and social care, both service providers and users will need a better understanding of age equality in health and social care and of the different arguments that can be put forward to justify or challenge age-related care. There also needs to be greater consensus about what is fair (or not) about age-based distinctions in access to and standards of care. In the absence of that understanding and agreement, it is hard to see how scrutiny, challenge and change can take place. This applies both to the implementation of voluntary good practice initiatives like the National Service Framework, and to the drafting and implementation of any future age equality legislation.

Interpretations of Equality in Health and Social Care

Age-based approaches to care can be justified on equality grounds. However, there are different notions of equality that come into play whenever people consider whether particular policies or practices are 'fair' to older people.[32] This is evident when we look at the five different principles of equality identified by Sandra Fredman and consider what the impact is when applied in practice:

1. **Equal treatment.** Here the aim is not to treat everyone the same but to treat likes alike. But the initial decision as to when two patients are alike requires complex judgments. Thus, it could be argued that everyone with the same health condition, such as a broken leg, are relevantly alike, and should therefore have the same access to and duration of care, regardless of their age. By contrast,

---

[31] E Roberts, J Robinson and L Seymour, *Old Habits Die Hard: Tackling Age Discrimination in Health and Social Care* (King's Fund, London, 2002).

[32] S Fredman, 'The Age of Equality', above ch 3.

it could be argued that the difference in age makes two such patients relevantly different, and that treating two such patients alike regardless of their age in fact amounts to a breach of the principle of equal treatment. In fact, it is not generally appropriate to standardise care in this way, given individual variations in severity of the condition, length of time needed to recuperate, and so on. Indeed, it would be most unfair to older people, given that they tend to take longer to recover from injury or illness.

Other ways of deciding when two groups are alike have been used. The principle of equal treatment can sometimes be used to justify organising services around particular age groups who are perceived to have similar needs or preferences. An example of such an age-related service are special hospital wards and physicians dedicated exclusively to the care of older people (or children). Similarly, specialist mental health services are provided in different ways according to whether the users are very young (Child and Adolescent Mental Health Services), whether they are adults aged 18–65, or are adults aged 65 and over (geriatric psychiatry) and social care day services provided for older disabled people offer a different range of activities and social engagement than those provided for young disabled people. It can be argued that a failure to take age into account here would disadvantage particular age groups. However, while it may be appropriate to differentiate care on age grounds, treating likes alike does not necessarily imply that the quality of service is high. To the contrary, specialist services can turn out to provide an equally poor service for all users of a certain age. This is an accusation that is sometimes made about the examples given above.

2. **Individual merit.** Here the aim is to treat all individuals on their merits, rather than according to characteristics like age, race or gender. Again, this is a principle that is not usually applied in health care. The exception is where decisions are made to reserve care or provide it more quickly to people who are actively engaged in the workforce. Some clinicians perceive people in work to be in some sense more deserving or valuable than those who are not, as they are making an economic contribution to society. This, of course, works to the detriment of retired people who may be denied access to interventions that are in very short supply or spend longer on waiting lists for routine surgery. Such age-related distinctions can be considered unfair, on the grounds that they ignore or give less value to other social contributions made by older people who are not economically active, such as caring for a disabled spouse or child, undertaking voluntary work for a charity, and so forth. In the final analysis, the principle of individual merit is a very weak justification for age-related differences in health care, as the NHS is intended to help people according to their need, not according to the economic or social contribution they make to society.

3. **Individual needs.** This is the most frequently invoked principle justifying differences in the care provided for individuals or groups. The National Service Framework for Older People states that 'treatment and care should be provided

on the basis of health needs and ability to benefit, rather than on a patient's age.' However, people's needs are related to age. Health need implies the existence of a disease or condition that threatens an individual's ability to function physically or mentally, to participate in social and economic activities, or to shorten life itself. The risks of these needs arising increases with age. Thus, it can be regarded as perfectly fair to immunise a child against common diseases like measles, mumps and polio and not to offer this protection to her grandmother, or to offer influenza injections to older individuals who are liable to become seriously ill and to develop complications like life-threatening pneumonia. This is fair because the risks of contracting particular diseases and the consequences of doing so are different at different ages.

Providing care on the basis of need alone would not be sensible, if it is known or thought very likely that an individual would not benefit from an intervention, for example, when a disease is so far advanced that it is untreatable. So, need has to be bound up with 'ability to benefit'.

The problem is that clinicians and policy-makers can make decisions using 'ability to benefit' criteria that work to the systematic disadvantage of older people. This happens because 'benefit' is defined in such a way that the level of benefit resulting from particular interventions is statistically associated with age, and the duration of benefit is likely to be shorter for older people than younger people (who will have more years of life).

The disadvantage for older people is evident when efforts are made to measure the cost-effectiveness of particular treatments, in order to inform decisions about allocation of resources to particular services. Health economists use measures called QALYs (Quality Adjusted Life Years) to assess the changes in length or quality of life brought about as a result of particular interventions. Even when it can be shown that older people benefit as much as younger people in terms of quality of life gained from say, an operation to remove a cataract, they will not enjoy the benefit for as many years as younger people will. These differential rates of health gain are then used to justify allocating fewer resources to health services for older people, on the grounds of cost effectiveness.

This cost-effectiveness argument can be challenged on socio-economic and moral grounds. In the first place, some assessment also needs to be made of the costs and benefits for society as a whole of even small improvements in the health of older people. For example, improved sight or mobility enables independence at home and reduces the need for social care services. In the second place, putting a greater value on the lives of young or old people is morally indefensible in a society that values all members equally.

When it comes to doctors deciding whether to treat individuals, their 'ability to benefit' will be a matter of clinical judgment. Where doctors make those judgments on assumptions (based on prejudice, experience or research evidence) that older people, by and large, are less likely to benefit from particular interventions, this acts against the interests of those individuals who are not like the 'average' older person. These judgments about 'ability to benefit' then result in older people with say, coronary heart disease or cancer, being less likely than younger people with the same conditions to be offered the medication, surgery or other therapy known to be effective in curing or minimising the impact of those diseases.

These age-related restrictions on access to health care are increasingly justified on the grounds that there is no evidence that such interventions are effective with people over 65 or more. This constitutes a 'double whammy' for older people: the absence of research evidence showing how effective various treatments can be, even for very old people, is a consequence of decisions made by drug companies and others to exclude people aged 65 and over from their research studies.

4. **Fair distribution.** Here the aim is to achieve equality of outcomes. It is a principle that can be used to justify allocating unequal amounts of resources to particular age groups in order to rectify health inequalities among the population. One example, mentioned earlier, is the policy exempting older people from paying for drug prescriptions. A failure to 'favour' this section of the population, it is argued, would result in disadvantage for older people (who are more likely to need medication and less likely to be able to pay for them). Here age is being used as a proxy indicator for ill-health and poverty, but in order to benefit—not disadvantage—older people.

Favouring one age group over another can also be justified in terms of inter-generational justice. Thus, allocating more resources to the treatment and care of children or young people while, at the same time, withholding or reducing the care provided for older people is seen as fair, given that over a life time, everyone will experience the advantages accruing to the young and the disadvantages experienced by the old. This is the 'fair innings' argument that is so often used to legitimise discriminating against older people in order to benefit children 'who have their whole lives before them'. Spending proportionately higher amounts of money on improving the health of the young is seen as a more efficient use of scarce resources, given the pay back in terms of the overall health of the population.

In practice, as we saw in Sandra Fredman's chapter, there are problems with the 'fair innings' approach, in that there is no consensus about the period of time that constitutes a 'fair innings' and it is left to individual doctors to judge when someone's time is up. There is no transparency about the age cut-offs being used—is it 50, 60 or 70? While many would regard it as right and proper to favour children in hypothetical examples involving doctors who have to decide whether to operate either on a child or an old man, there is little public support for policies that would automatically withhold or withdraw treatment from our relatives and friends just because they have grown old. It is, of course, an entirely different matter when individuals decide for themselves that they would prefer not to have medical intervention that might prolong their life.

Furthermore, it cannot be assumed that all older people received the same advantages when they were young; some will have developed poor health because of deprivations suffered in childhood.

5. **Equal rights.** Here the aim is to ensure that all individuals have equal opportunities to achieve particular outcomes. In health and social care, the desired effect of treatment, care and support is to enable individuals to have a quality of life characterised by maximum independence and the freedom to participate in those aspects of family and community life that they wish to engage in. It can be regarded as unfair to organise and deliver services in such a way that older people have less chance than others of achieving that quality of life. That can happen, for example, when the failure to provide rehabilitation services after illness or injury leaves older people more dependent than they need be, with no option but to leave the home they would prefer to stay in and enter some form of institutional care.

In practice, it can be difficult to define 'quality of life' in the detail that is required to judge whether it has been achieved or not. Perhaps more importantly, health and social services are not the only agencies that can enhance or impede individuals' independence and social participation. Housing, transport, education and other bodies also have a part to play. This can make it difficult to determine the extent to which the actions of health and social care bodies have contributed to the poor quality of life experienced by so many older people.

Equality is not the Only Consideration

Of course, when scrutinising age-related approaches to care and judging whether they are justified or not, equality considerations are not the only aspects to take into account. Equality criteria can be over-ridden by other considerations, such as value for money (where the cost-effectiveness of particular types of care for specific age groups is in question), or user preference. This is all quite legitimate, given that some limits on equality have to be imposed when there are trade-offs between conflicting criteria. It could, for example, be regarded as quite impractical and unreasonable to pursue equality objectives, regardless of cost. But it is important that these justifications are transparent to those challenging their validity, and are backed up with evidence about costs and benefits, or patient preferences. As Sandra Fredman argued in chapter three, for discriminatory treatment to be justified, the evidence must show that it is necessary for a legitimate purpose and proportional. Without that evidence, there is a danger that the explanations offered for treating different age groups differently may amount to no more than thinly disguised ageist prejudice.

In summary, it is perfectly possible to strive for age equality in health and social care and to test age-related policies against different principles of equality. These interpretations of equality will need to be applied when framing any new legislation relating to health and social care.

IS AGE EQUALITY LEGISLATION NEEDED?

Some would argue that the introduction of age equality legislation is neither necessary nor desirable. It is not necessary, they say, because the Government has only recently developed a policy prohibiting age discrimination in health and social care. It is early days yet but, if implemented properly, we can expect the NHS and local government to take steps that will put an end to age discrimination in local services. Some might even argue that new laws are not necessary, as some discriminatory decisions or actions can be challenged under the European Convention on Human Rights, which prohibits action that threatens individuals' rights to life.[33]

Others argue that new laws do not bring about greater equality. It would be better to invest in education and training that will bring about changes in the hearts and minds of people who discriminate against older (or younger) people. Legislation can be regarded as potentially dangerous, leading to unintended consequences not in the interests of older people. It might, for instance, encourage some doctors to engage in inappropriate heroic surgery and other defensive medicine for fear of being prosecuted on charges of unlawful age discrimination.

I want to argue that new age equality legislation is, with some provisos, both necessary and desirable. The recently introduced National Service Framework is essentially a voluntary initiative. It shows what good practice looks like and advises agencies of the steps they should take to check whether or not their provision amounts to good practice. But the monitoring mechanisms set up by the Department of Health to ensure that agencies are following the steps specified are rather weak and undemanding.[34] For instance, much reliance is placed on 'champions' who have no authority but are nevertheless expected to look after the interests of older people. The Department of Health expects all authorities to audit their age-related policies and to decide what action is needed within a specified time period. Civil servants charged with monitoring these 'milestones' accept that some authorities will fail to meet the deadline but are prevented from 'pushing too hard'.

It is not clear what happens to those agencies that continue to fall short of the standard set on age discrimination, or what individuals or groups who believe they are being discriminated against can do to seek compensation or any other form of redress.

A recent King's Fund research report[35] indicates that senior health and social care managers do not appear to be doing very much to 'root out age discrimination'. They are preoccupied with other pressing priorities, such as reducing

[33] European Convention on Human Rights Arts 2, 3, 5, 8, 14.

[34] Minutes of a meeting of the King's Fund Working Group on Age Discrimination, November 2001 (unpublished).

[35] *Old Habits Die Hard* (n 31 above).

hospital waiting lists or meeting the targets associated with other National Service Frameworks on cancer or coronary heart disease. These managers are ultimately responsible for implementing the National Service Framework for Older People but, by their own account, few report that they feel under any great pressure from either politicians or the public to identify and combat age discrimination. As Lord Lester has argued, with no effective enforcement measures to ensure compliance with the National Service Framework, it would be unwise to place much hope in the new policy achieving much success in improving age equality in health and social care.[36]

New age-equality legislation would tackle the shortcomings of the National Service Framework for Older People, making it unlawful to discriminate on age grounds alone. It would also clarify in specific terms what compliance with the law means, and would indicate the penalties that could be exacted on those bodies not acting within the law. In addition, the new law would entitle aggrieved parties to seek redress.

It is true that new legislation will not by itself eliminate age discrimination. Education and training programmes will also be needed to increase awareness and understanding and to change attitudes and behaviour. The legislation will need to be drafted carefully to avoid the unintended consequences of defensive medicine.

What Kind of Legislation?

To be effective in tackling age discrimination in health and social care, the new legislation will need to provide more protection than that offered by the Human Rights Act 1998 which brought the European Convention on Human Rights into domestic law. The protection of the 'right to life' in that Act sets a high threshold before the courts will find a breach of the Act, and will probably not be very effective in challenging age discrimination—although that remains to be tested in the courts.

Conventional anti-discrimination laws, like those relating to race, sex or disability, will not be adequate. These laws are notoriously slow in changing discriminatory practices, as they deal solely with individual cases, and would be singularly ineffective in ending institutionalised ageism. It would also be particularly difficult for individuals to prove that they had been discriminated against on the basis of their age, when decisions about their care are a matter of clinical judgment regarding need, ability to benefit and so forth.

It would be better to frame the legislation in a way that both prohibits age discrimination and imposes a duty on health and social care providers to promote age equality when funding, organising and delivering their care services. This would follow the example of the Race Relations Amendment Act,[37] which

---

[36] A Lester, *Age Discrimination and Equality* (Help the Aged, 2001).
[37] Race Relations Amendment Act 2000, s 71(2)–(3).

imposes a statutory duty on public authorities not only to eliminate unlawful racial discrimination but 'to promote equality of opportunity and good relations between persons of different racial groups'.

A similar duty related to age equality would require service agencies to identify the factors that can prevent older people from enjoying equal opportunities to have a quality of life characterised by independence and social participation. They would have to implement strategies to remove those barriers to equality within their own organisations. Health and social care agencies would need to be able to demonstrate how effective those strategies were proving to be, in case of challenge. They would have to collect and analyse information about referrals, treatment, care and support provided by age, so that they or others could compare patterns and trends in provision for older people with those achieved by similar organisations serving comparable populations. Local variations in provision can reveal evidence of 'hidden' discrimination resulting from the decisions and actions of hundreds of health professionals. Where discrimination is in doubt, these comparisons can at least raise questions about the reasons for the differences and demand explanations if challenged.

Given that older people can be discriminated against on grounds of age, gender, race, disability, religion and sexual orientation, it would make sense to develop new legislation that would require public bodies like the NHS and local authorities to promote equality on all six fronts. An Equalities Commission might be set up to monitor compliance, possibly on the lines adopted in Northern Ireland.[38] There is, of course, a golden opportunity to develop that legislation over the next year or so, given that the Government has to respond to the European Union Framework Directive prohibiting age discrimination in employment.[39]

The Costs of Age Equality in Health and Social Care

It is clear that the promotion of age-equality in health and social care will incur costs. In the first instance, there will be expenditure on regulatory, inspection and review bodies required to monitor and assess the extent to which public bodies are eliminating age discrimination. New legislation would also inevitably increase expenditure on lawyers or other adjudicators who would deal with challenges made by older people or their advocates. Increased investment would need to be made in the education and training of health and social care staff.

These costs are likely to be relatively small compared with the consequences of outlawing the rationing of services on age-based criteria. It is not inevitable that the elimination of age-related rationing would necessarily push up the costs of care. Rationing (or priority ratings) would merely be based on other criteria,

---

[38] Equality Commission for Northern Ireland, web site: www.eocni.org.uk
[39] *Age Discrimination and Equality* (n 36 above).

transferring restrictions onto other groups of people, for example, those considered to be in less acute need. However, ever-increasing public demands for more and better health care for everyone are likely to intensify the political pressures that will lead to higher expenditure on care services. This alarms politicians and civil servants keen to ensure that public expenditure keeps within reasonable bounds, and managers who have long relied on age-related rationing in order to balance the books. Concern about the costs of age equality can lead to people dismissing proposals for change as 'unrealistic'.

Before rushing to that judgment, it would be a good idea to consider the costs resulting from age discrimination in health and social care. Some costs are currently borne by older people themselves, who experience avoidable pain and misery, disability and even premature death by being denied access to timely and appropriate treatment, care and support. The costs also fall on families—especially female relatives—who take on responsibilities of caring for older relatives who are ill or disabled. These relatives may forego the benefits of a decent salary or pension due to their inability to hold down a full-time job. They also become socially isolated through lack of relief from their caring responsibilities. Families may be denied the help and support of grandparents. Finally, costs that are not incurred in the health sector fall on other sectors, notably on local authorities responsible for financing long-term care, and on the social security budget used to fund disability benefits and carers allowances.

Further work is no doubt needed to quantify the costs and benefits of delivering age equality in health and social care in order to judge what can be afforded. But it is hard to imagine anyone seriously arguing that it is not worth spending the money required to prevent older people being excluded from opportunities to participate in family and community life. Failure to promote age equality in health and social care will perpetuate the tendency for some older people to be treated as second-class citizens.

CONCLUSION

If the National Service Framework on Older People is implemented properly, we should see some reduction in discriminatory health and social care practices. However, it would be unwise to expect any radical change, given the difficulties of enforcing what is essentially a guide to good practice. New age discrimination legislation is needed to increase the motivation of staff to organise and deliver their services in ways that do not disadvantage older people, and strengthen the ability of older people and others working in their interests to challenge discriminatory practice and seek redress. Nor is it sufficient to introduce conventional anti-discrimination legislation. There is a strong argument for creating new laws that place a duty on health and social care agencies to promote age equality and require them to demonstrate that they do not discriminate unlawfully against anyone on grounds of age.

That is not to say that legislation by itself will achieve greater age equality. Education and training of staff will be needed to change hearts and minds, as will review and scrutiny procedures to monitor and assess achievements on age equality.

Clearly, the measures needed to achieve age equality in health and social care will incur costs. New resources will be needed to establish review bodies required to ensure compliance with the law, for new programmes of education and training, and—perhaps most important—to manage the consequences of ending rationing of services on age-based criteria. However, in assessing such costs, it is crucial to recognise and factor in the costs of age discrimination itself. These are paid by older people themselves, who experience avoidable pain and misery, disability and premature death by being denied access to timely treatment, care and support. Such costs also fall on families who take on the responsibility of caring for older relatives who are ill or disabled. Costs saved in the health sector also clearly fall on other sectors, notably on local authority social services responsible for financing long-term care, and on the social security budget used for funding disability benefits and care allowances.

Further work is needed to quantify the benefits and costs of promoting age equality in health and social care. However, there can be no doubt that new measures are needed to prevent older people's exclusion from opportunities to participate in family and community life. Failure to introduce new legislation is likely to perpetuate the tendency for older people to be treated as second-class citizens.

6

Age Equality in Access to Education

TOM SCHULLER

AGE, EQUALITY AND EDUCATION[1]

Introduction

'FOR A VERY small expence the publick can facilitate, can encourage and can even impose upon almost the whole body of the people, the necessity of acquiring those most essential parts of education.'[2]

This quote from Adam Smith contains a number of lines of argument central to the theme of age and equality in relation to education. It begins with typical allusion to cost-effectiveness. It asserts the nature of education as a public good. It distinguishes between different strengths of policy intervention, from encouragement to compulsion. Finally, it implies (knowingly or not) a genuinely lifelong approach to learning, since almost the whole body of people is included.

I shall develop all of these arguments, to different extents. The main lines of argument in this chapter are as follows:

1. Demonstrable inequalities exist in the age distribution of education, in almost every form.
2. In absolute terms older people's access to education has improved over the last decade or so. However, their opportunities relative to those of younger generations have not. Both absolute and relative trends need to be considered. Intergenerational equality is a key issue in education.
3. In any discussion of equality, age should not be considered as a factor on its own. It will always interact with other social variables, notably class and gender.

[1] Thanks to the Nuffield Foundation for supporting the project; to Jodie Reed for her valuable research assistance; to Sir David Watson for his illuminating response to an initial presentation of the paper; to Jim Soulsby and Stephen McNair for giving me access to unpublished work; to John Bynner and Richard Worsley for helpful comments on a first draft; and especially to Sarah Spencer for helpful comments throughout.
[2] A Smith, *Wealth of Nations* vol 1 book 2, quoted in A Sen, *Development as Freedom* (Oxford, OUP, 1999) 129.

4. Ends and means, intrinsic and instrumental aspects are intertwined. There are strong pragmatic reasons for promoting educational opportunity for older people; however the case will ultimately rest on intrinsic values, in particular on notions of personal autonomy and capability, as defined by Sen.[3]

The chapter therefore explores inequality and discrimination in education in respect of age; what forms it takes, and what might be done about it. As things stand there will be legislation on age discrimination, following the European Directive on Article 13. This will cover training as part of employment which is required to be covered under the Directive. I argue that the coverage should go wider than this, to include education generally.

DEFINITIONAL ISSUES

Education

Education here refers to all forms of organised learning. This can take place in formal institutions—schools, colleges etc—or in community centres or in the workplace. It can also take place in the home on an individual basis, through study packs or distance learning. There are of course fuzzy boundaries, for example where people are accessing self-help information through the Internet, or acting together in community settings. People have powerful learning experiences in a whole variety of modes and contexts. Informal settings are especially important for older people, who are less likely to aim for qualification-related learning. But we are talking here of learning activities with a degree of structure and intention which are to some extent governed or supported by public policy.

Age

Conceptualising the relationship between age and education presents particular problems. In general, the continuing identification of education with the initial phase in people's lives (however extended that may now be) means that from one point of view, discrimination against 'older' people starts very early. As I show below, the population over 25 has less access to significant forms of education, notably higher education. In the case of training, by contrast, patterns of age inequality emerge later in the age range.

'Older' people therefore means different things in different contexts. In the employment sphere it refers primarily to people aged 50–65. In the formal education system it may mean anything from 25 upwards. In the non-formal sector it is most likely to refer to people who have completed employment, but with an

---

[3] *Development as Freedom* (n 2 above).

age span of potentially five decades. Discrimination, and equality, will correspondingly reflect different experiences for different age groups.

Age discrimination can operate in reverse, with young people prevented by
law or practice from pursuing the options of their choice, which could take them
out of education. Although there is little pressure for actually reducing the
school leaving age, it is at least arguable that the requirement on young people
to stay in formal education deprives some of them of the most suitable learning
path. There is certainly a case for saying that the system's bias towards youth
disadvantages those young people who would benefit from a better balanced
system that allowed them to do their initial learning outside the formal system
and then return to it later when they are motivated. Systematic interleaving of
education, work and other activity is desirable, with lessons to be learnt from
other countries.

In general, I would argue that legislation and policy should discourage rather
than reinforce rigid age banding. They should therefore not be framed in such a
way as identifies quasi-universal age-groups, but use chronological age only as
appropriate in specific policy contexts.

Equality

Equality in relation to age and education cannot be sensibly conceived of in a simple linear mathematical sense, with each age group getting proportionately the
same amount of all forms of education. This immediately raises issues about how
to distinguish between equality between *groups* and between *individuals*; about
whether we focus on *access* to various forms of provision, on *content and pedagogy*, or on *outcomes*; and about the relationship between *need* and *entitlement*.
A key distinction is between equality in relation to *participation*—what proportions of which social groups take part in what forms of education—and equality
in relation to *public subsidy*—how much public money is going to which groups.

Inequality and discrimination are clearly connected, but inequality can occur
without discrimination. There are two rather different but interrelated lines of
enquiry into this relationship, which reflect a tension in policy and practice in
relation to age. One deals with the level of provision catering specifically for
older people, and attempts to reach some kind of judgment on its adequacy relative to provision for other groups. The other focuses on how far provision generally is age-blind, in the sense that it does not discriminate one way or another
in relation to older people. I am here more concerned with the latter.

We can also broadly distinguish between *direct* discrimination, where older
people are specifically (if not necessarily explicitly) discouraged from participating; and *indirect* discrimination, where such discouragement occurs as a result
of the nature of the provision.

Discrimination may occur at the *systemic* or policy level; or at the *provider*
level (institution, course or class). At the systemic level, there is potential

inequality in the level of *resource* provided specifically for education for older people compared with other groups; or in the *access,* which older people have to mainstream provision.[4] However in considering these issues it is important to avoid two potential traps. One is the danger that focusing strongly on older people will produce a form of ghettoisation, or divisive sectional lobbying on behalf of a particular group. Mixed-age and intergenerational learning, will not be helped by this. Social justice and mutual tolerance may even be out at risk, as the gilded exclusiveness of some gated Florida communities illustrates. The second is that factors influencing people's potential for learning and their learning achievements will be identified as associated with age, instead of being more rationally associated with other characteristics such as health.

Reasons for Inequality

General inequality at *systemic* level occurs for a number of reasons:

1. A general assumption that education is for the young

2. Assumptions about the capacity of older people to learn.

3. A concentration on the economic rationale for investment in education, with the corollary that those who have left the labour market for good are irrelevant.

4. The absence of a pressure group comparable to parents of young students

5. A lack of confidence and motivation on the part of older people, especially those with low educational levels, to articulate their needs and engage in education.

Some of the assumptions and attitudes are demonstrably wrong, and are a matter of ignorance or prejudice. Others involve matters of judgment or opinion, for instance about the nature and goals of education—whether the narrow economic imperative is justifiable, even on its own terms—or about the relative value of educating older rather than younger people where there is competition for a limited number of places. There are circumstances where logic, evidence and universal values point all in the same direction. In other cases, there may be some tensions and trade-offs. It would be wrong, in challenging the notion that old dogs can't learn new tricks, to pretend that older people do not have some limitations on their learning capacities compared with younger people. (The reverse is also true).

These factors also operate at the *provider* level, but inequality may result from other forms of discrimination:

---

[4] S Carlton and J Soulsby *Learning to Grow Older and Bolder* (NIACE, Leicester, 1999); J Soulsby, *'Education',* in *Age Discrimination in Public Policy: A Review of Evidence* (Help the Aged, 2002).

Issues to do with *entry requirements*, formal or informal: how far do they encourage or discourage people of different ages?

Issues to do with *curriculum and pedagogy:* How well do they reflect different needs and preferences? This includes assessment practices.

Issues to do with the *ethos* or *culture* of the institution: what is the implicit message it sends to older learners?

Issues concerned with *outcomes*: do the benefits of education flow equally to people of different age groups? This is largely out of the hands of educational providers, but is nevertheless a significant factor.

Evidence of direct discrimination against older people is fairly rare. Some financial regulations are discriminatory in that they debar older students from access to grants or other forms of support. This relates largely to implicit assumptions and calculations about investment and payback, discussed later on. Generally institutions either make no reference to age, or state a policy of encouraging mature students. Some medical schools refer explicitly to the length of their course and the expected length of service after qualification in their statement about mature students. At the institutional level, however, the decisive factors are more likely to be the attitudes of admissions tutors, the nature of the curriculum, the level of student support and the extent to which the education is compatible with other demands on the individual, primarily in terms of time and money.

Contrast with Inequality in Health Care

There are some interesting parallels to be drawn with the discussion of health in Janice Robinson's most useful parallel chapter.[5] They reinforce the need for a cross-sectoral approach to policy and legislation. However I want to suggest that at the macro level education differs substantially from health in at least three particular respects in this discussion.

First, there is a huge *implicit and systemic bias* in favour of youth in education. No policy-maker or thinking citizen could ignore older people in a general debate on health (which is a very different matter from saying that either category will deal adequately with the issue). At least some of older people's health needs are manifest and immediately recognisable. Forty per cent of the NHS budget is spent on those over 56.[6] The same is simply not the case for education, where older people's needs and preferences are commonly marginalised, and only a tiny fraction of the budget is devoted to them.

Secondly, there are very important issues to do with *intergenerational relations*. Achieving an appropriate balance in the distribution of educational opportunity across age groups is a difficult task, given patterns of expenditure

---

[5] J Robinson, above ch 5.
[6] S Fredman, above ch 3.

which shift continually across and within sectors. On the assumption of increasing prosperity, over time younger generations will when they die almost certainly have had more spent on their health than their predecessors had. However, younger healthier people will not displace older unhealthier people in the same way as younger more qualified people can do older people with fewer qualifications. Their improved health (if it does improve) will not generally impinge on the prospects and life chances of their elders, as their improved education (or at least increased qualification-holding) does.

Thirdly, *cumulative inequality* exists in both health and education, but with differences. The danger of continuous and growing polarisation within a single cohort as it ages is especially serious. Unhealthy young people are more likely to be unhealthy older people (or not to reach old age at all). This does not mean that they necessarily get more health care, since healthy people tend to have a class advantage in gaining access to health services; but their claims to health at any given point, and especially when they are older, may be more accepted. In education, the more you have had the more you are likely to get. Initially this is because successful school students are much more likely to go on to university or college, but also because people with good educational achievements tend to have higher motivation and skills in gaining access to training, and because employers are more likely to see them as a good investment. The increasing division of households into work and resource-rich and work and resource-poor is heavily influenced by labour market and economic factors. Any policy must be careful not to allow anti-discriminatory measures to accentuate polarisation *within* older age groups.

These latter two factors in particular mean that it is crucial to hold in mind the dynamics of the issue—the way it manifests itself both over the life course and between cohorts. A powerful example is the number of older people who were as children unable to take up grammar school or (in smaller numbers) university places because of lack of family funding. This has both a class and a gender dimension; working class people were much more likely to be unable to afford the uniform and other costs associated with a grammar school place, while even within middle class families girls were more likely than boys to forego opportunities. The claims of such people on the system remain, if one takes a full life course perspective. In respect of access to university, they have still today not faded from view.

Legitimate Limits to Age Equality

This gives some idea of the complexity of conceptualising equality in education—a complexity, it should be said, which it shares with health. If equality cannot be defined simply in terms of arithmetically similar participation rates for all groups, what kinds of inequality are reasonable, and might therefore justify direct or indirect discrimination?

First, there is an important sense in which it is accepted that education for young people should be compulsory but older people cannot be coerced into it. No one suggests that every older person should participate in education, on a universal basis. This is not trivial. It is the corollary of the basic position on capability and choice; but it also allows genuine debate about why compulsion is allowed, and up to what age.

Secondly, exclusion may be acceptable where a person is demonstrably unable to benefit from education. In so far as greater numbers of such cases may be found within the older population in respect of some forms of learning, then public support for such provision may discriminate. Training to be an astronaut is an extreme example, but the argument could hold even where access is open rather than competitive. However, the number of such instances is certainly less than might be expected, given the scope for adapting the environment. (There is an interesting parallel here with woman soldiers).

Thirdly, an older person's entitlement to publicly supported education may be constrained by the probability of that public investment being unlikely to show commensurate returns, ie where there is a reasonable case for saying that the public investment in the person's education would be disproportionate to the likely return. A 60-year-old would be unreasonable in asserting a claim to be able to start conventional medical training, even if they had gathered the appropriate qualifications in due time. There are reasonable trade-offs to be made, when places for medical students are limited. However, such cases would need to be strictly monitored, so that the estimates of probability were not too narrowly made, excluding older students unnecessarily. It is encouraging to hear of medical schools now admitting students of over 40 years old.

Fourthly, a similar argument may be allowed in relation to training sponsored by organisations. For example, it would be unreasonable for a person close to retirement to claim equality of treatment with a much younger person seconded for two years to do a major qualification.

Finally, there could be cases where an age-based claim for equality might be trumped by other equality-based claims. For example, a group of already well-educated older people might assert an age-based claim to provision tailored to their needs which would force an institution to devote resources to it which they could not then use to extend opportunities to disadvantaged younger people. This resembles an aspect of the forthcoming legislation on special educational needs and disability, where the notion of 'reasonable' awaits testing.

All of these will need exploration and testing in practical contexts. Overall, I argue that it is more important to focus on *systemic inequality* than *institutional discrimination*. That is to say, it is more important to aim at rebalancing the education system in favour of a more equal distribution across age groups than at targeting individual institutions. A better balance, with educational policies based on a genuinely lifelong perspective, will encourage institutions to do more and better work with older people. This approach is compatible, however, with forbidding institutions or local authorities to discriminate, for instance in admissions or grants policy.

POLICY FRAMEWORK

The identification of education with the first phase of life is very deep-rooted. Even now that large proportions of the population stay on in the education system until they become formally adult, the notion of 'student' is still very much associated, in the public mind and that of many policy-makers, with young people. In the post-compulsory sector, the average age of students in further and higher education has risen, but what this mostly signals is the prolongation of the initial studying period for young people.

There have been significant shifts in policy stance since New Labour came to power in 1997. A flurry of working groups and papers of various hues led to *The Learning Age*,[7] with a powerful foreword by David Blunkett as Secretary of State. As well as securing our economic future, he argued:

> Learning has a wider contribution. It helps make ours a civilised society, develops the spiritual side of our lives and promotes active citizenship. Learning enables people to play a full part in their community. It strengthens the family, the neighbourhood and consequently the nation. It helps us fulfil our potential and opens doors to a love of music, art and literature. That is why we value learning for its own sake as well as for the equality of opportunity it brings. To realise our ambition, we must all develop and sustain a regard for learning *at whatever age*.[8] (emphasis added)

Much has been done since then in the way of expansion and support for different forms of learning, appealing to different age groups. The Adult and Community Fund has repaired some of the damage perpetrated by the previous administration to community-based and local adult education (especially important to older people). Similarly, the Union Learning Fund has enabled good work to be done in opening up learning opportunities for people at work. One other positive step towards breadth of vision was funding from the DfES for a number of research centres, including one on the wider benefits of learning on which I report below, with age as one of its principal themes.

There has been no formal renunciation of Mr Blunkett's words. However, the focus of policy in relation to post-compulsory education has undoubtedly narrowed. One of the objectives of the DfES' strategy to 2006 is 'to encourage and enable adults to learn, improve their skills and enrich their lives.' This sounds generous enough, but the specific targets are mainly to do with qualification levels and vocational training. The only target which is potentially helpful to older learners who are not in the workforce is that relating to basic skills (to reduce

---

[7] Department for Education and Employment, *The Learning Age: a renaissance for a new Britain* (DfEE, Feb 1998).
[8] Ibid, Foreword.

the number of adults with literacy or numeracy problems by 750,000 by 2004) but even this is likely to favour younger people. To be bleak, the essential aspects of recent policy redefinition are a preoccupation with participation in higher education, including a crippling focus on 18–30 year olds; and an emphasis on certified and work-related learning. In short, there is strong evidence of a continued 'front-loading' of the education system, which diminishes the overall support for lifelong learning at every age and devalues forms of learning which are particularly valuable for older people.

This is reinforced even by the prospective legislation on age discrimination. As has been made clear in the other chapters, current law precludes discrimination in education on grounds of race, gender and disability (with various exceptions), but discrimination on grounds of age is lawful throughout the UK. In Northern Ireland, however, the 1998 Northern Ireland Act imposed a duty on public bodies, including education authorities, to promote educational equality on grounds of age (among other grounds). The Government proposes to introduce legislation to ban age discrimination in employment throughout the UK (though on a slow time-scale, by 2006) but has no plans to do so in relation to education. This confirms the narrower focus defined above. It reinforces a damaging division between work-related and other forms of learning, and suggests that discrimination beyond the age of retirement is unimportant. Central to policy-making is the making of choices between assumedly desirable alternatives. I have emphasised above that it would be highly undesirable for an age-sectarian resource struggle to develop, with the interests of older people set directly against those of younger generations. This is all the more the case if it applied to a fixed educational budget, in a zero-sum game. The debate needs to address priorities. In addition to the concerns about equity, which are the focus of this chapter, there are powerful arguments on efficiency grounds for favouring a more equal distribution of educational opportunity across age groups. People learn best when they are internally motivated. Extending the initial phase of education in order to increase the numbers of under-represented groups in universities and colleges has good moral grounds. But there is increasing evidence that one outcome is a growth in under-motivated students, with consequent low achievement and rising drop-out rates.

However, the alternative to this is not merely to enable people to enter further and higher education later on, when they are properly motivated. Higher education issues tend to dominate the debate, for crude political reasons. We need to look broadly at the system and weigh up the trade-offs to be made between adding some further points to the higher education participation rates of young people against provision of learning opportunities of a broad kind, at all levels and to different age groups. There can be little doubt where the higher levels of marginal utility are to be found.

Finally, the debate on age and education should be an ideal opportunity for a fruitful exercise in joined-up government. Some substantial policy analysis has been done on the position of older people in relation to the labour market or as active citizens.[9] Education has not been sufficiently tied into this. The proposal below for a Fifty-Five Educational Allowance (FFEA) is an ideal opportunity for displaying coordination between government departments responsible for education, employment, health, civic affairs and pensions.

RATIONALE FOR AGE EQUALITY

The rationale for greater equality derives from a broad set of concerns, which run from individual ones to those of a more collective nature. They cut across the public and private spheres of life. This implies, as Sandra Fredman argues in her comprehensive chapter, that a holistic approach is required, which takes into account the interaction between labour market and other concerns. In this section I look at the way in which benefits of education can be identified. I do this first in relation to health, family and civic participation, based on work carried out at the Centre for Research on the Wider Benefits of Learning.[10] I then deal with benefits in relation to the workplace. These are closely interrelated, notably through outcomes such as increased self-confidence, which are almost universal, cut across public and private spheres, and are not confined to those with little education.

One fundamental question is how issues of social efficiency interact with issues relating to personal fulfilment. I find Amartya Sen's notion of capability highly relevant to the discussion. He thinks of education as a kind of substantive freedom for the individual to achieve various lifestyles. The essence here is not what the person actually does; it is the fact that they have alternative functioning combinations from which they can choose what it is that they will achieve. Sen makes a crucial distinction between human capital and human capability:

At the risk of some oversimplification, it can be said that the literature on human capital tends to concentrate on the agency of human beings in augmenting production possibilities. The perspective of human capability focuses, on the other hand, on the ability—the substantive freedom—of people to lead the lives they have reason to value and to enhance the real choices they have.[11]

Much earlier,[12] he lays stress on a different relationship: the interaction between capability as significant itself for the person's overall freedom, and its importance in fostering the person's ability to have valuable social outcomes.

[9] Cabinet Office, *All Our Futures* (London, HMSO, 2000); Performance and Innovation Unit, *Winning the Generation Game* (PIU, 2001).

[10] The WBL Centre is a DfES-sponsored unit based jointly at Birkbeck and the Institute of Education (www.widerbenefits.net). The research referred to involved over 130 individual geographical interviews with adults of all ages, in three different parts of the country. Tom Schuller et al, *Learning, Continuity and Adult Life*, Centre for Research on the Wider Benefits of Learning, Report 3, London: Institute of Education (2002).

[11] *Development as Freedom* (n 2 above) 293.

[12] *Development as Freedom* (n 2 above) 18.

The combination of these two points seems to me to lay the foundation for equality in relation to education. An instrumental approach, based on human capital, could still generate powerful arguments for greater equality, and for tackling directly some of the forms of discrimination, which exist. But when we are thinking about age such an approach is enormously enhanced if it is underpinned by a more fundamental conception of capability, conceived of in terms of individuals' ability to choose.

Not every argument to do with equality points in the direction of simply increasing resources and opportunities for older people's education. I have already identified some cases where it may be reasonable not to guarantee access or direct resources in this way. There remains much thinking to be done on what kinds of trade-off or tension there might be, for example in relation to age limits (we might agree that the age limit on grants for higher education should be lifted above 50, but should it still be set at some age, eg 60, in the light of changing demographics?) or the problem of testing (chronological age is a very poor proxy in most respects, but what are the disadvantages of substituting other criteria for assessing suitability/potential?).

Wider Benefits of Learning: Sustaining and Transforming

Greater age equality can be justified by reference to a number of areas where education brings benefits not only to the individual, but to the wider community. One of the major outcomes of the fieldwork we have just carried out is the way in which education serves not only to transform people's lives, but to sustain them in the face of daily pressures and stresses.[13]

Figure 1: *The Effects of Learning*

---

[13] *Learning, Continuity and Adult Life* (n 10 above).

The vertical dimension of the matrix refers to the extent to which the effect of learning has been concentrated on the individual or has had a wider impact. The horizontal dimension refers to the extent to which the impact has been one of visible change, or of sustaining a life or community which might otherwise have deteriorated or collapsed. The key point is the extent to which education serves to hold together the social fabric in unspectacular but crucial ways. The arguments for greater equality do not depend only on individuals' opportunities to transform themselves, personally or occupationally, but on their capacity to sustain themselves, their families and their communities. The need for this capacity to be developed and maintained is a major rationale for greater equality, and is a common theme in what follows.

Improved Health

The health of older people is a major concern—primarily for themselves, of course, but also for their families and friends, and for the state. The most obvious aspect is the growing numbers of old and infirm, and the needs they have for physical care, now or in the immediate future. But people do not suddenly become old, and most of us do not suddenly become infirm. This means that any approach to the relationship between education and health needs to take a life-course perspective. It is no good attempting to resolve or mitigate health-related problems through education by starting only when the problems emerge.

Like education, health is unequally distributed.[14] Poorer old people are typically both less healthy and less well educated than their better off contemporaries. Simplifying, one can point to two ways in which changing our approach to education can address this. First, improving educational opportunities over the life-course for those who currently benefit least will give them a better chance of avoiding poverty and the health consequences of poverty, primarily through improving their labour market position. Analysing this is extraordinarily difficult, given the number of external influences on material success, though cohort data does offer great insights.[15] Given that there will always be lower paid jobs, improving some people's access to education as a means of escaping these entails others taking their place doing them. Improving the lot of some will have an adverse impact on others (a critical factor in evaluating the impact of expanding participation in higher education). It is, however, not a zero sum game. A general rise in educational levels will have some impact on the overall skill content of occupations. Greater equality in educational distribution, at all ages, will narrow the gap between top and bottom in later life.

[14] R Wilkinson, *Unhealthy Societies: The Afflictions of Inequality* (London, Taylor & Francis, 1996).

[15] J Bynner, *Improving Adult Basic Skills: Benefits to the Individual and to Society* (Research Report Department for Education and Employment) (DfEE Nottingham 2001); C Hammond, *Learning to be Healthy* (Wider Benefits of Learning Research Centre Report) (London: Institute of Education 2002).

Better education for all will endow them with the capacity to look after them-selves more effectively, at whatever level of material well being. More educated people have better access to information about the consequences of different types of health-related behaviour, for instance smoking, drinking and exercise. Secondly, education enables access to health services, in a number of ways. It helps people to understand the services available, to articulate their needs (face to face, or by telephone, letter or other means), and to assimilate what is being said to them by health professionals and others. This includes the ability to exer-cise pressure on public services and the public purse, for instance in retaining hospital provision in a given area. We have numerous examples of people reporting how much even a minor learning episode could help them in the rela-tions with health professionals.

It is crucially important to include mental health in the discussion. The phys-ical health needs of older people are often very evident, and this is accentuated by public images of older people in wheelchairs or beds, unable to care effec-tively for themselves. However this can easily overshadow mental health issues. Problems such as depression are both widespread amongst older people, and hugely underreported. According to Mind, about 70–80 per cent of older people with depression go unspotted in primary care practices, their symptoms being generally mistaken for other ailments.[16] Ironically, older people's greater propensity to physical ill-health serves to disguise possible mental health prob-lems, as they are simply less visible, and less likely to cause public disturbance. This covers up an enormous area of stress and distress, to the individuals and to their families.

Education has a particular part to play in preventing, reducing or resolving mental health problems among older people. It can do this in a number of ways: by giving people the skills to access information and knowledge individually; by enabling them to take part in discussion, at whatever level; by improving their self-confidence and self-image; and by giving them a structure to their daily or weekly lives. All of these, especially the latter, can give them a sense of purpose and future, which is hugely beneficial.

Pragmatically, the more people are able to maintain good health and personal autonomy, the fewer demands they will make on public services and on their families or neighbours. (This is not to say that all such demands are unwel-come). Investment in education may, paradoxically, be more cost-effective for older people than many other groups. One crude financial calculation is that if education enables postponement into dependency by one week, there is a mar-ginal saving (public or private) of several hundred pounds—current estimates of the cost of reasonable nursing home provision usually fall between £450 and £500 weekly. Alongside this is the financial and psychological saving to carers: direct costs plus those of (partial) exclusion from the labour market and from social participation.

---

[16] http://www.mind.org.uk/information/the_search.asp

There is one particularly strong policy implication here. Instead of medical services, many older people may benefit from access to educational opportunities. This is not a direct trade-off, of course—the two should go together. But imaginative initiatives such as Prescriptions for Learning[17] (where GPs recommend education courses rather than drugs) show how beneficial education can be to health, as well as saving significant amounts of time for medical staff.

This however underlines the need for a life course approach. Promotion of educational opportunity is better late than never; but it is much better timely, and universal, than late. Enabling older people who have never participated in education since leaving school to perceive the benefits of learning four, five or six decades later is not easy.

The conclusion is fairly clear. Older people need access to education in order to have their health needs met. Because their health needs are likely to be great, they will need more rather than less access to education, and for education to be appropriately designed. However any such expenditure is likely to pay off in greater capacity for independence, and for making efficient use of professional health services.

Interaction with Families

By families I mean broad family structures, including both 'reconstituted' and multigenerational families. Older people are located in a very diverse set of family relationships, which can change with startling rapidity.[18] The rationale for ensuring equality in education has a number of components.

First, older people are entitled to education as a means of enabling them to communicate meaningfully with their families. At a rather basic level, understanding modern trends (in technology or other fields) is not a necessary condition for good intergenerational communication, but it is likely to be helpful. This is not so much a matter of substantive knowledge as of active participation in social institutions, of which colleges and other educational sites are part. There is good qualitative evidence on how participation in learning opens up these lines of communication, to mutual benefit. We have many examples of how older people have been able, through education, to build up new forms of communication with their families, to mutual benefit.

Secondly, education enables older people to stay in contact with their families through ICT. In a mobile society, younger generations move away (though the extent of this is often exaggerated), and older people may not be able, physically or for financial reasons, to travel to see them. Currently, older people have fewer ICT skills and lower access to new technology. A DTI survey found that two-

---

[17] K James, *Prescribing Learning* (NIACE Leicester, 2001).
[18] L Blackwell and J Bynner, *Learning, Family Formation and Dissolution* (Wider Benefits of Learning Research Centre Report No 4) (Institute of Education Birkbeck, 2002).

thirds of all those who feel alienated by new technology are over 45.[19] Many of them lack the confidence even to address the issue. This is changing as the stereotype of technologically incompetent age dissolves, and the speed of this change will accelerate as cohorts of people at ease with new technology move into older age brackets. But there remains a pressing case for education, which will give older people the confidence to access ICT.

Thirdly, grandparents or other older family members can be an enormous source of needed stability and support in times of family stress, for example where divorce occurs. Formal qualifications are not necessary for them to act effectively in this regard, but participation in education and access to knowledge sources is likely to help. Above all, the self-confidence which education brings can be vitally useful here, as in other domains.

This argument may appear rather functional, even open to the charge that the case rests on exploiting older people as unpaid sources of social assistance. The point however, is not that older people are obliged to play these roles, but that they are entitled to the opportunities to do so. This exactly embodies Sen's notion of capability. It is significant for the person's overall freedom, and in fostering the person's opportunity to have valuable outcomes.

There is a further line of argument, which brings us back to the life-course perspective on equality. Women's childbearing patterns have changed enormously in recent years, with more and more women deferring having children. This may be for consumption reasons, but is primarily for occupational motives, so that they can establish a career before having children. There is increasing evidence that this can cause difficulties in having children for those who defer too long. There is no single solution to this dilemma; in particular, career paths will have to change to accommodate different trajectories. However, a more equal distribution of opportunity would mean that re-entry into education for women with young children was more fully enabled than it currently is. More women could then see that future professional careers would not be blocked by their not having gained high level qualifications early on.

As family structures become more complex, so the educational needs of older people grow in order for them to be able to participate in family life. There is a particular ethnic dimension here. High proportions of some ethnic minority elders are not only excluded from the labour market and many community activities, but find their family connections weakened by integration and modernisation. Education can, for them, be double-edged, as daughters gain independence and refuse to accept traditional roles. These groups are particularly unlikely to be able to articulate their needs easily, yet on equality grounds many of them will have triple or even quadruple claims.

---

[19] Department of Trade and Industry *Is IT for all?* (Department of Trade and Industry, 1999), cited in *Winning the Generation Game* (n 9 above) 65.

Social Capital

Much emphasis is placed on opportunities for older people to participate in civic activity, notably in Better Government for Older People. This fits with a growing trend to recognise the interrelationships between human and social capital.[20]

The evidence on general trends in civic participation is quite contentious, with differing views on whether it is growing or declining, following Robert Putnam's influential work on social capital in the US.[21] But there is no dispute that involvement in any organised civic activity is closely associated with education. One of the most striking findings of parallel work on social capital in the UK is that the gender gap in levels of civic participation has closed, so that rates of participation for men and women are now quite close, but the gap in social class has not, so that lower socio-economic classes continue to participate less. Hall attributes this directly to changing patterns of educational attainment.[22] Far more middle-class women now continue their education into university, but progress for working-class men and women has been very limited. This shows up in their respective likelihood of civic participation.

Part of the reason for the association is the intermediary factor of income and wealth. Educated people are more likely to have high incomes; and to come from families with some capital assets, usually in the form of property. This material comfort enables them to participate, for instance because they have access to a car for travel, or can more easily bear the incidental expenses of volunteering.

The evidence on age and civic engagement is mixed. Those aged 55–64 are less likely than other ages to be involved, and their involvement seems to be declining. The 1997 National Survey on Volunteering found that only 40 per cent of those aged 55–64 had volunteered in the last year, compared with 48 per cent of all adults, and the rate for this age group had fallen from 46 per cent in 1991. However, for those aged 65–74 it had risen, from 34 per cent to 45 per cent, and for the 75+ from 25 per cent to 30 per cent.[23]

This may bear out, to some extent, Peter Laslett's vision of Third Agers as social trustees, since they have the time as well as the experience to carry out such functions.[24] We are seeing more and more people with high qualifications and skills continuing to exercise these after they have finished employment, or at least full-time employment. However the distributional dimension is import-

---

[20] OECD, *The Well being of Nations* (Report) (Organisation for Economic Cooperation and Development, Paris, 2001); S Baron, J Field and T Schuller (eds), *Social Capital: Critical Perspectives* (Oxford, OUP, 2000).

[21] RD Putnam, *Bowling Alone: The Collapse and Revival of American Community* (New York, Simon & Schuster, 2000).

[22] P Hall, 'Social Capital in Britain' (1999) *British Journal of Political Science* 29/3, 417–61.

[23] J Davis Smith, *National Survey on Volunteering* (National Centre for Volunteering, 1998).

[24] P Laslett, *A Fresh Map of Life* (London, Weidenfeld & Nicholson, 1988).

ant here. A fulfilling component of later life may be much less available to those who do not have the skills or education-generated confidence to offer themselves as volunteers.

Education has a number of roles to play. First, it provides people directly with the skills, which enable them to participate and may be useful to voluntary organisations. Secondly, it provides the general confidence needed to participate in civic activity, formal or informal. Thirdly, it provides access to opportunities. One barrier to participation is lack of information about what is available. Especially for people who are not in employment, participation in education can provide access to networks through which information, and encouragement, comes.

Social capital extends well beyond formal types of civic activity. It refers to many different forms of involvement, as well as to attitudinal aspects, notably levels of trust. There is a strong link here to the previous section, in that a very high proportion of older people are carers, usually for other members of their family. Many of them have been debarred by this from participating, socially or occupationally, sometimes in the peak earning period of their lives.

Finally, this aspect is especially important given the apparent trend towards partial retirement and the so-called portfolio worker. Many older people wish to move to part-time employment, and maybe combine this with some voluntary or community work, spanning the spheres of paid and unpaid work. This is their preferred form of time mix, with potential benefit to both spheres.

Workplace Human Capital

I turn now to training, which falls within the European Union's Employment Directive covering age discrimination, and therefore under current proposals for discrimination legislation in 2006. *Winning the Generation Game*, from the Performance and Innovation Unit,[25] is a powerful statement of the case for changing attitudes and practice in respect of training older people. It contains a string of relevant recommendations, for example that Learning and Skills Councils should make training older workers part of their strategies and that Investors in People should pay specific attention to the needs of older workers— though it is worth noting that none of the training recommendations made it into the report's '10 key conclusions'.

There are several aspects to the relationship between age and education in the employment context. First is the way human capital, which is not formally certified, or which is not identified by modern qualification structures, is underrecognised in the allocation of training places. Although organisations may acknowledge experience as important, it is increasingly easy for them to rely solely or nearly solely on formal qualifications. There is evidence that people

[25] *Winning the Generation Game* (n 9 above).

over the age of 50 are more likely to be found in lower skilled jobs, regardless of their previous qualification or experience.[26] There is a lively debate on the relationship between qualifications, skills and job content, with some evidence that more and more people with high qualifications are in jobs which do not require these qualifications. Arguably preoccupation with higher education qualifications has devalued intermediate qualifications, to older people's cost.

Secondly, there is the prejudice which exists against older people's ability to benefit from learning opportunities. Older people may be less quick to respond to some of the dominant forms of testing in education. With age there is a shift from fluid to crystallised forms of intelligence, which means that people with more experience seek to locate what they learn in some kind of established cognitive framework, and they are less ready to memorise information unless it can be so located. This is often confused with a lower general capacity to learn. Employers and managers operate with misleading models of effective learning.

Thirdly, this prejudice is often internalised, with older people lacking the confidence to envisage themselves as successful learners. Therefore they do not present themselves as candidates for training or retraining, often stepping aside for younger people who are assumed to be better placed to benefit.

Fourthly, employers and policy-makers operate with assumptions that older workers have short payback times in relation to investment in their training. Older workers are more likely to stay in their current posts, whether or not they have upwards career trajectories, and payback times for many forms of training are anyway not extensive.

In one survey, almost one in two employers were reluctant to fund training for older staff for one or other of these reasons.[27] The result is bad for individuals and sub-optimal for organisations, which deprive themselves of both actual and potential human capital. More generally, econometric analyses tend to use only formal qualifications as their measure of human capital, and to trace returns to education over long periods, typically in the form of income differentials. Such analyses tend to privilege early investment in education, since these by definition have longer payback periods. But this obscures the extent to which such returns are a function of multiple factors, which are subsequent to the actual learning episode, and so exaggerate the relative effect of learning in the initial phase. Both public and private investment in later learning are correspondingly depressed.

Finally, training demonstrates yet again the power of cumulative inequality, as those who already have high levels of skill and qualification tend to have better access to further training. This has a particular gender dimension; except for professional levels, men get more training than women.

[26] S McNair, M Davies and J Soulsby, unpublished paper on 50+ and Skills in the SE Region (University of Surrey) 7.

[27] P Taylor and A Walker, 'The Ageing Workforce: Employers' Attitudes towards Older People' (1994) *Work, Employment and Society* 8, 569–91; *Winning the Generation Game* (n 9 above) 38.

Training is one of the areas in which direct discrimination against older people is most visible. It is therefore welcome that this at least is sure to be included as an area where legislation is planned. But a broad approach is needed to bring about the kinds of cultural change required. This will include changes in the mentalities and methodologies of evaluation.

Age Diversity: Learning from Each Other

Finally, a brief note on the strong arguments for maintaining a mix within the student population, in most contexts. Formal education has always exhibited a high level of age stratification, with students grouped together in tight age bands. This reduces the potential for students to benefit from the diversity of collective experience, which they might potentially embody.

There are two senses to this. First, is the mixing of ages within a classroom or course. Such diversity will not always make teaching easier, but many teachers will testify to the value that having a range of student experience brings to classroom dynamics. This is more true in some subject areas (social studies, humanities) than in others (mathematics, some sciences). Secondly, even where classes may be relatively homogeneous in age terms, having a range of ages present in an institution enhances the opportunities for different age groups to learn from each other socially, outside the classroom. This is a classic case where social capital depends on a suitable environment. Creation of a suitable institutional climate where respect for and understanding of other groups is valued is a significant aspect.

This is not to argue that all institutions should be mixed. Bodies such as the Universities of the Third Age cater specifically and effectively for some 120,000 older people in the UK alone. There could be some interesting questions in this context about where the age line is drawn, and about reverse discrimination.

CURRENT PROVISION AND PARTICIPATION

A full statistical account of age-related differences in education would occupy too much space.[28] Here I give a general overview, with three main components: first, some overall figures on participation in learning, drawn from the National Institute of Adult Continuing Education (NIACE) survey on adult learners; and then details at the top and bottom of the education range, on higher education and basic skills.

---

[28] See T Schuller and A M Bostyn, *Education, Training and Learning* (Report 3 for the Carnegie Inquiry into the Third Age, 1992) for an earlier attempt.

Table 1: *Current/Recent Participation in Learning, by Age, 1996 and 2001 Compared*

	1996	2001	Percentage change
Total sample	40	46	+6
17–19	86	82	–4
20–24	65	70	+5
25–35	48	57	+9
35–44	43	55	+12
45–54	36	48	+12
55–64	25	33	+8
65–74	19	22	+3
75+	15	12	–3

Source: Aldridge and Tuckett 2001

General Participation

The overall picture on participation in adult learning shows a direct relationship between age and participation.

For almost every age group there has been some improvement in their participation. However, older people are less likely to take part in any form of organised learning. Moreover, the NIACE survey shows a sharp increase in the gap between older groups—those aged 55 and over—and the rest of the population. In 1996 55–64 year olds were 11 percentage points less likely to participate than those in the immediately succeeding cohort; by 2001 this gap had increased to 15 percentage points. The gap between them and their immediate elders (65–74) had grown from 6 to 11 percentage points. And for those in the oldest age group, participation rates actually declined. The ratio between the participation rates of those aged 75+ and those aged 35–44 thus went from just over 1:3 in 1996 to under 2:9 in 2001.

However, another large-scale survey, the National Adult Learning Survey (NALS), while it confirms the general linear relationship between age and education, gives a rather different picture of trends. NALS records higher participation levels across all age groups, as it uses a broader definition of learning; and it reports a stronger increase in participation by 50–59 year olds than any other age group, from 67 per cent to 74 per cent (compared, for example, with an increase for 40–49 year olds from 78 per cent to 80 per cent). This reinforces the importance to older people of more informal modes of learning, which are not only sometimes unrecorded but also unrecognised.

Information and Communication Technology (ICT) is worth a particular mention. People with access to the Internet are twice as likely to be learning as people without.[29] A government survey at the end of 2001 showed visibly low use of ICT and the Internet by older age groups. Usage by all adults rose from 45 per cent to 53 per cent between October 2000 and October 2001, but from only 10 per cent to 11 per cent for those aged 65 and over. The figures for 55–64 were more encouraging, with a rise from 28 per cent to 37 per cent. But access to ICT is not only important instrumentally. Our evidence from the wider benefits of learning (WBL) research shows how acquiring and using ICT skills, however minimally, gives people of all age groups a sense of belonging and participating in the modern world, and therefore powerfully affects their sense of personal identity.

Higher and Further Education

The age profile of the higher education student population has changed in recent years. However, for the most part this results from a prolongation of the initial period of education, so that more people in their twenties are now enrolled in higher education as a completion of this initial phase.

Table 2 shows Universities and Colleges Admissions Service (UCAS) acceptances for 1996 and 2001. In interpreting these figures, and similar ones for

Table 2: *Number of UCAS Accepts by Age and Gender*

Age of Applicants	Year 1996		1996 total	Year 2001		2001 total
	Men	Women		Men	Women	
18	65,445	71,373	136,818	75,148	87,923	163,071
21	6,762	5,439	12,201	9,200	7,750	16,950
17 and under	4,325	5,018	9,343	4,295	5,285	9,580
19–20	41,634	39,391	81,025	53,556	55,191	108,747
22–24	11,059	8,467	19,526	12,339	10,406	22,745
25–39	14,738	16,094	30,832	13,315	16,659	29,974
40–49	1,868	3,003	4,871	1,748	3,577	5,325
50–59	444	511	955	486	713	1,199
60–69	117	96	213	136	173	309
70 or more	15	8	23	77	64	141
Grand total	146,407	149,400	295,807	170,300	187,741	358,041

Source: UCAS

[29] F Aldridge and A Tuckett, *Winners and Losers in an expanding system: The NIACE Survey on Adult Participation in Learning 2001* (NIACE Leicester, 2001).

enrolments in higher education and elsewhere, we need to be aware of where the major dividing lines are best drawn, since this is crucial if we are considering balance within the system. The numbers of those aged up to 24 rose by 24 per cent, from 258,913 to 321,093. The number of all those aged 25+ went up by just 54, from 36,894 to 36,948. As a proportion of the former figure, this represents a drop, from 14.2 per cent to 11.5 per cent.[30] This is arguably the most signific-ant dividing line, but the picture is reasonably consistent even if it is drawn at a different age point. The equivalent rise in those aged 40+ was 15 per cent, from 6062 to 6974. As a proportion of the under-25 group this represents a drop from 2.3 per cent to 2.1 per cent. In short, these figures suggest an increasing concen-tration of younger entrants (under 25), contrary to the proclaimed logic of a more equal access across the age range.

There is a gender dimension here, but a complex one in its interaction with age. From age 25 upwards women are more strongly represented than men in every age group (except most recently for those over 70). Moreover a higher proportion of young women now enter higher education. Men's participation continues to increase at the younger ages, but it has dropped in middle age (25–50). It may not be in higher education that the gender gap is most signific-ant, but it flags up an issue which is likely to develop impetus over time.

One of the reasons for decline in the numbers of mature students in higher education is student finance. Currently, the general regulation is that in order to qualify for a student loan you must be under 50 when your course starts. Some exceptions are made for those under 54 who make a 'firm commitment' to return to work. Over 50s are eligible for a grant towards their fees, and for a Disabled Students Allowance. The regulations are soon to change, removing age limits for eligibility for a dependant's grant, and support for travel, books and equipment. The recent White Paper, *The Future of Higher Education* (Cmnd 5735), introduces significant change into student finance but will not correct the age imbalance.

The picture in further education is somewhat different, but harder to be pre-cise about because of the diversity of provision and some difficulty in defining what courses students are attending. In the years from 1996/7–1999/2000 there was a substantial increase in the numbers of those aged 60 and over attending further education colleges funded by the Learning and Skills Councils in England, from 161,867 to 227,939, a jump of some 41 per cent. Given that the numbers of younger students have been flat or declining over the same period, this represents an increase from 4.4 per cent of the total to 6.2 per cent. But the extent to which support for colleges is geared predominantly to the acquisition of qualifications remains a major issue.

---

[30] The earlier growth of entry into higher education means the pool of potential mature students may be smaller, but this is a dubious explanation for the drop.

Table 3: *Basic Skills*

Age	% of Need	Number
16–25	14.7%	1,029,000
26–35	21.3%	1,491,000
36–45	17.4%	1,218,000
46–55	19.9%	1,393,000
56–65	26.8%	1,876,000
	100%	7,007,000

Source: BSA 2001[31]

Basic skills

At the other end of the educational spectrum, there are very large numbers of older people who lack basic levels of skill and qualification. More than one in four of the total number of adults with poor basic skills, about 1.8 million, are older adults between 56 and 65 years.

It is not only absolute numbers which should concern us; the relative point needs to be made also, since 33 per cent of those aged 50+ have basic skills problems compared with 20 per cent of the population as a whole. The document from which the table is taken observes that since many of these older people may have little interest in improving their basic skills as work and parental responsibilities are less motivating factors, solving our basic skills problem may not be as difficult as initially thought; hence the estimated costs may be rather lower than suggested in *A Fresh Start*, which set out the case for a major effort to improve basic skills.

If deliberate, this is a startlingly misguided statement. The largest group is the easiest to ignore! One has only to think about wrestling with the small print and the calculations in relation to the current pensions debate to appreciate some of the difficulties facing older people with these difficulties. A recent IPPR report[32] confirms the bewildering complexities of current pensions arrangements and the effect this has on people's capacity to control their own situation. Moreover the motivation to learn with grandchildren is a strong one, and should not be brushed aside in such cavalier fashion (see above, on families).

Discussion of basic skills reintroduces the question of priorities and trade-offs. On both equity and efficiency grounds there can be little doubt that basic skills provision deserves a very high priority indeed. It is perverse that so little

---

[31] BSA Benchmark information on the scale of need in different areas of England (Basic Skills Agency, 2001).
[32] R Brooks, S Regan and P Robinson, *A New Contract for Retirement* (London, IPPR, 2002).

attention is given to the issue in comparison with the acreage of newsprint devoted to higher education, but the political reasons for this are clear. But as the table suggests, there is a strong congruence here between need on the one hand and age-equitable policy on the other.

Training

The data on age and training is unambiguous. Older people have less access to training, at all occupational levels. This is on top of the fact that they have will generally have fewer qualifications than their younger counterparts, because they passed through the initial phase of education when it was narrower; and this has then been compounded by those with fewer qualifications having less access.

More generally, the 1997 National Adult Learning Survey showed that only 9 per cent of 50–59 year olds, compared to 17 per cent of all adults had undertaken taught learning with future work in mind, and only 14 per cent compared to 39 per cent had undertaken learning related to their current job.[33] NALS 2001 reports much higher figures for all age groups in respect of the broader category of 'vocational learning', but a steep decline occurs similarly at age 50+.

As for government training, my calculations are that by January 2002, of the total number of starts on the various forms of New Deal, 12,630 were by those aged 50+. This represents 17 per cent of the total 25+ starts, and 4 per cent of all New Deal starts.

Table 4: *Employees Receiving Job-related Training[1]: by Gender and Age[2], Spring 2001 United Kingdom, Percentages*

| | Males | |
Females		
50–59/64	8	13
35–49	13	18
25–34	16	19
18–24	23	25
16–17	20	21

[1] Percentage who received job-related training in the four weeks before interview.
[2] Males aged 50 to 64 and females aged 50 to 59.
Source: Labour Force Survey

[33] *Winning the Generation Game* (n 9 above) 66.

In short, the figures show unmistakably the inequalities *in current educational participation rates* across the age groups. Participation is of course a function of motivation as well as opportunity. But it is crucial to see these in combination with the *cumulative inequality* of educational opportunity. Most of those in the younger age groups will have greater access to learning as they move through life than their preceding generations at equivalent points in their lives. This is, in itself, entirely positive, as it signals general progress over time. But it accentuates the relative inequalities experienced by different generations. It also foreshadows major cumulative problems to be experienced by younger people with no qualifications, who as they age, are likely to suffer increasing exclusion relative to their contemporaries.

FIFTY-FIVE EDUCATIONAL ALLOWANCES

As one specific measure to address this deficit, I propose a Fifty-Five Educational Allowance (FFEA). The FFEA would have both symbolic and material value. It would signal to older people that learning is for them; and it would offer help with the costs of participation—modest, but sufficient to cover many short courses. After the Individual Learning Account debacle it will be necessary to think carefully about accountability and control, but such problems should not be unsurmountable. The likely benefits—hard though they may be to fit into narrow Treasury accountancy procedures—should be a substantial offset to the gross costs.

Around 15 million people are aged 55 or over in the UK today. Each year about 700,000 people reach their fifty-fifth birthday.

1. A £150 Educational Allowance for all over 55 would parallel the Winter Fuel Allowance, catering for people's intellectual and psychological well being as the WFA caters for their material comfort.
2. The FFEA could be triggered as part of the 'life check' proposed by the National Institute for Adult and Continuing Education, offering advice to older people on health, pensions and tax matters. This would help those without much previous educational experience to take advantage of it.
3. The FFEA should be a universal allowance, even though some people would benefit who would not strictly need it (as is the case with the WFA). The potential cost, of 100 per cent take-up, would be some £2.2 billion annually. However, take-up would be very unlikely to exceed 25 per cent (especially in the older groups). In all probability it will be very much lower, perhaps around 10 per cent. Gross expenditure might therefore amount to around £200 million, with a maximum of £4–500 million.
4. An additional allowance should be given to those who have no university degree, and had therefore not benefited from this form of major public subsidy throughout their lives. They should receive a one-off payment doubling the FFEA. It might be thought too expensive to introduce this immediately

for all 55+; so it could go first only to the 10 million aged 65+. Take-up for the older groups would be lower still, and would still be unlikely to exceed 10 per cent, ie £150 million as an initial one-off. The phasing in of the additional allowance could take place over 2–5 years, going 'backwards' until the 55-year-olds are reached.

Of the 700,000 reaching 55 annually, the great majority of current cohorts do not have degrees, and so would be entitled to the additional allowance. With a take-up of 25 per cent this would mean about an additional £25 million annually.

Net costs depend on assumptions about the savings, which involvement in learning might bring, and on how far our accountancy systems allow cost-benefit analysis. Saving Lives: Our Healthier Nation quotes an estimate of £32 billion as the cost of mental health to England. This seems a huge claim; let us deflate it by over half, to £15 billion. If, by stimulating more involvement in adult learning by older people, FFEAs resulted in a 1 per cent improvement in mental health—hardly a heroic assumption—they would save £150 million, or nearly a third of the cost estimated above. Other gains would include reducing the burden on carers, and on social services; plus increased productivity among older people.

The impact of the FFEA should be monitored with both quantitative and qualitative outcomes evaluated. The allowance could be introduced on a pilot basis until such evaluation has been undertaken.

There are significant issues to do with what types of learning would be sanctioned, and with accountability. It would run against the grain of my argument if the FFEA could only be used for formal types of learning. On the other hand, too open a definition makes it hard to control what is eligible for funding. We might expect voluntary organisations and local authorities (health and social services as well as education) to be major providers in addition to recognised educational institutions; but there should be scope for flexibility. Local control mechanisms will be most appropriate.

CONCLUSIONS

I have argued that education is vitally important to older people in ways which are largely unrecognised—to their health, including mental health, to their family life and to the quality of their civic, economic and social life. Equality of opportunity in relation to education is as important for older people as it is for the rest of the population.

There are a number of respects in which discrimination operates, overtly or covertly, and which need to be confronted. These include assumptions about older people's capacity to learn, and the payback period. However, we need to be careful about forcing some kind of binary division, where older people's needs are held up in discrete opposition to those younger generations.

The key to achievement of greater age equality in education lies in shifting the overall basis of educational policy towards a broad vision of lifelong learning. The fundamental lines of argument set out above, with their basis in Sen's notion of capability, are congruent with the arguments advanced by Sandra Fredman in favour of choice and participation as the basis for equality.

Even if this conclusion is accepted—that the primary emphasis should be on changing overall education policy to make it lifelong—it does not mean that legislation on discrimination is inappropriate. On the contrary, much of the argument above suggests that measures in relation to education should be part of the wider move against discrimination, and that education should therefore be included, along with employment and training, in discrimination legislation. The essential corollary is that age discrimination legislation should be broad and unified, so that rulings, policies and support are consistent with each other. This is essential to minimise the potential costs of discrimination legislation.

Education intersects with other areas, notably health, family life and civic activity. In one sense it could be regarded as fundamental to, or at least a necessary condition of, the capability for basic participation in society. For older people, to restrict education to training in an employment context is grossly inadequate.

A life-course perspective should promote a better general distribution of learning opportunities, longitudinally over the life-course but also across social groups. But it could also well be supported by entitlements. A specific educational entitlement for everyone who reaches their fifty-fifth birthday (FFEA—Fifty-Five Educational Allowance), weighted in favour of those who have had no university education, would be more constructive in changing patterns of demand and supply than the threat of litigation. The impact of the FFEA should be monitored with both quantitative and qualitative outcomes evaluated. The allowance could be introduced on a pilot basis until such evaluation has been undertaken.

Two factors make a powerful case for quick action. Cumulative inequality and the effect of generational change mean that there is a cohort of people who have had, throughout their lives, low access to education. Waiting for them to die off is not reasonable.

7

Children's Rights for Grown-ups

JONATHAN HERRING

INTRODUCTION

MUCH OF THE discussion in this book and elsewhere about delivering age equality has focused on the rights of older people. In this chapter, by contrast, the focus is on children and young people. It considers the grounds on which it is, or is not, legitimate to treat them less favourably (or more favourably) than adults.

In 1646 the Commonwealth of Massachusetts passed the Stubborn Child Statute under which repeatedly disobedient sons over the age of 15 could be put to death.[1] Those days are long gone. Children are no longer seen as the chattels of their parents, required to be obedient and quiet. Instead, in academic circles and increasingly in public discourse,[2] the talk is of children's rights.[3] The United Nations Convention on the Rights of the Child,[4] although not directly enforceable in English and Welsh courts, has given the calls for increased recognition of children's rights an added impetus. Further the EU directive on equal treatment on the grounds of age[5] seeks to tackle discrimination on the grounds of age in the context of employment, vocational training and the membership of employers' or workers' organisations. This applies to discrimination against the young and the old. As the Government considers how the implement this directive there will be debate over whether generally it is ever appropriate to discriminate against children and deny them the same legal rights as adults. In part this 'children's rights talk' is motivated by an increasing awareness of the wrongs done to children and a desire to protect them from those harms by giving them basic

---

* I am grateful to Stacie Strong for her comments on a draft of this paper.

[1] Referred to in G van Bueren, *The International Law on the Rights of the Child* (The Hague, Martinus Nijhoff Publishers , 1998) 73.

[2] See for example, the work of the Children's Rights Alliance for England.

[3] B Bennett Woodhouse, 'The Status of Children: A Story of Emerging Rights' in S Katz, J Eekelaar and M Maclean (eds), *Cross Currents* (Oxford, OUP, 2000) provides an excellent summary of the history of children's rights.

[4] See C Lyon, 'Children and the law- towards 2000 and beyond' in C Bridge (ed), *Family Law Towards the Millennium* (London, Butterworths, 1997) for a useful summary of the Convention and its potential impact.

[5] Council Directive 2000/79/EC, 27 November 2000.

rights. But in part there is also a recognition that children should be able to make decisions for themselves and should be encouraged to play a full role within society.

David Archard argues that: 'What it is forbidden to do to a human being because of its humanity it is forbidden to do to a child.'[6] This is relatively uncontroversial. Simply put: children have human rights, because children are humans. The debate is no longer over whether children have any rights,[7] but rather whether there is any justification for denying children all the rights that are available to adults. The debate has centred particularly on the question whether children should have the right to autonomy: 'the most dangerous but most precious of rights: the right to make their own mistakes.'[8] In a way this has produced, at least in the West, a skewed perspective on the rights of children. It is easier to find academic analysis on whether children should be allowed to have their noses pierced than children's right to clean water.[9]

This is, of course, largely due to the affluence of the West. Not that Britain needs to be complacent about the basic needs of children. The number of children recorded as living in poverty in 2000/01 was 3.9 million;[10] seven per cent of children suffer serious physical abuse at the hands of their parents or carers;[11] a quarter of 16-year-olds failed to achieve any GCSEs above a grade D in 2001;[12] one-third of British teenagers are overweight.[13] Many other shaming statistics could be produced and the United Nations Committee on the Rights of the Child had no difficulty in providing extensive criticism of the position of children within the UK.[14]

Despite the disturbing figures on the position of many children in Britain the academic focus on the right of autonomy can be justified on the basis of it being the key issue, which distinguishes the variety of theoretical approaches towards children. This chapter will seek to summarise the debates over the extent to which children should be given adults' rights. It will be structured in this way. First, some examples of the way in which the law distinguishes between children and adults will be given. The chapter will then outline some of the most popular theories of how the law should respond to children and, using them, consider

---

[6] D Archard, 'Philosophical Perspectives on Childhood' in J Fionda (ed), *Legal Concepts of Childhood* (Oxford, Hart Publishing , 2001) 47.

[7] Although see O O'Neill, 'Children's Rights and Children's Lives' in P Alston, S Parker and J Seymour (eds), *Children, Rights and the Law* (Oxford, Clarendon Press, 1998) for a powerful argument that we should be concentrating on the obligations of adults, rather than the rights of children.

[8] J Eekelaar, 'The Emergence of Children's Rights' (1986) 6 *Oxford Journal of Legal Studies* 161.

[9] I am as guilty on this as anyone: see J Herring, *Family Law* (Harlow, Longman, 2001) ch 8.

[10] Child Poverty Action Group, *Child Poverty Figures 'Very Disappointing'* (London, CPAG, 11 April 2002).

[11] NSPCC, *Child Maltreatment Survey* (London, NSPCC, 2000).

[12] New Policy Institute, *Monitoring Poverty and Social Exclusion* (York, Joseph Rowntree Trust, 2002).

[13] BBC News Online, 17 Sept 2002.

[14] For a sceptical discussion questioning whether the growth of interest in children's rights has practically benefited children see M King, *A Better World for Children?* (London, Routledge, 1997).

the justifiability of distinguishing between children's and adults' rights. It will examine some practical issues and consider how the different theories would respond to them. At the end of the chapter I will suggest that the debate on children's rights may have been looking at the question from the wrong angle. I will suggest that the strongest case for equality between adults and children is not to be made by emphasising the capabilities of children, but recognising the vulnerability of adults.

EXAMPLES OF WAYS IN WHICH CHILDREN ARE NOT TREATED IN THE
SAME WAY AS ADULTS

In this part examples will be given of the way in which the law discriminates against children by treating children and adults differently. This is not intended to be anything like a complete list,[15] but rather to provide a flavour of the many ways in which the law distinguishes children from adults. As will be seen, the distinctions between adults and children include not only denying children rights that adults have, but 'favouring' children by giving them rights that adults do not have, or saving them from duties.[16] It should be added that the divisions used here are contentious. What to one person is providing a child with a right to protection, to another is depriving a child of a liberty.[17]

Rights Available to Adults which are Denied to Children

There are a whole host of restrictions on what children can buy and when children can use dangerous pieces of machinery. Although officially 18 is the age at which minority ends, there is in fact no consistent pattern as to when a child is allowed to do something. To give but one example, a 16-year-old is deemed mature enough to consent to sexual relations with her or his MP, but not to vote for her or him! Here are just some of the things children cannot do lawfully.

1. Children are not able to enter a legally binding contract unless the contract is for the supply of necessities or is for a beneficial contract of service.[18]
2. Those under 18 are not permitted to vote.[19]

---

[15] For many more examples see Children's Law Centre, *At what age can I . . .?* (London, Children's Law Centre, 1999).

[16] A Platt, *The Child Savers: The Invention of Delinquency* (Chicago, Chicago University Press, 1969).

[17] T Campbell, 'The Rights of the Minor' in P Alston, S Parker and J Seymour (eds), *Children, Rights and the Law* (Oxford, Clarendon Press, 1992) 20.

[18] See *Family Law*, above n 9, 379–340.

[19] Children's Rights Alliance for England, *The Real Democratic Deficit: why 16–17 year olds should be allowed to vote* (London, Children's Rights Alliance for England, 2000). For a provocative analysis from an American perspective see J Rutherford, 'One Child, One Vote: Proxies for Parents' (1998) 82 *Minnesota Law Review* 1463.

3. Those under 16 cannot marry.[20]
4. Those under 16 cannot buy National Lottery tickets.[21]
5. Those under 15 cannot attend a '15 rated' film.

Rights Available to Children which are not Available to Adults

The law offers to children a range of rights and protections, which are not available to adults. Here are three:

1. There are a raft of criminal offences which protect children, where there is no equivalent offence for adults. For example, section 1 Children and Young Persons Act 1933:

   > If any person who has attained the age of 16 years and has responsibility for any child or young person under that age, wilfully assaults, ill-treats, neglects, abandons or exposes him or causes or procures him to be assaulted, ill-treated, neglected, abandoned or exposed, in a manner likely to cause him unnecessary suffering or injury to health (including injury to or loss of sight or hearing, or limb or organ of the body, and any mental derangement) that person shall be guilty of an offence.

   In the area of sexual offences many offences have been created specifically to protect children from sexual abuse.[22]
2. The Children Act 1989, Part IV enables local authorities to provide services or take into their care children in need or who are suffering significant harm. There is no equivalent obligation on local authorities in respect of adults.
3. Education must be provided for children under the age of 16 by local authorities[23] and parents are required to ensure that their children receive suitable education.[24]

Where there is a clash between the Rights of Children and Adults, Children's Rights are seen as Stronger

Where there is a clash between the interests of children and of adults the law generally[25] gives greater weight to the interests of children. Here are two examples:

---

[20] Matrimonial Causes Act 1973 s 11.
[21] National Lottery Act 1998 s 12.
[22] Most recently the Sexual Offences (Amendment) Act 2000.
[23] Education Act 1996 ss 10 and 14.
[24] Education Act 1996 s 7.
[25] But see *Family Law*, above n 9 at 340–1 for a discussion of when the welfare principle does not apply.

1. Where an application concerning the upbringing of a child is brought under the Children Act 1989, the child's welfare shall be the paramount consideration. This has been interpreted to mean that the court should consider only the interests of a child.[26] In other words the court can make an order promoting the interests of the child, even if it causes an adult significant harm.[27]

2. Under the European Convention on Human Rights where there is a clash between the rights of children and adults and these rights need to be balanced, then the rights of children are to be 'crucial'[28] or even 'paramount'.[29]

Responsibilities Adults have which Children do not

The law is very reluctant to impose positive obligations on children. Most notably, children who commit crimes under the age of 10 cannot be convicted of a criminal offence, however malicious or unpleasant the acts they perform.[30] Children are also exempt from various bureaucratic obligations, for example to fill in a tax return.

Responsibilities Children have which Adults do not

There are very few obligations, which are imposed uniquely on children. A child is required to attend education until she or he has reached the age of 16. However, the failure to attend school will lead to proceedings being brought against the parent of the child, rather than the child her or himself.[31] Another obligation unique to children is the power the courts have to impose curfew orders on young offenders, requiring them not to be in public places after a certain time.[32] Such orders cannot be made against adults.

---

[26] *Re KD* [1988] 2 FLR 139, *Re P (Contact: Supervision)* [1996] 2 FLR 314.

[27] However, see J Herring, 'The Welfare Principle and the Rights of Parents' in Bainham, Richards, Day Sclater (eds), *What is a Parent?* (Oxford, Hart Publishing, 1999) for a discussion of how the courts have still managed to place significance on parents' interests.

[28] Eg *Scott v UK* [2000] 2 FCR 560.

[29] *Yousef v Netherlands* [2002] 3 FCR 577.

[30] This low age of criminal responsibility was criticised by the Committee on the Rights of the Child in its concluding observations following its consideration of the United Kingdom's second periodic report under the UN Convention on the Rights of the Child produced on 4 October 2002.

[31] A Bainham, ' "Honour Thy Father and Thy Mother": Children's Rights and Children's Duties' in G Douglas and L Sebba (eds), *Children's Rights and Traditional Values* (Aldershot, Ashgate, 1998).

[32] Criminal Justice and Police Act 2001. See further Juvenile Offenders Unit, Local Child Curfew Guidance (http://www.homeoffice.gov.uk/yousys/ guidcurfew.pdf).

THE BASIC LEGAL POSITION OF CHILDREN

In this part three popular perspectives on how the law ought to respond to children will be outlined.

Paternalism

Paternalism promotes the view that the law should do all it can to promote the well being of children. At its heart is a view that children are vulnerable[33] and need protection from the dangers that are posed by the world, adults, other children and themselves. It often stems from a firm rejection of a view that children are sub-human, or the property of their parents. Reading the profoundly depressing accounts of the starvation, ill heath and abuse of children produces a deep desire to save and protect them. Children lack the knowledge, experience or strength to care for themselves, it is thought.[34] To paternalists therefore discrimination against children on the grounds of age can easily be justified on the basis of lack of competence to make decisions for themselves. This leads to legal responses that are designed, as far as possible, to ensure that only good things happen to children.[35] Legislation, then, should promote the welfare of children and protect them from the horrors that all too many children face. A clear example of such an approach is found in the Children Act 1989, which opens with what is generally known as the 'welfare principle':

> Where a court determines any question with respect to.
>
> (a) the upbringing of a child; of
> (b) the administration of the child's property or the application of any income arising from it,
>
> the child's welfare shall be the court's paramount consideration.[36]

Within paternalism there is, however, a controversy. Accepting that children are not in a position to make decisions for themselves and that decisions must be made for them by adults, who is to make the decision? Who is to decide what is best for children? Generally it is accepted that a child's parents are best placed to determine what will be in the child's welfare on a given question.[37] However, at the same time it is clear that some parents abuse their children and cause them manifold harms. There is therefore much dispute over the extent to which the state is

---

[33] J Fionda, 'Legal Concepts of Childhood: An Introduction' in J Fionda (ed), *Legal Concepts of Childhood* (Oxford, Hart Publishing, 2001).

[34] See F Harding, *Perspectives in Child Care Policy* (Harlow, Longman, 1997).

[35] B Hafen and J Hafen, 'Abandoning Children to Their Autonomy: The United Nations Convention on the Rights of the Child' (1996) 37 *Harvard International Law Journal* 449.

[36] Children Act 1989 s 1(1).

[37] K Smith, 'The United Nations Convention on the Rights of the Child: The Sacrifice of American Children on the Altar of Third-World Activism' (1998) 38 *Washburn Law Journal* 111.

entitled to 'interfere' with the way parents raise children in the name of promoting the child's welfare. The compromise reached under the Children Act is essentially that parents can decide how to raise their child as they think fit, unless that decision causes the child significant harm or the decision is challenged by another parent or person with a close link with the child.[38] In part this approach is explained by the fact that in many areas of life the courts do not know what is in a child's best interests. Consider, for example, *Re W (Residence Order)*[39] where a non-resident father[40] sought a court order to prevent the resident mother and her new partner from being naked in front of the children.[41] The Court of Appeal, in effect, held that as it could not be shown that the nudity harmed the child they would not prevent it, although they accepted they had no idea whether it was or was not in the interests of the child to see her carers naked on a regular basis. The matter could therefore be left to the resident parent to decide.

It should not be thought that paternalism rejects any notion of placing weight on the wishes of the child. Indeed in deciding what will best promote the welfare of the child the Children Act 1989 specifically requires the court to consider the child's wishes.[42] This makes sense. Whether or not attending ballet classes is in a child's best interests is likely to be heavily dependant on whether the child enjoys ballet. Even allowing a child to make a decision which turns out to be a mistake could be supported on the paternalistic basis that to do so will enable the child to learn from her or his mistakes. Allowing children to experiment with different hairstyles and dress (even if adults may see them as 'mistakes') enables the child to develop her or his own style. However, according to paternalism, allowing children to make some decisions for themselves is permitted because it is regarded by adults as good for children, rather than on the basis of any rights of children.

Although it is common to see a paternalist approach with its focus on welfare as diametrically opposed to a rights-based discourse,[43] in fact it is possible to phrase paternalistic approaches in terms of rights. It could be argued that children have the right to have their welfare promoted.[44] However, John Eekelaar,[45] for one, has rejected any suggestion of such a right:

> A claim simply that people should act to further my welfare as they define it is in reality to make no claim at all. Running behind these explicit propositions lies the suggestion that to treat someone fully as an individual of moral worth implies recognizing that that person makes claims and exercises choices: that is, is a potential right-holder.

[38] 'The Welfare Principle and the Rights of Parents' (above n 27).

[39] [1999] 1 FLR 860.

[40] The (rather clumsy) term family lawyers use to refer to a father who is not living with the children.

[41] The mother and her partner were naturists.

[42] Children Act 1989 s 1(3)(a).

[43] S Parker, 'Rights and Utility in Anglo-Australian Family Law' (1992) 55 *Modern Law Review* 31.

[44] J Eekelaar 'Families and Children' in C McCrudden and D Chambers (eds), *Individual Rights and the Law in Britain* (Oxford, OUP, 1994).

[45] J Eekelaar, 'The Importance of Thinking that Children have Rights' (1992) 6 *International Journal of Law Policy and the Family* 221, at 228.

Child Liberation

The essential claim of child liberationists is that children should have all the rights that adults have.[46] Supporters of such a view have become known colloquially as 'kiddie libbers'.[47] Holt has written that the law supports the view of a child 'being wholly subservient and dependant . . . being seen by older people as a mixture of expensive nuisance, slave and super-pet.'[48] Such a view of children as second class citizens must be rejected, he argues, and children recognised as having equal rights to adults. Childhood, he and many others have maintained, is a social construction.[49] There is no point in time at which in biological or psychological terms a person stops being a child and become an adult. Holt therefore concludes that children should have the same rights as adults to, inter alia, vote, determine their own education, engage in sexual activities and use drugs. To treat children and adults differently is improper discrimination on the grounds of age.

In response to the concern that children lack the ability to exercise such rights Holt agues that that assumption is a fiction, a rhetorical device, which enables adults to oppress children. True, children may make mistaken decisions, based on a lack of understanding of the relevant facts or experience of life, but adults do that all the time.[50] Some child liberationists simply deny that there is any difference in substance between the decision-making abilities of a child and an adult. Others are willing to accept that generally speaking there is a difference between children and adults, but argue that there is no rational place to draw the line. As only arbitrary distinctions can be drawn between those of different ages, they should not be made at all.[51]

Child liberationists reject paternalism arguing that to deny children's rights and instead focus on their needs demeans children. Bandman argues that rights 'enable us to stand with dignity, if necessary to demand what is our due without having to grovel, plead or beg'.[52] To have a right then is have a claim to something, rather than have to ask for something to be considered in one's best interests.

---

[46] J Holt, *Escape from Childhood: The Needs and Rights of Children* (London, Penguin, 1974); H Foster and D Freund, 'A Bill of Rights for Children' (1972) 6 *Family Law Quarterly* 343; B Franklin, 'The Case for Children's Rights: A Progress Report' *The Handbook of Children's Rights* (London, Routledge, 2000); C Smith, 'Children's Rights: Judicial Ambivalence and Social Resistance' (1997) 11 *International Journal of Law Policy and the Family* 103.

[47] R Mnookin, 'Thinking About Children's Rights—Beyond Kiddie Libbers and Child Savers' (1984) *Sanford Lawyer* 24.

[48] *Escape from Childhood: The Needs and Rights of Children*, above n 46.

[49] A James and A Prout, *Constructing and Reconstructing Childhood* (Basingstoke, Falmer Press, 1990).

[50] 'Children's Rights: Judicial Ambivalence and Social Resistance', above n 46.

[51] 'Philosophical Perspectives on Childhood' n 6 above; 'Legal Concepts of Childhood: An Introduction', above n 33 . See also N Postman, *The Disappearance of Childhood* (London, Vintage, 1994). H Bevan, *Child Law* (London, Butterworths, 1989) 11.

[52] J Bandman, 'Do Children have Any Natural Rights?' *Proceedings of the 29th Annual Meeting of Philosophy of Education Society* (1973) 234, 236.

Balancing Protection and Autonomy

It appears that the majority of commentators reject 'the extremes' of child liberation or paternalism and instead seek to develop a model which acknowledges both a child's right to be protected from harm and a child's right to make decisions for her or himself.[53] In other words a model which balances a child's right to self-determination and a child's right to be protected. One theory, which has received widespread support is that proposed by John Eekelaar.[54] He has developed an approach to children's rights which requires the law to protect three different interests that a child has:

1. *Basic interests*. These are interests that are central to a child's well-being. They would include the feeding, housing and clothing of a child. Basic interests also include promotion of the child's physical, emotional and intellectual care. The duty to ensure that these are provided falls on the parents or, failing them, the state.

2. *Developmental interests*. These are the interests that a child has to enable her or him to develop as a person. Eekelaar explains that 'all children should have an equal opportunity to maximise the resources available to them during their childhood (including their own inherent abilities) so as to minimise the degree to which they enter adult life affected by avoidable prejudices incurred during childhood.' Interests in education or socialisation may be included here. Eekelaar suggests that to a large extent these are not legally enforceable rights, but rather moral claims that can be made against the wider community.[55]

3. *Autonomy interests*. These are the interests that children have in being permitted to make decisions for themselves. Eekelaar defines these interests as 'the freedom to choose his own lifestyle and to enter social relations according to his own inclinations uncontrolled by the authority of the adult world, whether parents or institutions.' Here, then, Eekelaar seeks to protect the decision-making powers that a child has.

Eekelaar goes on to argue that where there is a clash between the autonomy interests and the other two, the developmental or basic interests would trump the autonomy interest. In other words children have an interest in being able to make decisions for themselves, unless such a decision would infringe their basic or developmental interests. Children would therefore be able to make what adults might think of as 'bad decisions', but only as long as those are not such bad decisions that they interfere with matters that are central to a child's well-being.

---

[53] *Child Law*, above n 51 at 11.

[54] For particularly useful analysis see M Freeman, *The Moral Status of Children* (The Hague, Martinus Nijhoff, 1997) and N Wald, 'Children's Rights: A Framework for Analysis' (1979) 12 *University of California Davis Law Review* 225. For an excellent summary of the different theories see A Bainham, *Children: The Modern Law* (Bristol, Jordans, 1998).

[55] One example could be the right of a child to a clean environment: M Fitzmaurice, 'The Right of the Child to a Clean Environment' (1999) 23 *South Illinois University Law Journal* 611.

It will be noted that Eekelaar describes his approach in terms of interests rather than rights. This is because, although he is confident that children have these interests, whether they are respected as rights depends, he suggests, on whether there is a general acceptance that these interests should be protected by the law as rights. Nevertheless, he argues that at least the state should treat children as if they had these rights.[56]

As can be seen from these three models it is the approach to the right of autonomy, which most clearly distinguishes these different views. The right of autonomy is the right to decide how you wish to live your life. If you wish to spend the whole of your life writing academic articles, watching television, or plane spotting you can. It is common to talk about each person having the right to pursue their vision of the 'good life' without interference of the state or others, unless, of course, that vision causes harm to others. This will generally be regarded as not only good for each individual but also good for society. Our society benefits from people having a wide variety of different hobbies, interests, and religious beliefs, for example.

But to what extent can and should children be given the right to decide what is for them a 'good life'? Paternalism holds it to be for parents or ultimately the law to decide what will be a good life for children until they have reached adulthood and can decide that for themselves. Child liberationists would fully support children's right to decide how they would like to live their lives. For John Eekelaar children should be allowed to make their own decisions and live by them, but within bounds. They would not be permitted to exercise a choice that would harm their fundamental needs and ability to develop as people.

DIFFERENCES BETWEEN ADULTS AND CHILDREN: ARE THEY DISCRIMINATORY?

Not every distinction is discriminatory. As has been argued in other chapters in this book, express distinctions on grounds of age may not be considered unlawful if they can be justified. We will now return to the distinctions that have been drawn between children and adults, examples of which were given above and consider how they might be justified.

Rights Available to Adults which are Denied to Children

Here are some reasons that have been advanced to explain rights available to adults might justifiably be denied to children

---

[56] J Eekelaar, *Regulating Divorce* (Oxford, OUP, 1991) 103. For a different theory which suggests that children have welfare rights, protective rights, rights grounded on social justice and autonomy rights, see M Freeman, *The Rights and Wrongs of Children* (London, Frances Pinter, 1983).

Paternalism

Paternalists would support denying children the rights that adults have. They would argue that to give children the same rights as adults to work, engage in sexual activity or enter contracts would simply lead to children suffering great harm at the hands of sweat shop owners, child abusers, or manipulative toy manufacturers. Many disctinctions between adults and children might therefore be readily justifiable. To let children make all the decisions we allow adults to make would not be to promote a child's welfare.

Jurisprudential Concerns

The second objection to giving children adult rights is jurisprudential in nature and will only be discussed briefly.[57] There are two main theories about the fundamental nature of rights. The 'Will Theory' argues that rights can only be exercised if the right-holder has the choice of whether to act in a particular way. This theory therefore has difficulties in accepting that young children could have rights, as they would be unable to exercise the choice. However, the alternative theory, the 'Interest Theory', has no such difficulty. This theory argues that rights exist for the purpose of protecting a person's interests and are not dependent upon the right-holder being able to exercise a choice.[58] Under the Interest Theory, therefore, there is no difficulty with the notion that children have rights.

'The Right to be a Child'

Some argue that the most important right for children is 'the right to be children'.[59] The argument is that children should not be expected to bear all the burdens and responsibilities of adulthood. There is, for example, evidence from psychologists interviewing children whose parents are divorcing which suggests that although children do wish to be listened to by their parents and the courts, they do *not* wish to be required to choose between their parents.[60] To give children rights and expect them to be autonomous decision-makers is to rob children of their childhood, it is argued. There is something here, it must be said, of an image of an idealised childhood—a time of innocence, free from the concerns and responsibilities of the adult world—that is a far cry from the poverty, bullying and abuse which is the lot of all too many children.

---

[57] For excellent discussions see W Lucy, 'Controversies About Children's Rights' in M. Freestone (ed), *Children and the Law* (Hull, Hull University Press, 1990) and N MacCormick, 'Children's Rights: A Test-Case for Theories of Rights' (1976) 62 *Archiv für Rechts und Socialphilosophie* 305.

[58] Eekelaar's theory is clearly dependent on the interest theory of rights.

[59] 'The Rights of the Minor', above n 17.

[60] B Cantwell and S Scott, 'Children's wishes, children's burdens' (1995) 17 *Journal of Social Welfare and Family Law* 337; J Trowell and G Miles, 'Moral Agendas for Psychoanalytic Practice with Children and Families' in King (ed), *Moral Agendas for Children's Welfare* (London, Routledge, 1999); M King, 'Playing the Symbols—Custody and the Law Commission' (1987) *Family Law* 186.

'Dynamic Self-determinism'

Imagine a six-year-old child decides not to go to school. A strict child liberationist might argue that the child's wishes should be respected. After all we do
not require adults to attend schools, so children should not have to either. One
challenge to the child liberationist response here is based on the concept of
autonomy. As already mentioned, the traditional liberal view is that people
should be allowed to pursue their vision of the 'good life' as long as that does
not harm other people. Although to allow the child not to attend school might
be respecting the six-year-old's autonomy at age six by the time she reaches the
age of 16 the range of options open to her will be severely restricted, without any
educational qualifications. In effect then it can be argued that in order to maximise her autonomy in adulthood, it may be necessary to restrict her autonomy
in childhood.[61]

John Eekelaar has adopted arguments of this kind in suggesting that the law
should promote a child's welfare by encouraging dynamic self-determinism. He
explains that:

> The process is dynamic because it appreciates that the optimal course for a child can-
> not always be mapped out at the time of decision, and may need to be revised as the
> child grows up. It involves self-determinism because the child itself is given scope to
> influence the outcomes.[62]

The aim of his approach is:

> To bring a child to the threshold of adulthood with the maximum opportunities to
> form and pursue life-goals which reflect as closely as possible an autonomous choice.[63]

This involves encouraging and enabling the child to make decisions but not to
the extent of seriously prejudicing her life choices in adulthood.

Eekelaar's approach, while emphasising the importance of allowing and
enabling the child to make decisions for her or himself also provides a way of
distinguishing between legitimate differentiation and unjustifiable discrimination. Children's autonomy in childhood should be restricted in order to maximise their autonomy later in life. It is interesting to note that Eekelaar's
argument provides a possible reason for distinguishing between the treatment of
those incapable of decision-making through youth and those incapable through
illnesses associated with old age. Eekelaar's emphasis on leaving the child with
an open future would have no application for an incompetent person near the
end of their life.[64]

---

[61] J Eekelaar, 'The Interests of the Child and the Child's Wishes: The Role of Dynamic Self-
Determinism' (1994) 8 *International Journal of Law and the Family* 42.

[62] Ibid at 48.

[63] Ibid at 53.

[64] *Family Law*, above n 9 at 567–68.

Approaches of the kind Eekelaar has developed are very appealing and have attracted much support. They are however susceptible to challenge. For example, they fail to explain why such an approach cannot be used to justify restrictions on rights throughout life.[65] A 20-year-old who enjoys a hedonistic lifestyle rather than undertaking study or career development may be said to be restricting her autonomy later in life, as may even be a middle aged person who is failing to provide finance for her or his retirement. There is also a danger with Eekelaar's approach that the interests of the child as she or he *is* will be subordinated to the interests of the adult she or he *will become*.

The 'Thought Experiment' Approach

Michael Freeman has suggested that one way of approaching children's rights is to ask:

> What sorts of action or conduct would we wish, as children, to be shielded against on the assumption that we would want to mature to a rationally autonomous adulthood and be capable of deciding our own system of ends as free and rational beings.[66]

He[67] suggests that adopting such a 'thought experiment' one would not have wanted to be given all of the rights that an adult has. Many people are grateful that their parents did not give in to every wish and whim they had as they were growing up. However, Freeman suggests that many people would have wanted their childhood wishes to be followed unless serious harm would result. Tom Campbell is concerned about such an approach and expresses his worries this way:

> It is easy from this sort of hindsight position to welcome sacrifices that were made in the happiness of the child because of the advantages that are now involved . . . The method of retrospective substituted judgment does not play fair and equally with the interests of the child as they are manifest in the experiences of childhood.[68]

Concern over Misuse of Children's Rights by Adults

There are also concerns that far from liberating children a child liberationist perspective might in fact lead to the oppression of children.[69] This is because children may be open to manipulation by adults who could persuade children to exercise their rights in a way, which benefits adults rather than children. As Locke put it: to give liberties to a child is to 'thrust him out among Brutes, and abandon him to a state as wretched, and as much beneath that of a Man, as theirs'.[70] An obvious example might be in the arena of sexual behaviour. The

---

[65] *Family Law*, above n 9 at 355.
[66] *The Rights and Wrongs of Children*, above n 55 at 57.
[67] John Eekelaar in fact uses such a test in support of his approach to dynamic self-determinism.
[68] 'The Rights of the Minor', above n 17 at 21.
[69] 'Abandoning Children to Their Autonomy: The United Nations Convention on the Rights of the Child'(n 35).
[70] J Locke, *Two Treatises of Government* (Cambridge, CUP, 1963).

reports of the sophisticated 'grooming' techniques adopted by paedophiles to encourage children to engage in sexual activity demonstrates the concerns involved in giving children full sexual liberation.[71] Child liberationists might reply that because children's rights are capable of misuse is not an argument that rights should therefore be denied to children.[72] Indeed the argument of potential misuse could be used against any disadvantaged group within society to deny them rights.

Children's Rights are Inappropriate in the Family Setting.

A further objection that can be raised against the child liberationist position is that children's lives and interests are inevitably tied up with their parents. Although adults are able to pursue their wishes and desires without others, especially for the very young it is not possible for children to pursue their own interests without involving adults.[73] It can also be argued that the language of rights is inappropriate in the context of intimate family relationships, where sacrifice and mutual support are the overriding values,[74] rather than the market place philosophy of individualism where rights as traditionally understood make more sense.[75]

This objection might be overcome if an approach to rights could be developed which recognised the importance of relationships.[76] For example, it can be argued that beneficial relationships between people are those where rights are respected and fulfilled.[77] So seen, rights are the foundation of relationships, rather than antagonistic towards them. Another reply would be to accept the apparent conflict between rights and relationships, but to argue that the value of both can be maintained. For example, Michael Freeman argues,

> [t]o say that rights are important, and important also for children, is not to gainsay the crucial part which other morally significant values, such as love, friendship and compassion, have and play in life's relationships.

Practical Difficulties over Enforcement

There are difficulties over the enforcement of children's rights.[78] The child may be too young to enforce the right her or himself. Although in some cases parents

---

[71] See Home Office, *Protecting the Public* (London, Home Office, 2002).

[72] S Wolfson, 'Children's Rights: The Theoretical Underpinning of the "Best Interests of the Child" ' in M Freeman and P Veerman (eds), *The Ideology of Children's Rights* (The Hague, Martinus Nijhoff, 1992).

[73] See J Fortin, *Children's Rights and the Developing Law* (London, Butterworths, 1998) 6.

[74] See K Czapanskiy, 'Interdependencies, Families, and Children' (1999) 39 *Santa Clara Law Review* 957 which emphasises the significance of the child's primary care giver to the child's welfare.

[75] In a wider context see M Regan, *Alone Together: Law and Meaning of Marriage* (New York, OUP, 1999).

[76] 'The Welfare Principle and the Rights of Parents', above n 27.

[77] J Eekelaar, 'Beyond the welfare principle' [2002] *Child and Family Law Quarterly* 237, at 234.

[78] A point recently recognised by the House of Lords in *Re S; Re W (Minors) (Care Order: Implementation of Care Plan)* [2002] 2 All ER 237.

will be able to enforce the right on the child's behalf, this will be of no use where the child is seeking to enforce a right against the parents themselves. Indeed there are concerns that if children are given the rights that adults have these rights will only be enforced at the behest of the child's parents, which will only be when to enforce those rights will pursue the interests of the parents.[79]

A different concern over enforcement is that some rights that are claimed for children are simply too vague to be enforced, or even if they have sufficient precision it is unclear who has the duty that corresponds to the right. An example may be Article 27 of the United Nations Convention on the Rights of the Child, which declares 'the right of every child to a standard of living adequate for the child's physical, mental, spiritual, moral and social development'. Such a right is too vague to be legally enforceable and the article does not make it clear who is under the duty to ensure that these rights are fulfilled.

Partly with these concerns in mind Onora O'Neill[80] has argued that the law would benefit from focusing on the obligations of parents rather than the rights of children. This is because the enforcement of obligations could be undertaken by a state authority if necessary, thereby avoiding the difficulty that would arise in deciding who had standing to enforce the right on the child's behalf. The disadvantage of this approach is the lack of empowerment of older children. As mentioned earlier, rights enable a person boldly to claim her or his entitlement and acknowledge that such a person deserves to be recognised as a right-holder.

Discrimination on the Grounds of Competence rather than Age

Even if you were persuaded by the arguments of those who oppose child liberation on the ground that children lack the capacity that adults have, you could still argue that adults and children should have the same rights although some people (be they adults or children) would lack the capacity to have or be able to exercise their rights.[81] In other words, although it may be proper to discriminate against people on the ground of capacity, it is improper to discriminate on the basis of age.[82]

---

[79] See the wider concern that rights benefit only the strong, eg E Kiss, 'Alchemy or fool's gold? Assessing feminist doubts about rights' in M Shanley and U Narayan (eds), *Reconstructing Political Theory* (Cambridge, Polity, 1997) and A McColgan, *Women under the Law: The False Promise of Human Rights* (Harlow, Pearson, 2000).

[80] 'Children's Rights and Children's Lives', above n 7.

[81] Art 12 of the United Nations Convention on the Rights of the Child is a little ambiguous on the question of whether age or competence should be the key criterion of assessing a person's competence. It requires that states,

> should assure to the child who is capable of forming his or her own views the right to express those views freely in all matters affecting the child, the view of the child being given due weight in accordance with the age and maturity of the child.

By referring to age *and* maturity the implication in Art 12 is that the state is entitled to give less weight to a child's views because of their age, regardless of their maturity.

[82] See for example, J Harris, 'The political status of children' in K Graham (ed), *Contemporary Political Philosophy* (Cambridge, CUP, 1982).

It is generally accepted that age is an arbitrary criterion.[83] On your sixteenth birthday you do not suddenly become competent when a few hours before you were not. In fact the move from childhood to adulthood is better seen as a developmental process than as one-off transformation.[84] There is no doubt that some 14-year-olds are as able as adults to make some decisions.[85] Indeed one recent survey of the material on competence of children suggested that the majority of children aged 14 had similar cognitive capacities in relation to decision-making as adults.[86]

The argument in favour of relying on competence rather than age is that to do so treats each person as an individual, rather than relying on stereotypical assumptions about age.[87] It does not treat a person under 16 as 'a child' but considers carefully whether she or he has the capacity to make that decision. Age discrimination is thereby avoided. Are there any sound arguments against such a proposal?

It has been suggested that age has the benefit of being a clear and impersonal requirement, which does not involve 'contested norms'.[88] The point can be made by referring to cases which have involved consideration of whether a child who refuses a blood transfusion on religious grounds is competent to do so. Some judges have taken the view that children raised within strict religious backgrounds should be deemed to lack capacity to make medical decisions because they have had only a 'narrow upbringing'.[89] Similarly, beliefs by such children that they would go to heaven if they died or that there might be a miracle saving them from death, have lead judges to decree that they lack a sufficient understanding of the nature of death to make the decision not to take life-saving treatment.[90] Such decisions on competence are controversial. Age at least avoids judges needing to make judgments of this kind. A similar concern is that tests of competence can disguise a paternalistic decision. A judge or doctor may assume that a child is competent if she or he reaches a 'right' decision; but incompetent if the decision is 'wrong'.[91]

---

[83] *Contra*, 'Abandoning Children to Their Autonomy: The United Nations Convention on the Rights of the Child', above n 35, who argue that the notion of autonomy in childhood is an illusion.

[84] P Graham, J Turk and F Verhulst, *Child Psychiatry: a Developmental Perspective* (Oxford, OUP, 1999); 'Legal Concepts of Childhood: An Introduction', above n 33. See also, *The Disappearance of Childhood*, above n 51.

[85] See P Alderson, *Consent to Surgery* (Oxford, OUP, 1993) and *Perspectives in Child Care Policy*, above n 34, for discussions of the extent to which children have the same reasoning abilities as adults.

[86] M Schmidt and N Reppucco, 'Children's Rights and Capacities' in B Bottoms, M Bull Kovera and B McAuliff (eds), *Children, Social Science, and the Law* (Cambridge, CUP, 2002).

[87] Chapter 3 by S Fredman in this book.

[88] J Haldane, 'Children, Families, Autonomy and the State' in D Morgan and G Douglas, *Constituting Families* (Stuttgart, Franz Steiner Verlag, 1994).

[89] *Re S (A Minor) (Consent to Medical Treatment)* [1994] 2 FLR 1065; *Re E (A Minor) (Wardship: Medical Treatment)* [1993] FLR 386; *Re L (Medical Treatment: Gillick Competency)* [1998] 2 FLR 810.

[90] Ibid.

[91] M Brazier and C Bridge, 'Coercion or Caring: Analysing Adolescent Autonomy' (1996) *Legal Studies* 84.

There are practical benefits of using age, rather than competence. Take the example of the sale of alcohol. An approach which permitted the sale to anyone who was capable of understanding the potential consequence of alcohol abuse and had the capacity to decide whether they wish to drink, would certainly make a bartender's job more difficult. Is she or he to question everyone who asks for an alcoholic drink to see if they have sufficient capacity to make the order? It is certainly easier for a bartender to have a strict rule that those under a certain age are not permitted to purchase alcohol. The age criterion also makes it easier for citizens who will be able to plan their lives on the basis that they are or are not to be assessed competent, rather than having to establish their competence on each new occasion.[92] Of course, a child liberationist may reply that arguments of this kind, based on administrative convenience, fail to provide an acceptable basis for denying a right.

Rights Available to Children which are not Available to Adults

Compared with the vast literature on whether children should have the rights that adults have, there has been comparatively little discussion seeking to justify children being given extra rights over and above those granted to adults. This is in part because giving children these special rights is relatively uncontroversial. The special rights given to children can fall into two basic categories: (i) those that reflect the inability of children to care for themselves (eg special protections under the criminal law) and (ii) those that are designed to enable the child to take up their position as an autonomous adult and responsible citizen (eg rights to education).[93] There are therefore few problems for those approaching the issue from a paternalistic perspective, except to explain why these same benefits should not be available to those adults who may have the same needs as a child in these regards. To some child liberationists these 'special rights of protection' are seen as in fact denials of freedom. So, the special protection under the criminal law that children are given in the area of sexual offences are seen by some not as special rights of protection, but rather an interference with sexual liberty. To those adopting Eekelaar's analysis the special rights given to children can be said to exist in order to protect the child's basic or developmental interests.

---

[92] L Teitelbaum, 'Children's Rights and the Problem of Equal Respect' (1999) 27 *Hofstra Law Review* 799.

[93] M de Winter, *Children as Fellow Citizens: Participation and Commitment* (Abingdon, Radcliffe Medical Press, 1997); J Roche, 'Children: rights, participation and citizenship' (1999) 6 *Childhood* 475.

Where there is a Clash between the Rights of Adults and Children, Children's Rights are seen as Stronger

To paternalists there is little difficulty in arguing that children's interests should be preferred over the interests of adults where there is a clash between them, although it was noted above that for some paternalists the child's welfare is best defined in terms of the views of the parents on the issue at hand. The benefit of the welfare principle in the Children Act 1989 (which declares that the welfare of the child is to be the court's paramount consideration) is that it ensures that the judge's mind is focused on the interests of child, which might otherwise be too easily overlooked. The child may well not be represented directly in court and may be the person with whom the judge can least readily empathise. Further, the child is the person who is least able to move away from the troublesome situation and is least to blame for the cause of it.[94] Even if there are no theoretical justifications for prioritising the interests of children over adults, the history of the treatment of children by adults suggests that it is not possible to over-emphasise the importance of the interests of children.[95]

Despite these points the predominance of children's interests over adults' is rejected by many. In particular it is seen as unacceptable that an order could be made which slightly promotes the interests of a child even if it causes an adult significant harm.[96] For Helen Reece,

> (t)he paramountcy principle must be abandoned, and replaced with a framework which recognises that the child is merely one participant in a process in which the interests of all the participants count.[97]

She suggests a simple balancing of the interests of children and adults, without any preference being given to the interests of children. Andrew Bainham[98] has suggested balancing the interests of parents, children and the 'collective family unit' by regarding the more important rights as 'primary' and the less important secondary. Where the rights cannot be reconciled, primary interests (be they of children or adults) should prevail over secondary interests.[99] John Eekelaar has suggested:

> The best solution is surely to adopt the course that avoids inflicting the most damage on the well-being of any interested individual.[100]

---

[94] 'Children's Rights: The Theoretical Underpinning of the "Best Interests of the Child" ', above n 72.

[95] 'Beyond the Welfare Principle', above n 77.

[96] See the discussion in 'The Welfare Principle and the Rights of Parents', above n 27.

[97] H Reece, 'The Paramountcy Principle: Consensus or Construct?' (1996) *Current Legal Problems* 26.

[98] ' "Honour Thy Father and Thy Mother": Children's Rights and Children's Duties', above n 31.

[99] He does not explain what should happen where two primary interests clash.

[100] 'Beyond the Welfare Principle', above n 77.

In other words the court would make the order which imposes the least harm on any of the adults or children concerned. This might mean not making the order, which is best for the child if that causes significant harm to an adult. However, in an important caveat he adds that:

> No solution should be adopted where the detriments outweigh the benefits for the child, unless that would be the result of *any* available solution, so that it is unavoidable.[101]

So, adults' interests can be taken into account in justifying making an order, which does not advance a child's welfare as much as another order would; but not to justify an order, which harms a child.

An alternative proposal is to re-conceptualise the welfare principle to involve what I have called 'relationship-based welfare' which conceives children's best interests as being promoted when they are raised in good relationships.[102] As family relationships inevitably involve give and take and require sacrifices of the individual members there may be occasions on which a decision is made which seen in isolation might harm the child, but which is a legitimate part of an on-going relationship which benefits the child. Such an approach would still place children's interests at the forefront, but argue that children's welfare is based in being brought up within co-operative relationships; relationships which must on occasion mean that decisions are made which, seen in isolation, might be thought to harm the child. John Eekelaar is, however, concerned by such an approach, suggesting that unless children's interests are clearly isolated and seen separately there is a danger they will be subsumed within the interests of others.[103]

Responsibilities Adults have which Children do not

The most significant distinction here is, as mentioned above, the fact that a child under 10 is not criminally responsible for his or her actions. There is more to this than simply saying that a child who commits a crime cannot have understood the consequences of his or her action, because in such a case the normal requirements of the criminal law would have been able to provide a defence. The defence of infancy is an acknowledgment that the child lacks the abilities, which are essential preconditions to an ascription of moral responsibility for their action.[104] They are not acting as 'moral agents'.[105] The key point is not so much

---

[101] Ibid at 243.

[102] J Herring, 'The Human Rights Act and the Welfare Principle in Family Law—Conflicting or Complementary?' (1999) 11 *Child and Family Law Quarterly* 223; 'The Welfare Principle and the Rights of Parents', above n 27.

[103] 'The Welfare Principle and the Rights of Parents', above n 27 at 238.

[104] G Douglas, 'The Child's Right to Make Mistakes: Criminal Responsibility and the Immature Minor' in G Douglas and L Sebba (eds), *Children's Rights and Traditional Values* (Aldershot, Ashgate, 1998).

[105] 'Philosophical Perspectives on Childhood' , above n 6.

a lack of factual knowledge but that children are not in a position to respond to the criminal law, adjusting their behaviour and respecting the values of the criminal law, in a way that an adult is.[106]

Responsibilities Children have which Adults do not

There are relatively few responsibilities that are imposed on children, which adults do not have to bear. This is not surprising. Children are generally thought to lack the capacity which is required to make it fair to impose obligations upon them and hold them responsible for failing to meet those obligations. Further, as mentioned above, there is the strong feeling that children should, as far as possible, have childhoods free from the burdens and responsibilities that adulthood brings. However, as Andrew Bainham[107] has argued, if children are deemed mature enough to have rights then they may also be mature enough to have responsibilities and duties.[108] Indeed to be given rights without any responsibilities in the way those rights are exercised might be regarded as inappropriate.[109]

SOME PARTICULAR CASES INVOLVING CHILDREN'S RIGHTS

This part will consider some particular cases where the law distinguishes children and adults. The topics have been selected because they demonstrate some of the issues, which have been discussed above.

Gillick and Consent to Medical Treatment[110]

In *Gillick v West Norfolk and Wisbech Area Health Authority*[111] a mother argued that it was unlawful for a health authority to advise doctors that they could give contraceptive advice and treatment to girls under the age of 16 without their parents' knowledge or consent. Mrs Gillick complained that for doctors to provide such treatment to her daughters would infringe her parental

---

[106] J Horder, 'Criminal Law: Between Determinism, Liberalism and Criminal Justice' (1996) *Current Legal Problems* 159.

[107] ' "Honour Thy Father and They Mother": Children's Rights and Children's Duties', above n 31.

[108] S Martineau, 'Reconstructing Childhood: Towards a Praxis of Inclusion' in A McGillivray (ed), *Governing Childhood* (Aldershot, Ashgate, 1997).

[109] T Campbell, 'Really equal rights? Some philosophical comments on "Why children shouldn't have equal rights" by Laura M Purdy' (1994) 8 *International Journal of Children's Rights* 259.

[110] For a useful general survey of the law see 'Coercion or Caring: Analysing Adolescent Autonomy', above n 91.

[111] [1986] AC 112.

rights.[112] The majority of their Lordships found it was not unlawful for a health authority to advise doctors that they could give contraceptive advice. The majority of their Lordships held that once a child has sufficient understanding and intelligence to make decisions for her or himself she can give legally effective consent for medical treatment. In such a case the doctor could provide the treatment to the child, despite the opposition of her or his parents. Applying this to the facts of the case, if an under 16-year-old girl sought contraceptive treatment from her doctor, the doctor could provide the treatment if the girl had sufficient understanding concerning the issues involved, without the approval of her parents; indeed despite the opposition of her parents.[113] Following this case the concept of '*Gillick* competence' has developed. This expression defines a child who has sufficient understanding and maturity to take the relevant decision. Lord Scarman explained that it required the child to have sufficient awareness of the,

> moral and family questions, especially her relationship with her parents; long-term problems associated with the emotional impact of pregnancy and its termination; and . . . the risks to health of sexual intercourse at her age, risks which contraception may diminish but cannot eliminate.[114]

At the time *Gillick* was seen as recognising the child's autonomy right: permitting the child to decide for her or himself whether to have medical treatment.[115] However, this interpretation has proved ill-founded.

Decisions of the Court of Appeal since *Gillick* have made it clear if a *Gillick* competent child consents to treatment a doctor can provide medical treatment, but if the *Gillick* competent child refuses to consent to the treatment the doctor can still provide the treatment if the doctor has the consent of a person with parental responsibility,[116] or a court authorises the treatment.[117] If necessary, force can be used to compel a child to receive treatment against his or her wishes.[118] Putting the point in terms of rights a child has a right to consent to treatment, but does not have a right to refuse treatment.

Although at the time of *Gillick* the case was seen as a milestone in the recognition of children's rights,[119] the present law is illogical from the perspective of

---

[112] There was no suggestion that Mrs Gillick's daughters wanted or were likely to seek such treatment or advice.

[113] Section 8 of the Family Law Reform Act 1969 created a rebuttable presumption of lack of capacity for children under 16.

[114] *Gillick v West Norfolk and Wisbech Area Health Authority*, above n 112 at 189. The test for competence for adults appears much lower: eg *Re JT* [1998] 1 FLR 48 (a woman with learning difficulties who suffered from renal failure was competent to refuse dialysis) and in *Re C* [1994] 1 All ER 819 (a chronic paranoid schizophrenic was competent to refuse to have gangrenous leg amputated).

[115] 'The Emergence of Children's Rights', above n 8.

[116] *Re L*, above n 90.

[117] *Re C (Detention: Medical Treatment)* [1997] 2 FLR 180.

[118] Ibid.

[119] 'The Emergence of Children's Rights', above n 8.

children's rights and could be cited as a clear example of discrimination against children on the basis of age. To say that a child is competent enough to say 'yes' effectively, but not 'no' makes no sense. Not only is it odd to say that one is competent to answer a question, but only if one gives a particular answer; it is also bizarre because the law protects the less important right (the right to be able to give consent to medical procedures), but does not protect the more important right (the right not to have medical procedures imposed against your wishes).

The law however makes perfect sense if seen from a paternalistic perspective. The cases made it as likely as possible that treatment will be provided. A doctor can operate with the consent of either the competent child, or the person with parental responsibility or the court. Neither the parent nor child has a veto, which might prevent the provision of the treatment, which is presumed to be beneficial to the child.[120]

It can be seen then that in these cases the courts, although attracted to the liberationist notion of allowing children to be able to make medical decisions for themselves, were not willing to do so in a way which would allow children to threaten their lives or significantly impair their well-being. Such a result will be praised by paternalists and might be supportable under the Eekelaar model, at least where, without the proposed treatment, the child will suffer significantly. However, to child liberationists the present law is unjustifiable. They might refer to *Re E (A Minor)(Wardship: Medical Treatment)*[121] where Ward J explained that a child under 18 could not 'martyr himself'. In that case a 15-year-old boy refused blood transfusions on religious grounds. Without the transfusions he would die. His parents, sharing his religious beliefs, agreed with his decision. The High Court overrode his refusal and authorised the blood transfusions. Once he reached the age of 18, he refused further blood transfusions and died. Gillian Douglas has written of that decision:

> His case highlights the illogicality of the law's distinction between adults and minors—while a competent child can be kept alive in her best interests, as soon as she reaches adulthood, her refusal of further treatment becomes effective.[122]

Corporal Punishment

A person with parental responsibility for a child is entitled under common law[123] to administer corporal punishment on the child if that punishment is 'moderate and reasonable'.[124] However, the extent of this defence has been restricted following the Human Rights Act 1998 and the decision of the

---

[120] It is submitted it cannot always be assumed that what a doctor proposes is in the interests of a child (see *Family Law* n 9 above at 366).

[121] *Re E (A Minor) (Wardship: Medical Treatment)*, above n 90.

[122] G Douglas, *Introduction to Family Law* (Oxford, OUP, 2002) 76.

[123] The defence is preserved by Children and Young Persons Act 1933 s 1(7).

[124] *R v Hopley* (1860) 2 F&F 202.

European Court of Human Rights in *A v United Kingdom*.[125] In that case a step-father was acquitted of an assault causing actual bodily harm after he hit his nine-year-old son with a cane. He successfully pleaded the defence of reasonable chastisement. The European Court of Human Rights held that the existence of the defence of reasonable chastisement in English and Welsh law meant that the state was failing to protect children's rights to protection from torture and inhuman and degrading treatment under Article 3 of the European Convention on Human Rights. Following that decision the Court of Appeal in *R v H*[126] held that, when considering whether chastisement was reasonable, the jury had specifically to consider the nature and content of the treatment, its duration, its physical and mental effects, and the age, sex and state of health of the victim.

Despite these recent developments there is still a startling distinction between adults and children here, which must be considered discriminatory. The merest touch of an adult without their consent can amount the criminal offence of battery, yet a parent can hit a child and not be guilty of a criminal offence. Michael Freeman writes:

> Nothing is a clearer statement of the position that children occupy in society, nor a clearer badge of childhood, than the fact that children are the only members of society who can be hit with impunity.[127]

Why does the law allow this distinction? To child liberationists, corporal punishment is unjustifiable: it should be as illegal to hit a child, as it is to hit an adult. Paternalists might reply that it is simply because corporal punishment is good for children. However, the evidence is now very much weighted in favour of the view that corporal punishment does not benefit children.[128] More influential on governments may be the fact that many parents do in fact use corporal punishment on children.[129] Corporal punishment is clearly found by many parents to be a swift and apparently effective means of discipline. To make illegal an activity which is so widespread and is condoned by a high proportion of the population would be politically controversial.[130] It may be that the law wishes to be indulgent towards parents recognising the 'rough and tumble of home life'.[131] The law does not wish to impose too heavy burden on

---

[125] (1999) 27 EHRR 611.

[126] [2002] 1 Cr App R 59.

[127] M Freeman, 'The Convention: An English Perspective' in M Freeman (ed), *Children's Rights: A Comparative Perspective* (Aldershot, Dartmouth, 1996) 100.

[128] Useful surveys of the available material are found in P Newell, 'Global progress on giving up the habit of hitting children' in B Franklin (ed), *The New Handbook of Children's Rights* (London, Routledge, 2002) and D Orentlicher, 'Spanking And Other Corporal Punishment Of Children By Parents: Overvaluing Pain, Undervaluing Children' (1998) 35 *Houston Law Review* 1478.

[129] According to Department of Health *Protecting Children, Supporting Parents: A Consultation Document on the Physical Punishment of Children* (London, Department of Health, 2000).

[130] The Government in its review of the law on corporal punishment (*Protecting Children: Supporting Parents* (above n 130) has ruled out the possibility of outlawing all corporal punishment and has indicated that it will consider legislating to make it clear what forms of punishment are or are not permissible.

[131] *Surtees v Kingston-upon Thames BC* [1991] 2 FLR 559, at 583–4.

parents, given the trials and burdens of parenthood. Such concerns may be thought to be lessened by the fact that in Sweden, Finland, Denmark and Austria corporal punishment has been prohibited.[132]

The Government in its review of the law on corporal punishment has ruled out the possibility of outlawing all corporal punishment and has indicated that it will consider legislating to make it clear what forms of punishment are or are not permissible. Paternalists are split on the issue. To some, children need protecting from corporal punishment, which can be seen as a form of abuse. However, others, especially those who are willing to assume that parents know what is best for their children, would be wary about interfering with the parental decision on this issue.

Sexual Relations

The law on children and sexual relations require a delicate balance. On the one hand there is the need to protect children from sexual exploitation. On the other those sympathetic to the liberation of children would support the right of children to experiment sexually. The present law is generally regarded as restrictive. A child under the age of 16 cannot consent to indecent assault.[133] Further, it is an offence to commit an act of gross indecency with or towards a child under the age of 16 or inciting a child under that age to commit such an act with oneself or another.[134] This means that even sexual 'petting' where one of the parties is under 16 is illegal.

In part the debate is over the extent to which sacrifices in the rights to sexual freedom of children are justified in the name of the protection of children. But even from a paternalistic perspective there is still the question of what is 'good and bad sex for children.'[135] This in turn reflects the ambiguities over society's response to children's sexuality. One the one hand, there is the perception that children are sexually innocent, an innocence which is precious and must be preserved; and on the other there is the reality that society, through advertising, fashions, and pornography uses sexual images of children.[136]

---

[132] Committee on Economic, Social and Cultural Rights, E/C12/1/Add.79, May 2002 and Human Rights Committee, CCPR/C/SR.1961, Oct 2001.

[133] Sexual Offences Act 1956, s 14(2) (girls) and s 15(2) (boys). There are specific offences of having sexual intercourse with a girl under 16 (Sexual Offences Act 1956 s 5) or under 13 (Sexual Offences Act 1956 s 6).

[134] Indecency with Children Act 1960 s 1.

[135] See R Stainton-Rogers and W Stainton-Rogers 'What is Good and Bad Sex for Children?' in M King (ed), *Moral Agendas for Children's Welfare* (London, Routledge, 1999).

[136] D Haydon, 'Children's rights to sex and sexuality education' in B Franklin, *The New Handbook of Children's Rights* (London, Routledge, 2002).

Access to Courts

If children cannot apply to courts to enforce their rights then those rights are of little practical importance.[137] Significantly the Children Act 1989 permits children to apply for orders under that legislation, if they have leave of the court.[138] This could even include a child applying for a residence order, which would permit the child to live with someone other than her or his parents.[139] In considering whether to give leave to hear such applications the key question is whether the child has sufficient competence to bring the proceedings.[140] In fact, the courts have been very reluctant to permit children to bring such proceedings: the child is found to lack the maturity to instruct her or his solicitor on the issues that might arise during the hearing;[141] or the issue is too trivial to justify having a court hearing;[142] or the issue is said to be better dealt with by the parents and child resolving the issue themselves, rather than by court intervention.[143] Even where the child seeks to intervene in proceedings between her or his parents they may well not be permitted to do so,[144] the concern being that to allow the intervention would increase animosity between the parties.[145]

The lack of ready access to courts for children to enforce their rights and the absence of a Children's Rights Commissioner in England[146] are major stumbling blocks for those who wish to use children's rights to improve the legal and practical position of children. The courts appear to place greater weight on concerns that children may be being manipulated by others into bringing actions, or that the child may be traumatised by her or his time in court, or arguments that children have rights of access to the courts, or a right to be heard when a court is making a decision concerning his or her future.

---

[137] J Masson, 'Representations of Children' [1996] *Current Legal Problems* 245.

[138] Children Act 1989 s 10(8)(9).

[139] Children Act 1989 s 10(8). See M Freeman, 'Can Children Divorce Their Parents?' in M Freeman (ed), *Divorce—Where Next?* (Aldershot, Dartmouth, 1996).

[140] *Re S (Contact: Application by a Sibling)* [1998] 2 FLR 897; *Re H (Residence Order)* [2000] 1 FLR 780.

[141] *Re SC (A Minor) (Leave to Seek Section 8 Orders)* [1994] 1 FLR 96.

[142] Ibid.

[143] *Re S (A Minor) (Independent Representation)* [1993] 2 FLR 437.

[144] *Re M* [1995] 2 FLR 100; *Re H* [1993] 1 FLR 440.

[145] Advisory Board on Family Law, *First Annual Report*, 1998, para 4.12. It may be that in the future Art 6 of the European Convention on Human Rights (protecting the right of access to the courts) will mean that the courts will be more likely to grant leave. See *Sommerfeld v Germany* [2002] 1 FLR 119.

[146] G Lansdown, 'Children's Rights Commissioners for the UK' in B Franklin (ed), *The New Handbook of Children's Rights* (London, Routledge, 2002). Wales has a Children's Commissioner: Children's Commissioner for Wales Act 2001.

CHILDREN'S RIGHTS FOR ADULTS

Much of the debate about the justifiability of distinctions depriving children of rights has focused on whether children can be shown to have the competence of adults. Although hard to gauge, the majority of academic commentators appear to accept that the vulnerability of children and their dependency on adults (usually their parents) to meet their needs and desires mean that children cannot be granted exactly the same rights as adults. To do so would enable adults to exploit a child's vulnerability and might disrupt the family relationships upon which the child's well-being is usually so dependent.[147] Further, a child's lack of knowledge, experience, and decision-making ability mean that the child's choices should not automatically be followed and instead a competent person or court should make at least some decisions on the child's behalf. Although exactly which decisions should be made for children and which left to children themselves is much disputed. Many would agree with Bingham MR who in *Re S (A Minor) (Independent Representation)*[148] stated:

> First is the principle, to be honoured and respected, that children are human beings in their own right with individual minds and wills, views and emotions, which should command serious attention. A child's wishes are not to be discounted or dismissed simply because he is a child. He should be free to express them and decision-makers should listen. Second is the fact that a child is after all a child. The reason why the law is particularly solicitous in protecting the interests of children is that they are liable to be vulnerable and impressionable, lacking the maturity to weigh the longer term against the shorter, lacking the insight to know how they will react and the imagination to know how others will react in certain situations, lacking the experience to match the probably against the possible . . .

Although much of the academic debate has been over whether children are as competent and self-sufficient as adults, it is revealing to ask the question from the other end. Are adults not vulnerable and open to abuse? Are adults not dependent on others for pursuing their vision of a good life and dependent on the cooperation of others to pursue their goals? Are adults not all too often lacking in the necessary knowledge and experience for making important decisions, often 'blindly' following the advice of professionals? In many ways adults are as vulnerable, dependent on others, and lacking in competence to make important decisions as children. I would suggest that the difficulties that arise in granting adult rights to children are not due to children's lack of capacity, but the fact that adult rights often presuppose an autonomous individual adult.[149] The

---

[147] Janet L Dolgin, 'The Fate Of Childhood: Legal Models Of Children And The Parent-Child Relationship' (1997) 61 *Albany Law Review* 345.

[148] *Re S (A Minor) (Independent Representation)*, above n 144.

[149] M Minow, 'A Feminist Approach to Children's Rights (1986) 9 *Harvard Women's Law Journal* 1.

image of the self-sufficient, independent, fully competent adult is an 'ideal' which is far from realistic for many adults.

This is not an argument for limiting adults' rights, but rather rethinking them. Any conception of rights requires a recognition that adults' lives usually involve a network of cooperative relationships. Any successful version of rights must be one that respects and upholds these relationships, while at the same time protects individuals from the vulnerability that results from close relationships.[150] Rights must be rights that make sense in the relationships of give and take and interconnection that make up most of our lives. This means that it is often not possible to take a snap shot of a one-off situation and ascertain who has a right to do what, but instead the relationship between the parties must be looked at as a whole and it must be decided whether, in the light of the relationship, between the parties the right is one that can be claimed within that relationship. At the same time, rights need to protect those who are exploited in intimate relationships. An apparently autonomous decision made as the result of an exploited relationship need not be regarded as truly autonomous. I would suggest that, for example, the fact that the criminal law on sexual relations between adults cannot be applied to children, reveals the failure of the criminal law to protect adults who are exploited in sexual relationships.[151]

We are beginning to see the law recognising both the benefit and vulnerability of relationships in rights discourse. Article 8 of the European Convention on Human Rights requires the state to respect the right to private and family life. This notion of respect includes not just a negative requirement of not interfering in family or private relationships, but also can include a positive requirement that thestate seek to foster and maintain family relationships. For example, when a child is taken into care the state is required to take positive steps to foster the relationships between the child and her or his family unless to do so would cause great harm to the child.[152] The recognition of the potential for exploitation within relationships can be found in the development of the doctrine in *Barclays Bank v O'Brien*[153] which seeks to protect a person who signs a guarantee of a loan taken out by another person with whom they are in a close emotional relationship. Another would be the decision of the House of Lords' in *R v Hinks,*[154] which accepted that a woman who befriended a vulnerable man and dishonestly acquired his property through exploitation of their relationship[155] could be convicted of theft, even if such a transfer could be regarded as valid under civil law.

---

[150] M Minow, 'Interpreting rights: an essay for Robert Cover' (1987) 96 *Yale Law Journal* 1860.
[151] See J Herring, 'Does Yes means Yes?' (2002) *Singapore Law Review* (forthcoming).
[152] *K and T v Finland* [2001] 2 FCR 673.
[153] [1994] 1 AC 180.
[154] [2000] 4 All ER 833.
[155] A Bogg and J Stanton-Ife, 'Theft As Exploitation' (as yet unpublished paper). I am grateful to the authors for letting me have sight of this paper.

David Archard suggests that there are features of childhood, which are especially valuable: innocence, wonder and trust. But he then lists those features, which are not valuable: dependency and vulnerability. I disagree,[156] but there is not space here to discuss the positive aspects of dependency and vulnerability.[157] What can be asserted briefly is that dependency and vulnerability are a normal part of life for many people.[158] As Anne McGillvray explains:[159] 'Dependence is not a defect, which proscribes rights. It is an attribute of all human relationships.'[160] Once co-operative, care-giving relationships among vulnerable people (rather than autonomous individuals) are seen as the basis around which rights work, the difficulties with children and adults having the same rights to a large extent fall away.[161] Once adults are recognised as dependent and as vulnerable as children, they can share the same rights that children deserve.

CONCLUSION

As Andrew Bainham points out, 'it should be acknowledged that the substance of the relationships between children and the adult world are, in the final analysis, of greater significance than any theoretical description applied to them'.[162] In all the heat generated by the discussion of the rights of children and the extent to which children should be given the rights of adults, it should not be forgotten that the legal terminology given to children and their relationships with their parents, families and the wider world matters little compared with the reality of children's lives. Talk of children's rights is only of use if it results in practical measures being taken to improve the lot of children in Britain[163] and worldwide.[164]

[156] 'The Human Rights Act and the Welfare Principle in Family Law—Conflicting or Complementary?'(n 102). For a development of similar ideas in relation to pregnancy see J Herring, 'The Caesarean Section Cases and the Principle of Autonomy' in M Freeman and A Lewis (eds), *Law and Medicine* (Oxford, OUP, 2000) and in relation to organ transplantation see J Herring, 'Giving, Selling and Sharing Bodies' in A Bainham, S Day Sclater and M Richards (eds), *Body Lore and Laws* (Oxford, Hart Publishing , 2002).

[157] C Gilligan, *In a Different Voice: Psychological Theory and Women's Dependence* (Cambridge Mass, Harvard University Press, 1982); S Sevenhuijsen, *Citizenship and the Ethics Of Care: Feminist Considerations on Justice Morality and Politics* (London, Routledge, 1998).

[158] Ibid.

[159] A McGillivray, 'Why children do have equal rights: in reply to Laura Purdy' (1994) 2 *International Journal of Children's Rights* 243.

[160] Most children are dependent on their parents for the basic requirements of life. But this is not always the case. The Department of Health estimates that there are as many as 50,000 young people caring for their parents, and bearing significant levels of domestic, social and economic responsibilities.

[161] K Federle, 'On the road to reconceiving rights for children: a post-feminist analysis of the capacity principle' (1993) *De Paul Law Review* 983.

[162] *Children: The Modern Law*, n 54 above at 81.

[163] On 4 October 2002 the Committee on the Rights of the Child issued its Concluding Observations following its consideration of the United Kingdom's (UK) second periodic report under the UN Convention on the Rights of the Child, setting out an extensive list of the ways the UK was failing to protect children adequately.

[164] M King, ' "You have to start somewhere" ' in G Douglas and L Sebba (eds), *Children's Rights and Traditional Values* (Aldershot, Ashgate, 1998).

This chapter has focused on the question of whether it is legitimate to give children fewer rights than adults or whether such distinctions are discriminatory. The most popular way of considering this question has been to debate whether children have the same level of competence as adults and to consider the vulnerability of children. Those arguing for equality of rights between children and adults tend to play up the autonomy of children and downplay their vulnerability and dependency. The argument sketched very briefly at the end of this chapter has suggested that a stronger case for equality of rights can be based on recognising the dependency and vulnerability of adults, rather than seeking to prove the competence and self-sufficiency of children. A system of rights that recognises the fundamental role that mutually dependent cooperative relationships play in the lives of adults and children; that respects and upholds those relationships; and that protects people who are exploited by inappropriate relationships is a good system of human rights: not just for a few powerful autonomous individuals, but for the majority of dependent and vulnerable people, be they adults or children.

8

Age Discrimination Law: Some Remarks on the American Experience

LAWRENCE M FRIEDMAN

THE UNITED STATES Congress passed the Age Discrimination in Employment Act (ADEA) in 1967, during the Presidency of Lyndon Johnson.[1] Three years earlier, Congress had passed the most important civil rights law of modern times in the United States—a law which, among other things, outlawed race and sex discrimination on the job.[2] The ADEA was a response to a somewhat similar problem, or what was perceived as a problem: employers seemed to be prejudiced against older workers. They wanted young blood and only young blood. If an older worker, it was said, was fired or laid off, it was hopeless to think about getting a new job. Age discrimination, in other words, was rampant in society, at least in the workplace.[3]

The ADEA in its 1967 version, protected workers between the ages of 40 and 65. Employers were not allowed to discriminate in hiring, firing, or conditions of work. The law also outlawed discriminatory job advertisements;[4] discrimination in pay, and in use of company facilities. Sixty-five was chosen as the upper limit, probably because at that time it was the usual or at least a very common retirement age. Federal old age pensions typically began at 65, under the Social Security Act, first enacted in the 1930s. The upper limit under the ADEA was raised to 70 in 1978; and then, in 1986, the age cap was removed altogether. This meant, in theory, that an employer cannot refuse to hire an able and willing worker who is, let us say, 85 years old. But practically speaking what the latest change meant was the abolition of mandatory retirement. Essentially, then, the ADEA protects older workers from discrimination in getting and

---

[1] 29 U.S.C. 621.

[2] The Civil Rights Law of 1964 was, of course, far broader, and covered public accommodations, housing, and education as well. These other types of discrimination are not included in the ADEA. There had been proposals to add 'age' to the civil rights law of 1964, but these proposals were defeated, in part out of an impulse not to load the civil rights law with too many issues at once. See LM Friedman, *Your Time Will Come: The Law of Age Discrimination and Mandatory Retirement* (Russell Sage Foundation, 1984) 14.

[3] K Segrave, *Age Discrimination by Employers* (London, Jefferson N.C., 2001).

[4] The EEOC regulations prohibit even such phrases as 'college student,' or 'recent college graduate'. (29 CFR s 1625.4).

keeping a job; and from losing a job because of age, or because of a retirement rule. These aspects of the law are obviously linked. It is certainly a kind of age discrimination to fire a good and willing worker simply because she has reached the age of 65, or 70. But the ban on age discrimination, and the ban on mandatory retirement, are in some ways analytically and socially distinct, and I will discuss them separately.

The federal law is administered by the Equal Employment Opportunity Commission (EEOC), a federal agency.[5] The EEOC also has responsibility for job discrimination on the basis of race, sex, religion, and the like. Age discrimination is only one of its charges. The ADEA was the first major piece of federal legislation on the subject of age discrimination. But it did not come entirely out of the blue. For example, civil service rules, from 1956 on, had banned age discrimination in hiring for employees of the federal government.[6] Some of the states passed laws on age discrimination before the national government did; and some, like California, got rid of mandatory retirement before this was done on the national level (California's law went into effect in 1978).

Many of the states have created administrative agencies for enforcing age discrimination laws (usually among other things). Apparently, every state now has some sort of age discrimination law of its own—the last holdout was Alabama, which enacted its law in 1997.[7] Many of the state laws imitate the federal statute, but there are often significant differences. For example, the federal law applies to employers with more than 20 workers;[8] in some states, however, the law is stricter. In California, the statute applies to employers with five or more employees. A few states have statutes, which prohibit 'age discrimination' against anybody over the age of 18; and some do not specify *any* particular age. These statutes presumably protect a 30-year-old against age discrimination, although the decisions on this point are not at all uniform. I will return to this point. The state laws are especially important today for workers who work for state governments. The Supreme Court has recently held that people who work for a state government cannot sue their government under the ADEA; they are relegated to their local remedy.[9]

---

[5] The federal law has been administered by the EEOC since 1978. Before 1978, it was administered by the Wage and Hour Division of the Department of Labour.

[6] D Neumark, 'Age Discrimination Legislation in the United States' Working Paper no 8152 (National Bureau of Economic Research, March 2001).

[7] RF Gregory, *Age Discrimination in the American Workplace: Old at a Young Age* (New Brunswick, NJ Rutgers University Press, 2001) 16.

[8] Originally, the Act applied to companies with 25 workers or more; in 1974, the number was reduced to 20.

[9] *Kimel v Florida Board of Regents*, 528 U.S. 62, 120 S. Ct 631 (2000). The Supreme Court held that it was beyond the power of Congress to allow private citizens to sue their state for age discrimination. Since age was not a protected category under the Fourteenth Amendment, Congress could not authorise this kind of lawsuit as a way of putting meat on the bones of a Fourteenth amendment right. The Court said, too, that this hardly left state workers powerless—they could sue under state law, after all.

AGE DISCRIMINATION ACT

The ADEA applies only to employment. There is a separate federal law, the Age Discrimination Act (ADA), which was enacted in 1975.[10] It applies to all programmes and activities that receive support from the federal government. These programmes and activities are not allowed to discriminate 'on the basis of age.' Any age, by the way; not just old age. Obviously, Congress could not have meant to affect *all* federal programmes that drew age-lines; otherwise, old age pensions themselves would be illegal, and so would federal programmes like Head Start which are only for little children. Not to worry: ADA, according to the statutory text, does not apply to actions that 'reasonably take into account age as a factor necessary to the normal operation . . . of the program or activity;' or to 'benefits or assistance.' This leaves the ADA mostly words; and in fact it is much less important than the ADEA. It is not, however, totally toothless. A medical school, for example, which gets much of its money from the federal government, cannot simply adopt a blanket rule that nobody over 30 need apply.

The European initiatives, which I will discuss shortly, are concerned only with employment; and I will concentrate on employment. Clearly, employment has been the major area where older people feel the bite of discrimination. Nobody claims that restaurants slam the door on people with grey hair; or that landlords refuse to rent to anybody over 40. Education is another matter; and here, as I mentioned, the ADA is of some utility. And some of the state laws cover housing, or public accommodations. Whether this is at all necessary is another question.

For many years, there was nothing in Europe equivalent to the ADEA or ADA. Now there is some activity, in a few countries, and very notably, a directive of the European Union, mandating age discrimination laws for all member nations. The preamble, I note, states that the directive is 'without prejudice to national provisions laying down retirement ages' and the actual provision on age discrimination is, as I read it, a bit vague. It allows member states to take actions, which are 'objectively and reasonably justified by a legitimate aim, including legitimate employment policy,' and it recognises 'labour market and vocational training objectives.'[11] This is certainly wishy-washy enough. It is, in fact, a question whether this directive really forces a country to do anything much at all about age discrimination. I have no idea what 'legitimate employment policy' is supposed to mean. Time will tell whether the directive, or the laws member states enact to put it into effect, will have some real impact. For now, however, it seems likely—though not certain—that a member nation could comply with the Directive, and still keep its rules on mandatory retirement.

[10] 89 Stat. 724 (Act of November 28, 1975); 42 U.S.C. 6101.
[11] Council Directive (EC) 2000/78 on establishing a general framework for equal treatment in employment and occupation [2000] OJ L303/2.

NON-DISCRIMINATION IN THE FEDERAL CONSTITUTION

The ADEA outlaws age discrimination in the job market. In many ways, the statute parallels the laws on race and sex discrimination; but there are some significant legal differences between the texts and interpretation of the various discrimination laws. The Supreme Court has decided that the federal Constitution forbids race and sex discrimination. Specifically, the Fourteenth Amendment to the Constitution is the governing text.[12] This means that states are forbidden to discriminate, even without any specific federal statute outlawing discrimination. Race and sex are 'suspect' categories, in the Court's jargon- race more suspect than sex. Laws that discriminate on the basis of race get what the Court calls 'strict scrutiny,' a beady eye, like the glance of the basilisk, which almost no statute can survive, if it draws a race line. A law that discriminates on the basis of sex, or draws some sort of gender line, gets 'intermediate scrutiny,' which is not quite so fatal.

Age discrimination falls into neither of these rarefied categories: at any rate, the Supreme Court so decided in 1976, in a case brought by a Massachusetts state police officer.[13] Murgia, the complainant, had been forced to retire at 50. This rule, he argued, violated his right to equal protection of the laws, under the Fourteenth Amendment. He lost the case. The Court refused to apply the concept of 'strict scrutiny' to age discrimination; or, really, any scrutiny at all. The tough tests- the 'scrutinies'—were appropriate only when a statutory classification 'interferes with the exercise of a fundamental right or operates to the peculiar disadvantage of a suspect class.' There was, however, no fundamental right to serve Massachusetts as a police officer, or in fact to hold any government job. Nor did the statute discriminate, really, against 'the elderly.' Instead, the statute drew a line 'at a certain age in middle life'. The elderly, said the Court, did not constitute in themselves a class needing protection- unlike racial minorities. Old age, after all, is 'a stage that each of us will reach if we live out our normal span.' Most of the justices, of course, had long since already reached it.

The Supreme Court has never revisited this question, and *Murgia* is presumably still good law. Age discrimination, in short, is not prohibited by the federal constitution. As far as the job market is concerned, this does not matter very much. Congress outlawed age discrimination in employment, by passing the ADEA; and the constitutional issue is for most workers therefore quite irrelevant.

---

[12] On race discrimination, the key case was *Brown v Board of Education*, 347 U.S. 483 (1954); the first case that held unconstitutional a state law, on grounds of sex discrimination, was *Reed v Reed*, 404 U.S. 71 (1971)—this was seven years *after* Congress had passed a civil rights law that included sex discrimination.

[13] *Massachusetts Board of Retirement v Murgia* 427 U.S. 307 (1976).

IMPACT OF ADEA

The ADEA is now more than 30 years old. It is certainly not a dead letter. Far from it. The Employment and Equal Opportunities Commission (EEOC) has a great deal of age discrimination business. Between 1 October 2000, and 30 September 2001, there were 80,840 charges filed with the EEOC. Of these, 21.5 per cent or 17,405, were complaints about age discrimination.[14] A person who thinks he or she is a victim of age discrimination can file a complaint with the EEOC, which has field offices in various cities in the United States. The EEOC will investigate the claim. If it decides that there is some substance to the complaint, it will try to work things out with the company. If this attempt at conciliation and settlement fails, the EEOC can either take the case to court itself; or, in cases where it chooses not to, it can give workers so-called 'right-to-sue' letters, and let them go to court on their own. The letter ends the matter at the EEOC, but without prejudice.

A person can also start the process by filing a complaint with his own state agency. If so, the state agency will usually handle the complaint on its own, but will also notify the EEOC. Similarly, if the charge is filed with the EEOC, but is also covered by state or local law, the EEOC will keep the matter under its wing, but will let the local agency know. It is not easy to tell how many complaints are filed with state agencies; but the numbers in some states are significant, and have been for some time. In California, a report for 1988–89, of the Department of Fair Employment and Housing, which handles race, sex, and other forms of discrimination as well, showed 1,134 cases filed which alleged age discrimination—15 per cent of the total number of complaints.[15] Whether some, or most, of these were also filed with the EEOC is not stated. But it is clear enough that the state agencies are fairly busy organisations. Indeed, a newspaper article in 1999 claimed that at that date, age discrimination claims in California were running at the rate of 3,000 a year.[16]

Each year, as we said, there are thousands of complaints to the EEOC. Most of them are dismissed, or simply dropped. Many of them settle. Only about 1 per cent of them end up in court. But this is still enough each year to build up a massive body of case law. Many of these reported cases, of course, turn on technical or procedural issues. But there are also some issues of substance. Under the statute, the ban on age discrimination is not absolute. The text of the ADEA makes specific reference to seniority systems, and clearly indicates that a

---

[14] Public Employment Law Report, May 2002; race accounted for 35.8% of the filings, sex/gender, 31.1%.

[15] Department of Fair Employment and Housing (Annual Report 1988–89) 14, Table 3; 18, Table 10. Interestingly, there were 22 complaints of discrimination in housing based on 'age'. One wonders what these were exactly.

[16] SA Capps, 'Davis Signs Bill Aiming to Protect Workers Over 40' *Modesto Bee* (Modesto, USA, 3 August 1999) 1.

seniority system as such does not violate the law. The law and the courts also allow age-limits for a few jobs that touch on public safety—long-distance bus drivers, or airline pilots.[17] And the law does not protect executives or high policy-makers.[18] A company can dismiss its chairman of the board at 65 or 70, if it wishes. Also, an employer is not guilty of violating the act, if the actions of the employers were based on 'reasonable factors other than age.'[19] This phrase, of course, is rather opaque. Suppose a company is having some financial troubles. It decides to 'downsize.' It decides, further, to get rid of some relatively senior high-paid employees. They complain of age discrimination. No, says the company, the point was not how old you are, but how expensive you are. Seniority, age, and fat paycheques are strongly correlated, however. Has the company violated the act? Was its action based on some 'reasonable' factor other than age? There is, so far, no definitive federal answer.[20]

An important Supreme Court case, decided in 1993, does shed some light on the issue. In this case, *Hazen Paper Company v Biggins*,[21] the company fired Biggins, who was 62 years old. The company had a pension plan, which vested after a worker had served ten years. There was some suggestion that Biggins was fired just before his pension would have vested. A suspicious mind might even conclude that this was *why* he was fired. But the Supreme Court held that pension status, though it might be 'correlated' with age, was 'analytically distinct' from age. Firing somebody because they had so many years of service was a decision, therefore, not necessarily based on 'age.' The company might have violated federal laws about pensions; but it had not violated the ADEA.

State law does not necessarily go along with this decision. A law in California, enacted in 1999, specifically states that it may be considered 'age discrimination' to use 'salary as the basis for differentiating between employees when terminating employment,' that is, if the use of salary as a basis 'adversely impacts older workers as a group.'[22]

---

[17] On long-distance bus drivers: *Hodgson v Greyhound Line, Inc.*, 419 U.S. 1112 (1975). The airline pilots must retire at 60. They have been fighting this rule, so far unsuccessfully.

[18] 29 U.S.C.A 631 (c) (1).

[19] Another defence is the so-called 'BFOQ' defence. It is an excuse if age is a 'bona-fide occupational qualification'. But the courts have construed this defence very narrowly (in sex discrimination cases, for example). With regard to age discrimination, courts have been sympathetic only when the question is one of public safety.

[20] But California law is otherwise, see n 22 below.

[21] 507 U.S. 604 (1993).

[22] California Government Code s 12941.1. The statute also specifically authorises the 'disparate impact theory of proof . . . in claims of age discrimination,' and tells the courts to interpret the age discrimination laws 'broadly and vigorously,' just as they do laws 'against sex and race discrimination.' Moreover, the statute specifically rejects *Marks v Loral Corp.*, 57 Cal. App. 4th 30 (1997), which held otherwise as to 'disparate treatment.'

Disparate Impact

A related question, which overlaps this one, concerns the so-called 'disparate impact' doctrine. Suppose a company adopts a policy that has a worse impact on workers over 40, than on younger workers. Does the burden of proof now shift to the company to justify this policy? Must the company now show that the policy was necessary for some good and valid reason other than discrimination? For age and sex discrimination, the answer in analogous cases is yes.[23] For age discrimination, the answer is maybe. Some federal courts say yes, some federal courts say no. The *Hazen* case left the question open. The Supreme Court recently refused to decide the issue.[24] California's courts said no, but the legislature overturned this decision and said, most definitely, yes. Those courts that reject disparate impact make it fairly tough to win an age discrimination case. You have to show that the boss fired you *because* of age; that there was deliberate, intentional discrimination. This is no easy task. If you are lucky, you can find a smoking gun—some tactless personnel director who told you he was clearing out old fogies, or that the company had to get fresh blood. But not all plaintiffs are so lucky. For the others, they may face an uphill battle.

Take another situation. A company needs, or thinks it needs, to downsize. It decides to get rid of older workers. They cost more money than the young ones. The company offers them a substantial bribe to take early retirement—a package of benefits, often including cash, if they will please leave the premises. Is this age discrimination? No, say the courts, if the plan is truly voluntary; yes, if it has an element of coercion—take this package or else; or if the company makes clear that the employee is going to be terminated, one way or another; and so he might as well take this generous offer. This situation is, at least in part, now covered by statute, as we will see later on.

ADEA's Critics

Economists, and lawyer-economists, on the whole, have not been terrifically friendly to age discrimination law. Richard Posner feels that the 'age discrimination law is largely ineffectual'; and to the extent it is 'effective it has a perverse effect. . . . The age discrimination law is at once inefficient, regressive, and harmful to society.'[25] Some of these scholars are hostile to discrimination law in general. But there are also some who at least claim to think race and sex discrimination laws are ok, yet oppose age discrimination laws. They have noticed

[23] A key case was *Griggs v Duke Power Co.*, 401 U.S. 424 (1971).

[24] See L Greenhouse, 'Supreme Court Taps Cases to decide 3-Strikes Issue' *New York Times* (New York, USA, 1 April 2002).

[25] RA Posner, *Aging and Old Age* (Chicago, University of Chicago Press, 1995) 319. Not all economists feel that age discrimination laws are inefficient. See D Neumark and WA Stock, 'Age Discrimination Laws and Labour Market Efficiency' (1999) 107 *Journal of Political Economy* 1081.

that most plaintiffs in age discrimination lawsuits seem to be white males. Moreover, most of these plaintiffs are white males who had good , high-paying, high-status jobs. Studies of age discrimination cases in courts have consistently found this to be true.[26] A study published in 1984 analysed 153 federal court cases under the ADEA.[27] Eighty-one per cent of the plaintiffs were men. Most of them were in their 50s. Fifty-seven per cent were 'professional/managerial'; only 25 per cent were blue-collar workers.[28] And most of these plaintiffs complained about job termination. Thirty-six per cent had been let go, and another 31 per cent involuntarily retired. Very few cases were about a failure to hire. The law, according to the authors of the study, had become the 'primary device used by white male professionals and managers to attack arbitrary personnel decisions.'

This lays the ADEA, as a working body of law, open to criticism. Why give a cause of action to this particular group? Most lawsuits, to this day, continue to show these characteristics: the plaintiffs are professional men or managers whose contracts have been terminated, and are unhappy about the situation. In a study of cases at the level of the Courts of Appeal, for 1996, 76 per cent of the plaintiffs were men. Women made more of a mark at the level of the district courts, and the trend over time seemed to be an increase in the percentage of women litigants; but men were still a substantial majority. And the litigants were people who had had good jobs: in the 1996 study, 43 per cent were management, 30 per cent were non-management but white collar, only 9 per cent were blue collar, at the level of the Courts of Appeal. And, again, the overwhelming majority complained about being fired or dismissed: 73 per cent of the cases.[29]

These facts suggest (to some people, at any rate) that there is no good reason to allow these lawsuits. Laws against discrimination are supposed to help the oppressed and the powerless. But, as one economist put it, 'Whatever the justification for protecting white males age 40 or over, it cannot be that they have been excluded from political and economic power.'[30] This, I think, somewhat misses the point. Yes, many or most people with wealth and power are over 40. Business executives are usually over 40, and are rich, and rather powerful. An executive's decision to fire somebody who is 50 can nonetheless be a product of prejudice or stereotype. Age discrimination, socially, is quite different from, say, race discrimination. As Howard Eglit has pointed out, age bias is situational: a biased personnel manager might refuse to hire a 60-year-old, but still welcome

---

[26] M Schuster and CS Miller, 'An Empirical Assessment of the Age Discrimination in Employment Act' (1984) 38 *Industrial and Labour Relations Review* 64; G Rutherglen, 'From Race to Age: The Expanding Scope of Employment Discrimination Law' (1995) 24 *Journal of Legal Studies* 491.

[27] 'An Empirical Assessment of the Age Discrimination in Employment Act', above n 26.

[28] HC Eglit, 'The Age Discrimination in Employment Act at Thirty: Where It's Been, Where It Is Today, Where It's Going' (1997) 31 *U Richmond L Rev* 579, 599–612.

[29] Ibid at 613–14, 623–30.

[30] 'From Race to Age', above n 26.

the same 60-year-old 'as a neighbour or tenant.'[31] Senior white men are perfectly capable of discriminating against other senior white men. Intra-group discrimination is not at all unusual. Landlords with small children are capable of discriminating against families with small children, in renting apartments. Women are capable of discriminating against other women on the job.

Judges, who are mostly professional people over 40, and mostly men, are also in the same demographic category as the typical plaintiffs. That should make them sympathetic—one might think. In fact, they seem not to be. In many courts, plaintiffs face tough doctrinal hurdles. The judges seem much friendlier to race and sex discrimination cases, than to age discrimination cases. Richard Posner—a judge, and well over 40—is one of these unfriendly judges, at least in his written *oeuvre*. The people who carry out employment policies, he says, 'are at least 40 years old and often much older.' It would be odd if they had a 'generalized antipathy toward old people.' And if older workers have trouble finding new jobs 'at high wages,' it is because their wages in the old job 'reflected firm-specific human capital that disappeared when they left.'[32] But, as we said, a 'generalized antipathy toward old people' is not the issue. Posner himself, and other judges, clearly do not feel, for whatever reason, that most of the plaintiffs have a legitimate claim. The judges certainly do not form a brotherhood of seniors.

Perhaps the judges are right, in their suspicion of age discrimination cases. Legally speaking, at any rate. It is hard to know the truth about discrimination in the job market. In the first place, studies based on actual lawsuits—and reported, published opinions at that—may not tell the whole story, or even the most important part of the story. The lawsuits represent, necessarily, difficult and perhaps borderline cases. This is true of discrimination cases generally. Crass and overt discrimination rarely ends up in court; it gets found out and remedied long before this. The plaintiffs, we must remember, are men and women who have a 'right to sue' letter, but the EEOC had already decided not to pursue the case any further. Not surprisingly, the vast majority of the plaintiffs in federal court are losers. There is some dispute about the actual percentages, but it seems pretty clear that the companies win at least two thirds of the cases, and perhaps as many as four out of five.[33] In short, most of the men and women who get as far as federal court will go away empty-handed.

Most of the cases, as we mentioned, are about firing, not hiring. It is entirely possible that the ADEA has helped some older workers get their jobs in the first place. For some industries, the evidence is completely obvious. Flight attendants are one example. The airlines once insisted that they had to be young—and also female. This is now history. And, under the ADEA, no employer can have a

---

[31] 'The Age Discrimination in Employment Act at Thirty, above n 28 at 619, n 112.

[32] *Aging and Old Age*, above n 25 at 320–21.

[33] See the discussion in 'The Age Discrimination in Employment Act at Thirty', above n 28 at 657–58. Plaintiffs who get to a jury are more likely to win than those who do not, however. And women plaintiffs do somewhat better than men.

deliberate, overt policy of hiring only young people. There is a fair amount of grey hair serving coffee on airplanes nowadays—female and male.

Impact on Employment Practices

Case law is not necessarily the same as the law in action. Employers are certainly aware of the ADEA. They know that they are not supposed to discriminate on the basis of age. They know that they are not supposed to run ads asking for young workers. Even expressions like 'recent college grads' are suspect. Some of them do not even ask for your birth-date, at least in a job interview. Companies know they have to be careful. In hiring and firing, personnel people have to watch their language. Does this mean that age discrimination has simply gone underground? Not entirely, of course. And the role of older people in society itself has been changing. People live longer and healthier lives. Older people do not necessarily 'act their age' any more. They lead more active lives. They are even supposed to have sex lives. All this, despite all the talk about a youth culture and the lack of respect for the elderly. The demographic and social facts are bound to affect attitudes towards old age. Some of this attitude change is bound to percolate into the job market. Hence the rich body of case law, though it tells us some interesting things, does not necessarily instruct us about the ways in which age discrimination law really works in the world of business.

Case Law

The case law, as it stands, would probably surprise the people who drafted the law. At that time, almost all the talk was about hiring. Older workers had trouble getting jobs. Companies wanted only younger workers. If you were over 40, or 50, you ended up on the slag heap. But the case law, as we said, is not about hiring at all, at least not often; it is mostly about firing, retiring, and letting go.[34] Complaints of this nature are by far the most common charges before the EEOC, as well as in court.[35] So much so, that some have argued that the ADEA has come to have an entirely new meaning. It is now a law about fairness, about wrongful discharge.

A few examples from the case law might be useful. In *Jackson and Serment v E. J. Brach Corporation*, a 1999 case in the Seventh Circuit of the federal system,[36] two men sued their former employer, a candy company. One of them,

---

[34] JJ Donohue and P Siegelman, 'The Changing Nature of Employment Discrimination Litigation' (1991) 43 *Stanford Law Review* 983.

[35] 'Age Discrimination Legislation in the United States', above n 6. This is true also for Title VII of the Civil Rights Act (race and sex discrimination, mostly): about a quarter of all complaints fall into this category, almost twice as many as the next largest category (terms of employment).

[36] *Jackson and Serment v E J Brach Corporation*, 176 F. 3d 971 (CA 7, 1999).

Jackson, was an African-American. He was 50, and he had worked for Brach for more than 27 years. The other plaintiff, Serment, was Hispanic, and had worked for Brach for 30 years. They both had supervisory jobs. The candy company was not doing too well; it decided to downsize. It let both Jackson and Serment go. The two levelled a barrage of complaints against the company, including age discrimination and race discrimination. Not so, said the company; we let Jackson go, because he was a weak performer. We got rid of Serment because he was redundant. At this point, the two men had a daunting problem of proof. To win, they had to show that these arguments were lies—pretexts; that bias was the cause of their termination. This they could not do—not to the satisfaction of the court. The trial court dismissed their case; and the appeal court affirmed.

Two supervisors, downsized; they complain, go to court, and lose their case. A typical result of a typical case. But it is easy to understand their anger. Twenty, thirty years for a company: and now it sends them packing. One is told he is incompetent—the other that he is useless. Would it be human nature, in this day and age, to take this lying down? Legally, the claims were probably groundless, as the courts said. But they were utterly sincere. And understandable.

In another case from the same year, in the eighth circuit, William L Montgomery sued the John Deere Company, his former employer.[37] Again, Montgomery accused the company of a whole series of wrong motives: age discrimination was only one of them. Montgomery, who, we are told, was 'part Cherokee Indian', was another long-time employee; he went to work for the company in 1966. Montgomery was diagnosed in 1980 as a narcoleptic. In 1989, he was assigned to work in the safety department of one of Deere's factories. His job was to administer various programmes of hygiene and safety. In 1992, he was reassigned to 'the environmental compliance area'. This was a new field for him. His work was apparently unsatisfactory, and in 1994, the company let him go. He was 52 years old, and had the title of 'senior engineer analyst'.

Montgomery, too, lost his case. He too was unable to meet the burden of proof. He was unable to convince the court—any court—that 'Deere's declared reason for firing him was a pretext for age discrimination.' Montgomery had other arguments, too, besides age discrimination; but the court brushed them aside as well. One of the judges, however, who concurred, could not help expressing his opinion; he fully understood Montgomery's 'frustration. He was a loyal employee who performed his job for over 28 years. Why was he suddenly discharged as he neared retirement age?' Montgomery's lawyer, the judge thought, used a 'shot-gun' approach, advancing all sorts of claims, hoping one of them would work. This technique backfired. But the result, said the judge, 'leaves the plaintiff feeling an injustice has been done and, although I lack a legal basis for saying so, I am not so sure that I disagree.'

---

[37] *Montgomery v John Deere & Company*, 169 F. 3d 556 (CA 8, 1999).

A remarkable statement. Injustice has been done. Yet there is no 'legal basis' for curing it. But history suggests that when enough people feel a sense of injustice, a legal basis *will* emerge, one way or another. Law is supposed to be *about* justice. In any event, it does seem true that much of the case law is really about this issue of fairness; it is about what we call wrongful discharge—whatever the formal legal claim. So far, this is a losing battle—the fight against unfairness in the workplace. In the present political climate, it seems unlikely to make much of a mark in the near future. But the *feeling* is there; and it makes a difference in behaviour, if not yet in law; and it foments complaints, claims, and ultimately actions at law.

Economic Impact

A number of economists have studied the ADEA and tried to measure its impact. These studies, on the whole, pay very little attention to the *social* meaning of age discrimination law. The literature is obsessed with whether or not age discrimination law is 'efficient'. Some think it is; some think it is not. Employers, when the ADEA was passed, were worried that it would cost them money. They were worried, too, that it would tie them up in red tape. These fears were certainly not foolish. It is obviously cheaper and easier to hire and fire whoever you want whenever you want. In the *Brach* case, discussed earlier, the company, as we said, had decided to downsize. The Vice President of Human Resources issued a directive to the supervisors: in downsizing, they must use 'job-related criteria'. They were not to consider race, sex, age, religion, disability, citizenship, sexual orientation, and a number of other factors; and were to pay special attention to employees over 50 with 20 years or more of service.[38] This cautious note was not enough to save Brach from the lawsuit we discussed; but perhaps it spared Brach other lawsuits. And the directive obviously reflected company policy; and that policy, in turn, was shaped by company awareness of the legal regime it faced. At one time, the company would not have bothered to create the office of 'Vice President of Human Resources'. This additional staffing, and additional caution, is not costless. But it also signifies, what is clear from other evidence, that laws against discrimination may have *some* impact on the behaviour of companies in the market.[39]

---

[38] *Jackson and Serment*, above n 36.

[39] How much impact is a difficult question; in some cases the company efforts may be purely symbolic. See, in general, LB Edelman, 'Legal Ambiguity and Symbolic Structures: Organizational Mediation of Civil Rights Law' (1992) 97 *American J of Sociology* 1531. Yet on the whole the creation of these offices and slots within the company bureaucracy is bound to have some effect.

Justice

In any event, we should not judge the ADEA on a cost basis alone. This is not a branch of antitrust law. Efficiency is not the be-all and the end-all here. Freedom from discrimination is, plain and simple, an aspect of civil rights, of human rights. It is part of a whole complex of rules and regulations, which have bubbled up out of society, and which respond to norms, attitudes, ideas about right and wrong, fairness and unfairness. There is a growing social consensus that people should be judged as individuals, and on their merits. If it is unfair to refuse a job to a woman, a black man, or a person in a wheelchair who wants to work, and can do the work, it must also be quite unfair to slam the door on a 45-year-old who wants a job; or to fire him when he reaches a certain age.

Age discrimination law is thus part of the whole package of civil rights, and of the whole culture and ethos of civil rights. There is no question that there is less race and sex discrimination in the United States than there was, say, in 1950. The number of complaints to the EEOC stays high, but most of these, too, are dismissed, like the age discrimination complaints. What the high rate of complaints suggests is that people are in general more sensitive to injustice; or less willing to accept what they consider injustice. Their problem is finding a hook to hang their claim on. Meanwhile, the law, on the whole, is moving in the direction of more, not less, anti-discrimination law. Sexual orientation has been added to the prohibited list in some places. And a very strong law protecting the disabled was passed about a decade ago in the United States. Under this law (the Americans with Disability Act), employers are not to discriminate against people with disabilities, provided, of course, that they can do the work.

Sweeping, general rules against disabled people are presumptively illegal. In 1995, Jimmie Dean Stillwell, a man born without a left hand, sued the Kansas City Police Department.[40] Stillwell had been a licensed, armed security guard, since 1976. In 1992, the Kansas City Board of Police Commissioners refused to renew his license. They claimed that one hand was not enough for such 'defensive tactics' as 'handgun retention, lateral vascular neck restraint, knife defence, and handcuffing'; and that a one-handed guard would be 'more likely to use deadly force on another person than a guard with two hands.' Stillwell, for his part, insisted he could do the job. He based his claim on the Americans with Disabilities Act. The Appeal court was sympathetic. The ADA requires 'a case-by-case analysis of disabled individuals and the benefits or jobs they seek.' The Kansas City rule, a 'blanket exclusion of all one-handed license applicants,' was a violation of the ADA. The job of the board was to decide, 'whether or not an applicant can perform the duties of a police officer, not whether the applicant has two hands.' The board was ordered to rescind its rule. Stillwell had to be given a chance to prove he could do the job.

[40] The case is *Stillwell v Kansas City, Missouri Board of Police Commissioners* 872 F. Supp. 682 (1995).

The ethos of this case is strikingly like the ethos that underlies age discrimination laws. It is the ethos that requires giving everybody a chance to show that they can do the job; rules that are too general, that exclude this kind of individual showing, will have to go. Some of the cases make this point quite clearly. In a 1993 case, a federal court considered a rule from the state of Massachusetts: all state employees over 70 had to take and pass a physical exam. The court struck down the rule.[41] Of course, individualised assessments are more troublesome than blanket rules; and they cost more money. But in an age of individualised rights, with a growing and spreading culture of human rights, an age that rejects rules based on status and 'immutable' characteristics, judging people one by one and on their own merits seems to satisfy a deeply felt and widespread social norm.

I mentioned earlier that in some states the law outlaws age discrimination, but says nothing about a minimum age. One of these states is New Jersey. In a case in 1999, *Bergen Commercial Bank v Sisler*,[42] the plaintiff, Michael Sisler, was 25 years old. Sisler got a job at the Bergen bank, but in the course of a conversation with the chairman of the bank, revealed the dreaded news that he was only 25. The chairman (according to Sisler) seemed shocked, and warned Sisler not to tell anybody else this terrible secret. After some months, the bank fired Sisler and replaced him with a 31-year-old. The New Jersey Supreme Court held that Sisler, provided he could make out his case, had a valid claim; and sent the issue back down for trial. Nobody would seriously argue that the Sislers of the world suffer from disadvantage. Our cultures in fact are supposed to worship youth. But more and more the culture also worships fairness, and redefines fairness in a way that makes Sisler's claim, and Stillwell's claim, and all the claims here discussed, more attractive and even, in many cases, legally viable.

Changing Attitudes

Age discrimination laws, like laws against race and sex discrimination, may also in the long run produce changes in attitude, and ultimately, in behaviour—quite apart from the behaviour forced on companies by the law. Big companies, as we pointed out, have to pay attention to discrimination laws. They have to hire special staff, they have to tell personnel what to do and how to do it. This creates, inside companies, a bureaucracy with an interest in the implementation of anti-discrimination policies. The *Brach* case, as we said, illustrates this point.

The Western world has changed, and greatly, since the ADEA first became law. I looked at some of the material submitted to Congress during hearings, in 1967, on the proposed age discrimination law. American Airlines submitted a

---

[41] *EEOC v Commonwealth of Massachusetts* 987 F. 2d 64 (CA 1, 1993).

[42] 723 A.2d 944 (N. J. 1999); See CA Stewart, 'Young, Talented, and Fired: The New Jersey Law Against Discrimination and the Right Decision in *Bergen Commercial Bank v Sisler*' (2000) 84 *Minnesota L Rev* 1689.

statement defending its policy. That was a policy to hire 'young ladies' at 20, as stewardesses; they could hold this job only until age 32. At that point they had to be reassigned. The stewardess, said the airline, is the 'welcome aboard' of the airline industry. She symbolises 'the youth and vitality of the airlines.' The job is very desirable, in that it provides opportunity to travel—and a chance to meet men. The job leads 'directly to marriage for a large majority of the stewardesses.' Moreover, stewardesses need 'physical agility and endurance.' No one, said the airline, could 'reasonably contend that stewardesses should be retained until . . . 65.' After all, between 38 and 50, women are 'subject to changes in metabolism and in the endocrine, circulatory, digestive, nervous and cutaneous systems, symptoms of which would interfere with the desirable performance' of their job. Hence it was only right and proper to transfer them out of this 'Welcome Aboard' job at 32.[43]

This amazing statement has, of course, more to do with gender stereotypes than with age stereotypes, although there is enough of both in the statement for any taste. No company today would dare make such a statement. As a public position, it is as obsolete as the assertion that the earth is flat or the sun revolves around the earth. But 1967 was only 35 years ago—a little over one generation. It is likely the men (they must have been men) who wrote the statement are still alive and functioning. Culture can change a lot in a short time; behaviour can change a lot; and the law often gives both culture and behaviour a good swift shove in a certain direction.

At least since the days of the civil rights revolution, society has been travelling towards what I have called plural equality. Anti-discrimination laws have been an essential part of the story: they have been the tough, skeletal structure that gives substance to the vague, free-floating norms of fairness and equality. The countries of the EU have obviously been moving in the same direction. Of course, each country moves at its own pace and in its own way. When the United States embarked on the experiment of prohibiting age discrimination, it was almost alone in the world. Then Canada joined in. Now there are other countries as well, including some European countries. I note that the current text of the Australian labour code forbids firing any employee because of 'race, colour, sex, sexual preference, age, physical or mental disability, marital status, family responsibilities, pregnancy, religion, political opinion, national extraction or social origin.'[44] New Zealand is another country which has banned age discrimination. The EU Directive seems to be flowing with the current of the times.

Age discrimination is, to be sure, different from race and sex discrimination, in all sorts of ways (and they, in turn, are different from each other). Employers,

---

[43] Age Discrimination in Employment, Hearings before the General Subcommittee on Labour of the Committee on Education and Labour, House of Representatives, 90th Congress (August, 1967) 473–77. The bans on hiring male flight attendants did not survive litigation in the federal courts. *Diaz v Pan American Airlines*, 442 F. 2d 385 (5th Cir., 1971); see DL Rhode *Justice and Gender: Sex Discrimination and the Law* (Cambridge Mass, Harvard University Press, 1989) 94–95.

[44] Industrial Relations Reform Act 1993 s 170DF(1)(f).

and others who are opposed to age discrimination laws, and laws against mandatory retirement, often point out, and quite correctly, that age does make a difference, which race most certainly does not. People, unlike fine wines, do not improve with age. There are no 80-year-old soccer stars or ballet dancers. Dementia is highly correlated with age. Elderly people cannot walk as fast, remember as much, or lift boxes as heavy as they did when they were younger. Nobody would be so foolish as to deny that people tend to lose some of their strengths as they get older. But it is also true that women are on average shorter, lighter, and weaker than men. Sex discrimination laws do not insist that a boss must hire 50 per cent women on a job that requires tremendous stamina and muscle power. The laws simply insist that a woman must have a chance to prove herself. The same is true in other areas: the one-armed man, for example, has the right to show what he can do. Why should age be a more inaccessible barrier?

THE END OF MANDATORY RETIREMENT

This is a subject on which I admit to a certain amount of personal involvement. What got me interested, in the first place, was an incident in my own family. My mother became a widow when she was in her late fifties. Like many women of her generation, she had quit the work force when she got married. She made a home and raised three children. When my father died, he left no money to speak of. My mother had a social security pension, but was otherwise dependent on her children. Her reaction was to go out and get a job, selling yarn and other knitting goods in a Chicago department store. Of course, she needed the money. But she also loved the job. And she was good at it. She was, I am sure, a superb worker; and totally reliable. Then, one day, when she reached 65, she was summarily dismissed, in accordance with a rigid company rule. She never found another job. That incident triggered in me a sense of outrage. Outrage, in a professor, leads to research, and research to publication. I even engaged in a modest amount of activism, on behalf of the American Association of University Professors, who were fighting to get rid of mandatory retirement. That was years ago. I have now lived long enough to enjoy what my mother was unable to enjoy: keeping my job, past what used to be considered the 'normal' age of retirement.

The issue of mandatory retirement was hotly debated in the United States, in the 1970s. The debate was particularly sharp in higher education. Universities, including my own, were positively foaming at the mouth. It would be a disaster, they insisted, not to be able to get rid of older professors. They advanced a whole series of arguments, all of them (in my view) totally specious. There is no point in rehashing these arguments. Many were based on empty stereotypes. Perfectly reasonable people seem to believe that older people never get or entertain new ideas, that you can't teach an old dog new tricks, that no scientist or mathematician over 30 ever had an innovative thought, and that there is nothing like a bunch of older people to render an institution sclerotic.[45] Organisations need fresh blood, they say, or they will wither and die. I call this the vampire theory. I know of no hard evidence to support it. There are plenty of anecdotes, to be sure—everybody can tell a good story about somebody who has lost it, or who has gone past his sell-by date, as the British like to put it. Fewer people seemed to be concerned with the other side of a coin. What does a business or an institution *lose*, when it gets rid of good workers prematurely? After all, two can play the anecdote game—one can tell many stories about men and women, who, at 80, or 90 or even 100, are active, travelling, living a rich, full life; and who are often still on the job.

Universities and other employers also argued that it was better, and less cruel, to have a flat rule, than to single out somebody, tell them they were doddering, and force them out after a painful scene. I have never understood this argument. A flat rule is simply cruel and unfair to everybody, rather than to isolated individuals. In any event, it is a fantasy to imagine that there is an actual problem here. People, whose bodies fail them, or whose minds give way, do not want to keep on working. Work becomes painful, a nightmare. They want to quit. Of course there are exceptions. But not many.

Indeed, there are some interesting natural experiments on the impact of a no-retirement rule. The United States Supreme Court is one of these natural experiments. There is no retirement age; appointment is for life. Many, many justices have stayed on the Court past their eightieth birthday, including some of the most noted justices, John Marshall, Louis Brandeis, Hugo Black, among others. One of the greatest justices of them all, Oliver Wendell Holmes, Jr, was over 90 when he retired. In the two centuries or more this institution has been in existence, there have been at most two or three instances of justices who stayed on, or tried to stay on, when their powers failed them. On the other hand, men over 80 have written some of the most famous and notable decisions.

Of course, Justice of the Supreme Court of the United States is not a typical occupation. But there are all sorts of clerical, academic, professional, and white-collar positions where the work can be done just as well by healthy, intelligent men and women who are 70 or older. Jobs where the work is physically very demanding are different; but, as I said, few of these workers *want* to stay on, or can, when their strength gives way. And those who can do the job, and who want to keep doing it, should of course have the right to do so.

---

[45] The American Council of Education, an association of colleges and universities, sent a letter to a subcommittee of Congress, which was then considering ending mandatory retirement, asking for a 12-year moratorium. In some fields, the letter said, 'the major contributions of an individual often are made toward the beginning of his or her career.' No evidence was cited for this statement. Younger faculty were needed to challenge 'old as well as new ways of thinking,' and to provide 'new perspectives.' Moreover, the bulge in university hiring in the 1950s and 1960s presented the schools with a demographic crisis. Letter of Robert H Atwell, President, American Council of Education, dated 10 March 1986, in 'The Removal of Age Ceiling Cap under the Age Discrimination in Employment Act' Joint Hearing before the Subcommittee on Employment Opportunities, Committee on Education and Labour (Ninety-Ninth Congress, 1986) 57.

At any rate, all these arguments against ending mandatory retirement were, in the end, unsuccessful in the United States. The age cap was removed; and the sky has not fallen in. The universities had one small success: they succeeded in delaying the starting date; they won a seven-year reprieve. They hoped to produce evidence, during that interim, that they could use to persuade Congress to exempt them from the law. But the tide was running against them. A number of states abolished mandatory retirement on their own. Their state universities— the University of Florida, the University of Wisconsin, among others—had already given up any fixed retirement age. Nothing terrible had happened. Most professors did retire. Some did not. The seven-year period came and went; and the universities now are subject to the law, like every other employer.

The EU Directive, as I noted, *may* allow member states to hold on to mandatory retirement, even if they act against other forms of age discrimination. This was true of American law as well—at first. It has been a pattern elsewhere. New Zealand is a good example. A law of 1993, which went into effect in 1994, banned age discrimination in employment, but only up to the age of retirement. But from 1999 on, the upper age limit was dropped.[46] Whether other countries with age discrimination laws are going to follow the same trajectory is hard to know in advance. On the one hand, if you once establish as a principle, that people of a certain age have rights, and enforceable rights, and they are not to be shoved aside for younger people, that too many candles on the birthday cake does not make you a pariah, the logic of getting rid of mandatory retirement becomes pretty strong. After all, mandatory retirement is a form of age discrimination, indeed, it may be *the* form of age discrimination par excellence. But of course, politically, anti-discrimination law has to play itself out in each country in a unique and individual way. In many countries, unemployment is a major problem; millions of people are looking for jobs, and not finding them. They are not likely to favour anything which seems to clog the job market even further. On the other hand, many of these countries are choking to death, financially, because the welfare state has become so expensive. One reason is that it was never designed to take care of people who retire at 60, and live on to 95.

Impact of the Ban

What has been the impact, in the United States, of the ban on mandatory retirement? It is hard to give a definitive answer. Here are some interesting statistics. Between 1963 and 1999, labour force participation rates for men who were 62–64 declined from 76 per cent to 47 per cent. Among men who were over 70, it declined from 21 per cent to less than 12 per cent. For women over 55, labour force participation actually increased; but for women over 70, the participation

---

[46] A Fitzgibbon and R Roberts, 'Removal of the Compulsory Retirement Age' [Feb 1999] *New Zealand Law Journal* 36.

rate is something on the order of 5 per cent. The oldest workers, then, the men and women over 70, are not a substantial factor in the labour market. There had been a trend toward earlier and earlier retirement. But this trend levelled off after 1980.[47] In the last few years, the percentage of older workers still on the job may have actually increased slightly. The laws against mandatory retirement might be a factor; these laws may be acting as a brake on the trend towards early retirement. There are other factors at work as well. Men who mine coal or dig ditches wear out at an earlier age than salesmen or teachers. As manufacturing and mining jobs decline, and white-collar jobs increase, we would expect the number of workers who want to stay on also to increase. People are also in general living longer, as I mentioned. And they are healthier. Dead and dying people are not a factor in the job market. Social attitudes may also be changing. A survey of workers who were 34–52 years old found that 80 per cent percent expected to keep on working after age 65.[48] Beyond a doubt, maybe of these workers will change their mind when they really do reach 65. The attitude, however, is worth noting. Right now, and in the predictable future, most men and women seem to want to retire in their sixties; and do so.

It is not clear by the way, what it means to say a person 'retires'. Many people simply change jobs; they retire from one thing and go on to another. Many people go from full-time work to part-time work. Apparently, a third or more of the cohort of older workers retire only partially; they keep on with some sort of work for more than five years. One study found that about one retired worker out of four re-enters the work force.[49] There are some occupations with very early retirement—the army, for example; some police and fire departments. Men and women who are 50 are unlikely to sit in a rocking chair. They take other jobs. Not enough is known about this 'partial retirement.' Much of the research has more or less assumed that retirement was an either-or thing: you left your job, *and* the labour force, at the same time. Recent research, as we said, shows that is not necessarily so.[50] I suspect that 'partial retirement' will become more and more important, and more widespread, as longevity increases, and modern medicine helps keep people healthy for longer periods of time.

The law does allow employers to bribe older workers into retiring, by offering them money or other benefits. This has become, in some areas, fairly common practice. It is quite standard in universities, for example. Perhaps half of them offer cash or other prizes to faculty members willing to take early

---

[47] These figures are from Federal Interagency Forum on Aging-Related Statistics *Older Americans 2000: Key Indicators of Well-Being* (Indicator 10); the source is wysigy://1/http://www.agingstats.gov/chartbook2000/economics.html (consulted, 27 March 2002).

[48] JF Quinn 'Has the Early Retirement Trend Reversed?' (Working Paper no 424 Social Security Administration 1999) 9.

[49] JA McMorrow 'Retirement Incentives in the Twenty First Century: The Move Toward Employer Control of the ADEA' (1997) 31 *Univ of Richmond L Rev* 795, 800.

[50] JF Quinn, DA Myers and RV Burkhauser, *Passing the Torch: The Influence of Economic Incentives on Work and Retirement* (Kalamazoo MI, WE Upjohn Institute for Employment Research, 1990) ch 5.

retirement.[51] A statute of 1998, which applied specifically to tenured faculty at colleges and universities, allowed the employer to offer extra benefits for retiring, even though these benefits 'are reduced or eliminated on the basis of age,' that is, you get more if you retire at 60, less if you retire at 65, nothing if you retire at 70.[52] For companies that are really serious about making space for younger workers, buying off the seniors will be more and more the tactic of choice.

The end of mandatory retirement has certainly made <u>some</u> difference in society. The only question is, how much. Some workers are better off, financially and psychologically, because they get to keep the jobs they want to keep. Others are, frankly, better off because the employer has handed them a wad of cash to get them off the job. My own suspicion is that the law, in the end, is good for employers as well as for employees. Older workers are, mostly, good workers. Some companies have experimented with hiring mostly older people; they have had excellent results.[53] Jobs are more important to older workers, very often, than to younger workers, who may see the job as a stepping stone, or even as a distraction. I am not talking about brain surgeons or coal miners, but the millions of secretaries, salespeople, service workers of all sorts, bank tellers, mail clerks, truck drivers. The benefits from the law, from the abolition of retirement, are real enough; but they are almost impossible to quantify. How do we measure the gain to thousands of people who feel happier, better off, because they have a job, because they have structure in their lives, and a reason to get out of bed in the morning, or because they have social interactions with other people at the office, or because they feel still useful and productive? This benefit is an aspect of social justice. It is hard to capture in a mathematical model, and hard to measure or even define it. But as I and many others can testify, it is a thrilling and authentic social fact.

---

[51] RG Ehrenberg 'Career's End: A Survey of Faculty Retirement Policies' *Academe* [July/Aug. 2001]. Some universities negotiate with faculty members who want to continue teaching, and allow them to stay on and teach part-time, while drawing retirement benefits.

[52] *Public Law* 105–244, 112 Stat. 1581 (act of 7 Oct 1998), at 1834, amending s 4 of the Age Discrimination in Employment Act, 29 U.S. C. 623. The amendment applies to 'employees who are serving under a contract of unlimited tenure,' with regard to 'supplemental benefit upon voluntary retirement.'

[53] *Age Discrimination by Employers*, above n 3 at 168–69.

9

Comparative European Perspectives on Age Discrimination Legislation

COLM O'CINNEIDE

INTRODUCTION

As THE UK considers the options for the introduction of legislation prohibiting age discrimination in employment, it is useful to examine how other European countries are responding to the challenge posed by an ageing population. More specifically, since Council Directive 2000/78/EC (the 'Framework Equality Directive') requires all EU member states to introduce comprehensive legislation prohibiting age discrimination in employment and occupation,[1] it is valuable to consider the legislative models of our European partners. The aim of this chapter is to assess the current situation in a number of European countries, and to determine what useful lessons can be drawn.

Comparative approaches can provide useful and contrasting material to assist the UK in framing its own age discrimination legislation and policy, particularly given the lack of any simple or clear trans-European legislative model. Indeed, the embryonic state of age discrimination legislation throughout the EU makes the limited comparative experience that does exist all the more valuable. The chapter will focus on comparative experience within the EU, with particular emphasis on the relevant Finnish, Dutch and Irish legislation.

This comparative experience demonstrates that particular complexities exist in framing age discrimination legislation. A range of issues exist as to the scope of any such legislation and of any permitted exceptions, the degree of justification required to bring discriminatory behaviour within one of these exceptions, and the extent of any additional measures that are necessary to enhance the impact of the legislation. This set of policy choices makes it essential to identify the core principles and social policy goals that should underpin this legislation and any accompanying age equality measures. The argument will be made here that an individual, rights-centred approach to age equality provides clear

---

[1] The Directive's provisions in respect of discrimination on the grounds of religion and sexual orientation are to be implemented by December 2003: an additional 3-year period can be availed of by member states to implement its provisions in respect of disability and age. See Art 18, Directive 2000/78/EC L 303/16/2000.

guiding principles that can give a coherent shape to the legislation. This approach is also more consistent with the development of equality norms and the recognition of the crucial importance of individual human rights, than more minimalist approaches that give greater leeway to the use of age as an acceptable ground for discrimination.

EUROPEAN AGE EQUALITY STRATEGIES PENDING IMPLEMENTATION
OF THE EU DIRECTIVE

Pending national implementation of the Framework Equality Directive by the end of 2006, existing legal protection against age discrimination is very limited throughout the EU. Such protection as does exist is frequently directed towards protecting older workers in employment, a response to the changing employment situation of older workers throughout the EU. Employment policies directed towards encouraging early retirement and easing older workers out of the labour market have been recently reversed in favour of encouraging participation and eliminating discriminatory factors. These measures are frequently *ad hoc* and limited in nature, and reflect the fact that the primary concern of policymakers is to deal with the more troubling economic and social consequences of age discrimination, while minimising alterations to existing business and public sector policies. Thus, a non-intrusive standard of review is applied; legislation is generally restricted to employment; and the legislation includes sizeable specific exemptions or a general, broad justification defence.

This limited 'minimalist' approach can be contrasted with the 'rights' based approach taken in Canada and the Republic of Ireland (though as discussed below, the Irish approach is not without its problems). Such an approach recognises age discrimination as on a par with other forms of discrimination. It therefore prefers a more intrusive standard of review, particularly in respect of justification, and affords age equality legislation a wide scope (in particular extending it to goods and services).

Voluntary Measures

Most member states have developed national programmes involving a combination of tax breaks, fiscal incentives, training schemes and publicity initiatives to put this policy shift into effect.[2] These have had limited or occasionally even

---

[2] France and Sweden have, for example, introduced a system of compulsory extra payments to the unemployed insurance fund for the dismissal of long-serving employees over the age of 50. Portugal has developed a number of measures including incentives for hiring older workers, targeted training and education, as well as utilising publicity drives to encourage the recruitment of older workers, along with Germany, Denmark and Finland.

counter-productive effects.[3] Similarly, national and sector collective agreements have increasingly incorporated special protection provisions for the benefit of older workers, with again limited results.[4] The extent and comprehensiveness of the different national programmes varies considerably: many consist of a series of limited policy adjustments and publicity campaigns, while others, in particular Finland's National Programme for Older Workers, involve a coordinated and comprehensive government-led package of measures agreed with the social partners.

Being largely voluntary in nature, these incentive schemes and collective agreements are limited in terms of impact as well as being limited in scope, applying as they do usually only to older workers already in employment. Many collective agreements across the EU also serve to reinforce age distinctions, often providing for seniority-based pay scales and mandatory retirement.[5]

Legal Protection

Most of the constitutions of EU member state contain an equality clause,[6] often supplementing a general prohibition of unjustified discrimination with specific references to the right of equal treatment on the grounds of race, sex and other criteria. With the exception of Finland, age is not specifically listed in these

---

[3] In France, the penalty contribution for laying-off older workers, known as the 'Delalande' contribution, appears to have had a very limited impact, with evidence that it may actually discourage the taking on of employees over the age of 50, since any subsequent lay-off may prove too costly. Younger employees are also seen as bearing the knock-on effects of the requirement. See Report on France, *Industrial Relations and the Ageing Workforce: a Review of Measures to Combat Age Discrimination in Employment*, European Industrial Relations Observatory (EIRO) 2000, at www.eiro.eurofound.ie/2000/10/study/TN0010201S.html Spain introduced in 1997 social security allowances for companies hiring unemployed workers over the age of 45. This has had very limited results, with employers preferring to hire younger workers: *see Report on Spain*, in *Industrial Relations and the Ageing Workforce: a Review of Measures to Combat Age Discrimination in Employment*, European Industrial Relations Observatory (EIRO) 2000, at www.eiro.eurofound.ie/2000/10/study/TN0010201S.html

[4] In 1999, for example, a national joint pact for older workers was agreed in Austria by the government and its social partners, providing for financial incentives to employ older workers and for more flexible working time. See European Industrial Relations Observatory (EIRO), *Austria: An Employment Pact for Older Workers?* at www.eiro.eurofound.ie/1999/03/feature/AT9903135F.html German sectoral agreements frequently provide for special conditions and protection against redundancy to workers over 55 with a certain degree of experience. Belgium's social partners agreement in 1998 goes further by requiring employers to avoid discriminating against job applicants in respect of any of the grounds specified in Art 13 of the EC Treaty, including age. In several countries, such as the UK, Sweden and Ireland, individual public or private sector employers have agreed age-friendly policies in the context of collective agreements.

[5] The Dutch social partners, for example, have recently called for the age discrimination legislation to provide that that a general dismissal age lower than 65 is objectively justified as long as it is established in a collective agreement, to preserve existing mandatory retirement packages contained in collective agreements. The Dutch Government has argued that this is incompatible with the Directive: see n 36 below.

[6] Examples include Art 3, para 1 of the 1948 Italian Constitution and Art 3(3) of the German Basic Law.

clauses as a prohibited ground of discrimination.[7] Such general equality clauses nevertheless provide a degree of limited protection in most EU states against unjustified discriminatory treatment by the state or its organs.[8] However, the tendency is for age to be categorised with other 'non-suspect' discriminatory grounds as not requiring strict judicial scrutiny. The looser standard of 'rationality' is applied, which only requires the state to demonstrate an objective and non-arbitrary reason for its differential treatment for it to satisfy the relatively low standard of constitutional review applied. The lack of explicit reference to age discourages attempts to use the constitutional provisions to litigate cases of discrimination, and the limitation of most constitutional guarantees to the public sector further reduces their impact.

These open-ended constitutional guarantees have been supplemented and extended to the private sector throughout the EU by more comprehensive anti-discrimination legislation. However, with the exception of Finland and Ireland, prior to the enactment of the Directive, age was not included as a ground of discrimination in the equality legislation of any EU state. Such protection as did exist in a few states was limited to two categories, the explicit prohibition of age limits in recruitment and implicit restrictions on the use of age as a ground for redundancy. France in its Labour Code L311–1 prohibits upper age limits in vacancy notices, and Belgium has in Article 3 of the Act of 13 February 1998 on Employment Promotion prohibited the use of explicit or implicit maximum age limits in recruitment and selection. The impact of this legislation is obviously limited by its narrow scope, and its application to direct discrimination in recruitment rather than indirect forms of age prejudice.[9]

Several other states indirectly provide limited protection against age discrimination in redundancy decisions by virtue of legislative requirements that dismissals are made only for 'objective' reasons, or that they be made in accordance with 'social criteria' that aim to direct the burden of redundancies away from socially vulnerable workers, such as older workers.[10] Article 53 of the Portuguese

---

[7] Art 13 of the Portuguese Constitution, for example, guarantees the principle of equality regardless of gender, parentage, race, native language, place of birth, religion, political conviction and personal ideology, education, economic status and social condition, but does not refer to age.

[8] Section 9 of the 1996 South African Constitution and of the Canadian Charter of Fundamental Rights and Freedoms contain similar equality clauses. Protocol 12 to the ECHR, which was been opened for signature and ratification, provides for a similar general equality guarantee to be added to the ECHR. The UK has indicated that it does not intend to sign or ratify the Protocol for the foreseeable future.

[9] Belgium has recently enacted new legislation designed to implement the Framework Directive, including its age provisions: for a summary of its provisions, see www.antiracisme.be/en/racism/future3.htm (last accessed 25 November 2002).

[10] The German and Austrian unfair dismissal laws require that dismissals be objectively justified and redundancy selection be carried out in accordance with set social criteria, providing a degree of protection for older workers with families. Similarly, the Italian 'social shock absorber' legislation requires personnel lay-offs to be carried out with the lowest 'social shock' determined by fixed criteria: seniority of service and dependent family members are among the relevant criteria, protecting older workers. The presence of the 'social shock absorbers' and cultural factors have lead to claims that older workers are disproportionately protected at the expense of younger workers in Italy, and

Constitution guarantees the right to job security and prohibits dismissals without 'just cause', while France and Spain in their labour codes prohibit dismissals that cannot be objectively justified, with age alone not qualifying as an objective justification. Such legislative requirements are frequently backed or supplemented by provisions in collective agreements.[11]

These legislative measures suffer from limitations of scope, being largely concerned with protecting workers actually in employment rather than those excluded from the labour market by age discrimination. Also, because age is not explicitly barred from constituting an 'objective' ground for dismissal, age criteria may still be lawfully used in certain circumstances as a factor in dismissal decisions, and the extent of these circumstances remains very unclear. In addition, some of these legislative measures and collective agreements also actually lock in place and encourage age-based patterns of employment, by providing for seniority-based pay scales and compulsory retirement. Many member states still have a strong consensus between the social partners that redundancies and downsizing should be orientated towards older workers, who are compensated with generous early retirement schemes.[12]

This has fed the perception that age equality is an economic labour market issue rather than an equality issue, with the appropriate response being ad hoc legislation complementing collective agreements in reducing the disadvantages faced by older workers in employment rather than comprehensive equality legislation. Allied to varying labour market factors across the member states,[13] and a reluctance to legislate in areas traditionally subject to collective agreements, this has resulted in patchy protection for workers in employment against redundancy and very limited protection against age discrimination in recruitment, conditions or training, and a lack of recognition of age as an equality issue.[14] Reliance on collective agreements also results in age discrimination in areas not covered by the agreements being ignored, and lack of legislation has resulted in

---

labour market entry does remain the major problematic stage in the particular conditions of Italy: see Report on Italy, *Industrial Relations and the Ageing Workforce: a Review of Measures to Combat Age Discrimination in Employment*, European Industrial Relations Observatory (EIRO) 2000, at www.eiro.eurofound.ie/2000/10/study/TN0010201S.html

[11] German law also introduces protection for older employees in its legislation governing works councils in workplaces. The German Works Constitution Act (*Betriebsverfassungsgesetz*, BetrVG) requires that employers and works councils ensure that older employees are not discriminated against in redundancy decisions and in training.

[12] Belgium, for example, has retained its collective early retirement provisions, permitting employees to take generous early retirement if the employer recruits an unemployed younger worker to fill their place. It consequently has an employment rate for older workers considerably below the European average: only 22% of persons aged between 55 and 65 are employed, according to Belgian Federal Ministry of Employment and Labour statistics, 1999.

[13] For the ongoing concern in Italy in respect of limited opportunities for labour market entry for younger workers, see Report on Italy, *Industrial Relations and the Ageing Workforce: a Review of Measures to Combat Age Discrimination in Employment*, European Industrial Relations Observatory (EIRO) 2000, at www.eiro.eurofound.ie/2000/10/study/TN0010201S.html

[14] As an illustration of this, Luxembourg's discrimination law as amended in 1997 and 2000 listed over a dozen grounds of impermissible discrimination, but age was not included.

a very low awareness of age equality issues and EU-wide patterns of age discrimination in recruitment, pay, employment and conditions, as well as in
access to goods and services.[15] This 'minimal' approach, treating age discrimination as a labour market issue rather than as an infringement of equality and
fundamental rights has been a significant influence on the final shape of the
Directive, and in particular the very permissive scope of the labour market
objective exception in Article 6.

THE DIRECTIVE: EXISTING RESPONSES

There has been as yet a limited response to the requirements of the Directive
throughout much of the EU. However, all EU states have begun the process of
introducing age discrimination legislation to satisfy the Directive's requirements, with most aiming to have the legislation in force by the end of 2003.
Denmark has begun implementing the Directive by inserting age into the
definition of discrimination in its equality legislation.[16] The Danish anti-
discrimination legislation only applies where similar protection against
discrimination is not provided for by collective agreements, as is usual with the
'Danish model' of industrial regulation.[17] France, Belgium and Austria have
also extended existing legislation to cover age. Implementation elsewhere has
been slow, but Finland, The Netherlands and Ireland have all implemented or
are in the process of implementing comprehensive age discrimination codes
founded upon a discrimination law model rather than a labour market regulation model, and offer the most valuable comparative experience for the UK.

AGE EQUALITY IN FINLAND

Within the EU, only the constitution of Finland specifically identifies age as a
prohibited ground of discrimination.[18] However, as in constitutional equality

---

[15] See European Commission, *Towards a Europe for all Ages—Promoting Prosperity and Intergenerational Solidarity* Com (1999) 221.

[16] European Industrial Relations Observatory (EIRO), www.eiro.eurofound.ie/2001/02/InBrief/DK0102113N.html

[17] This use of collective agreements to implement directives has proved contentious: see European Industrial Relations Observatory (EIRO), at www.eiro.eurofound.ie/2000/01feature/DK0001164F.html, and is particularly problematic in the context of anti-discrimination law, with the requirement in both EC law and under Art 26 of the ICCPR and Art 2 of CERD to provide an effective remedy. Employer organisations in Denmark were initially opposed to the Framework Directive's requirement that legislation prohibiting age discrimination be introduced, arguing that it undermined the particular Danish model of using collective agreements to implement EU legislation and would be incompatible with existing collective agreements providing for positive benefits for older workers. Danish trade unions, on the other hand, tended to welcome the Directive. See Report on Denmark, *Industrial Relations and the Ageing Workforce: a Review of Measures to Combat Age Discrimination in Employment*, European Industrial Relations Observatory (EIRO), 2000, at www.eiro.eurofound.ie/2000/10/study/TN0010201S.html.

[18] Art 6(2).

guarantees in general, this provision is relatively limited in its application to the private sector. Finland has supplemented its constitutional provisions in the private sector with comprehensive provisions in its Penal Code in 1995 (prohibiting invidious age discrimination in access to goods and services) and the Contract of Employment Act 2001, which requires the impartial treatment of employees and job seekers, and non-discrimination in pay and conditions. Under the Act, age discrimination in employment is only permissible for objective and 'acceptable' reasons, an open-ended test that will have to be fleshed out by judicial application of its provisions in line with the terms of the Directive. Age limits for particular posts are prohibited, but employment contracts can stipulate a particular required retirement age when an employee becomes entitled to a pension. Positive action is permitted, to redress existing disadvantages. Collective agreements cannot vary or depart from the terms of the legislation. Complainants can bring cases to the courts, with the Labour Protection Authority having the power to monitor and advise complaints and employers on compliance.

The effect of the Finnish age discrimination legislation has been to eliminate most forms of open and manifest discriminatory behaviour by employers in recruitment, pay and dismissal.[19] The impact of the legislation on less obvious and direct forms of age discrimination has been more mixed, and statistical and anecdotal evidence shows that it has had limited effect in removing age as a factor from employer decision making.[20] This may partially be due to the open-ended justificatory defence, and the difficulties in proving age discrimination, highlighting the disadvantages of an open-ended discrimination standard.

Nevertheless, the legislation has been acknowledged as having a substantial impact in the context of the overall policy approach of the Finnish Government. Due to demographic trends and concerns about future labour market shortages, as well as clear evidence of substantial levels of discriminatory treatment,[21] Finnish age policy is now directed towards encouraging greater participation by older workers and their retention and reintegration into working life.[22] Implementing this policy shift has required the development of a coherent policy package aimed at retaining older workers within the workforce across a wide range of policy areas, including taxation, education, pensions and industrial relations. In this context, the age discrimination legislation is viewed as playing a vital symbolic role in demonstrating social disapproval of age prejudice, and in

---

[19] Communication between the author and Dr Maati Sihto, Senior Researcher in the Monitoring and Evaluation Unit of the Finnish Ministry of Labour, 3 May 2002.

[20] Ibid.

[21] See Ministry of Labour, 'Experiences of Age Discrimination in Work and Recruitment' (1999), discussed in Report on Finland, *Industrial Relations and the Ageing Workforce: a Review of Measures to Combat Age Discrimination in Employment*, European Industrial Relations Observatory (EIRO), 2000, at www.eiro.eurofound.ie/2000/10/study/TN0010201S.html

[22] This represents a substantial shift from the previous policy approach of meeting the expectations of older workers and trade unions by actively encouraging and facilitating early retirement. See M Sihto, 'Increasing Older Persons' Employment in Finland: In Search of a New Strategy' (1999) 10(3) *Journal of Ageing and Social Policy* 65.

changing attitudes by educating via legal prohibition on the inappropriateness of using age as a proxy for other relevant qualities.[23] Notably, employers and trade unions have been united in welcoming the legislation as playing an important role in the National Programme for Older Workers.[24]

The Finnish experience clearly shows the need for age discrimination legislation to be linked with coherent policies aimed at combating ageism and the factors that contribute to the exclusion of older persons from the labour market, education, health care and other areas of social activity.[25] Discrimination legislation in isolation will arguably only have limited effect, especially since the acceptability of age as a differentiating factor is so deeply rooted.

Nevertheless, making sure that the machinery of age discrimination legislation is effective is also crucial. In this respect, the usefulness of Finland's legislation as a model in the UK context is limited: its approach, and in particular its justification provisions, are different from the UK's approach to anti-discrimination law in general, with its preference for tightly-framed exceptions rather than the more open-textured Finnish approach to establishing justification. The requirement in Canada's Human Rights Act that 'bona fide occupational qualifications' be demonstrated to justify age discrimination is similarly open-ended, and is dependent on judicial interpretation and application to flesh out its meaning. This has produced considerable uncertainty as to its scope, which favourable judicial decisions such as *Etobicke* establishing a clear, strict standard of scrutiny have only recently begun to redress.[26]

AGE EQUALITY IN THE NETHERLANDS

As in Finland, the introduction of age discrimination legislation in The Netherlands to supplement existing discrimination law, while meeting the requirements of the Directive, also fits well with Dutch policy towards the participation of older workers in the labour market.[27] The Dutch Government and the social partners have begun to develop strategies to promote labour market participation by older workers, with the government repealing the 'directive for

---

[23] See n 57 below.

[24] See Report on Finland, above n 21, and Dr Sihto, above at n 19.

[25] Research conducted for the then UK Department for Education and Employment suggests that countries such as The Netherlands and Sweden that have successfully reduced early exit from employment have done so by a combination of active labour market policies, government pension and social security support and the development of a common approach with employers. See *Factors Effecting Retirement* (Dept of Education and Employment Publications, 2000).

[26] For this, see Morley Gunderson, 'Lessons from Canada' in Z Hornstein (ed), *Outlawing Age Discrimination: Foreign Lessons, UK Choices*, Transitions after 50 Series (York, The Joseph Rowntree Foundation, July 2001); see http://www.jrf.org.uk/knowledge/findings/socialpolicy/711.asp

[27] The proportion of older persons employed in The Netherlands is much lower than in other industrialised countries, with labour market participation of those over 55 being about 25%. Report on the Netherlands, *Industrial Relations and the Ageing Workforce: a Review of Measures to Combat Age Discrimination in Employment*, European Industrial Relations Observatory (EIRO), 2000, at www.eiro.eurofound.ie/2000/10/study/TN0010201S.html

the elderly' (Ouderenrichtlijn) in 1994, which permitted companies to include a disproportionately high number of older workers in collective redundancies. The government also established the Landelijk Bureau Leeftijds-discriminatie (LBL) in the same year to act as a national office to combat age discrimination.[28] Framing age discrimination legislation has however proven a complex process.

The New Age Discrimination Legislation

The Dutch Constitution is similar to the many other European written constitutions discussed above in containing a general equality guarantee, but The Netherlands again applies a 'rational' rather than 'strict' standard of review.[29] The Equal Treatment Act was introduced in 1994, prohibiting discrimination in employment, education and the provision of goods and services on the grounds of religion, belief, political orientation, race, sex, nationality, sexual orientation and marital status. Age was not included, and is therefore not covered by existing legislation. Since 1997, in response to recommendations by the employer-trade union Labour Foundation (Stichting van de Arbeid, STAR)[30] and the pressure exercised by LBL and other bodies, the Dutch Government has worked on drafting legislation against age discrimination.

The contents of a limited Bill were agreed in July 1997 with the social partners, forbidding age discrimination in recruitment and selection procedures, but with the exceptions to the Bill and the grounds that could constitute objective

---

[28] The LBL was established in 1994 because of serious concerns about the problem of ageism and age discrimination, and following pressure from the National Advisory Council on Policy for the Elderly and the older people's unions that stressed the necessity of a national office to combat age discrimination. The objectives of the LBL are the promotion and stimulation of research activities concerning the legal and social aspects of age discrimination, initiating actions and stimulating cooperation with organisations to combat age discrimination, and supporting other organisations that combat age discrimination. See http://www.leeftijd.nl/

[29] Art 1 of the 1983 Dutch Constitution provides that all persons in The Netherlands shall be treated equally in equal circumstances, and unfair discrimination on the grounds of religion, belief, political opinion, race, sex, or on any other grounds is prohibited. Age is not explicitly mentioned, but unjustifiable age discrimination can fall within the open-ended scope of application of this Article. However, an attempt to bring a constitutional challenge against the requirement that drivers over 70 had to pass a medical examination every five years to retain their licence was recently defeated, with the government held to have shown sufficient justification. See the LBL news archive, www.leeftijd.nl

[30] STAR in 1997 produced a position paper emphasising the importance of age equality in the workplace, with a particular focus on the provision of adequate training opportunities for older workers. See European Industrial Relations Observatory (EIRO), 'The Netherlands: Debate Centres on New Policies for Older Employees' at www.eiro.eurofound.ie/1997/08/feature/NL9708125F.html STAR's initial recommendations proposed encouraging employers to recruit or retain older workers by a strategy of 'demotion', allowing employers to offer these workers a downward adjustment of wages or functions. This attracted strong criticism from the Dutch trade union federation, and the final recommendations contained an agreement that employers would be barred from excluding older employees from policies to improve labour market participation on the grounds of the wage costs of older workers.

justification being left undefined and open-ended.[31] In particular, the ability of employers to discriminate against older workers on the grounds of costs or high wages remained unclear. The Bill's limited scope and vague provisions attracted considerable criticisms from non-governmental organisations (NGOs) and Parliament, and was withdrawn.

A second Bill was introduced in November 1999, with a considerably greater scope, banning direct and indirect age discrimination in recruitment, selection, promotion, vocational activity, training and labour mediation. However, the Bill contained nine very broad justification defences to direct discrimination.[32] The LBL welcomed this Bill as an improvement on the first, but queried why dismissal and working conditions were exempted, as well as questioning the scope of the exceptions provided for company and social interests. In particular, they were concerned that this exception would permit a 'balanced age structure' to constitute an objective justification, which could justify extensive age discrimination towards younger and older workers.

Accompanying the Bill, the Dutch Government initiated a general consultation on the legitimacy of existing age limits in the civil service, legislation and local authorities, as well as in the private sector. The use of age limits by various associations was questioned, in particular age limits on soccer referees imposed by the Dutch soccer association (KNVB).[33]

This consultation delayed the Bill, and it was still under discussion in the Dutch Parliament when the Framework Directive was agreed and came into effect in December 2000. The Directive was broader in scope than the proposed Dutch legislation, which did not apply to working conditions and dismissal. As a consequence, the Bill was withdrawn and re-worked, and a 'Bill on equal treatment on the ground of age in employment' was presented to the Parliament in December 2001. Delayed by the recent Dutch elections and change of government in June 2002, and the subsequent collapse of the new government, the legislation is expected to become law by December 2003.

---

[31] The LBL described the Bill's provisions as providing that 'age limits are not allowed unless they are allowed'. Previously quoted on the LBL website www.leeftijd.nl/update/ (accessed 21 July 2002).

[32] The exceptions set out in Art 3 of the Bill were as follows: 'considerable company or service interests' (which are not solely financial), the protection of health and safety, genuine occupational qualifications, requirements that are necessary due to the 'private nature' of the working relationship, age limits in selection and recruitment that are objectively necessary for the nature or goal of the position being recruited for, age limits in training and vocational activity that are also objectively necessary for the nature and goal of that training, and age distinctions required by international law. Art 9 made two further specific exceptions for employment or labour market policies designed to advance the labour market participation of particular age groups, and for differences in compensation under the minimum wage and holiday allowance legislation (which has special provisions for those between 15 and 23).

[33] In January 2000, three soccer referees won a legal challenge against the KNVB, which required that all referees had to retire at 47 with minimal exceptions, even though all referees were annually tested on their fitness and knowledge of the rules. The Court of Justice in Amsterdam held that the tests were a sufficient safeguard, and that consequently the age limit was unnecessary: see the LBL news archive, www.leeftijd.nl. An age limit of 70 for those manning polling stations was also successfully contested by the LBL, the government agreeing to remove the limit.

Unlike the Irish and US legislation, there are no minimum or maximum age-limits mentioned in the Bill which will be applicable to employees of all ages, and will therefore protect younger people. The scope of the Bill at present mirrors that of the Directive, with the result that access to goods and services is excluded. This has attracted strong criticism from the LBL and age NGOs, who are campaigning for comprehensive legislation. The government has justified the different treatment of age from the other equality grounds recognised in Dutch law on the grounds that age is of a different character than the other grounds and does not in constitutional terms constitute a '*prima facie* suspicious criterion' for distinction. The complexity of legislating in relation to goods and services has also been cited: as demonstrated by the Irish and Commonwealth experience of applying age discrimination codes to goods and services, the complexity of this process appears to be considerably exaggerated.

The definitions of direct and indirect discrimination in the Bill are taken directly from the Directive and the equality case law of the ECJ. In providing when either form of age discrimination is justified, the Dutch have altered their approach in the 1998 Bill and have inserted a general 'objective justification' test, based upon the Directive's own general objective justification defence and similar to the Finnish test. The complexities of listing all the possible exceptions in the 'new' areas of dismissal and employment conditions were cited as the justification for departing from the approach of the 1998 bill, which specifically listed the relevant exceptions. The LBL and NGOs have again been very critical of this, arguing that adopting the open-ended Directive test will greatly lessen the impact of the legislation. Similar concerns were raised in the parliamentary debates.

In addition to this general objective justification test, the Bill contains three explicit grounds where a specific direct distinction on the ground of age is allowed:

1. Differences of treatment on the ground of age, based on legitimate employment or labour-market policy to promote vocational integration of certain age-groups;[34]
2. Mandatory retirement on entitlement to a pension under the General Old Age Pensions Act, or at an older age;
3. The fixing of ages for admission or entitlement to retirement benefits and the use of age-criteria in actuarial calculations, as permitted by the exception in Article 6 (2) of the Directive.

The Dutch Government was of the opinion that the exception for dismissal on reaching pensionable age can be objectively justified under the Directive.[35] The

---

[34] This is compatible with the positive action provisions in Art 7 of the Directive.

[35] In response to criticism in Parliament, the government cited in support of this exception the general acceptance for the age of 65 years as the endpoint of working life in Dutch society, reflected in the entitlement to a non-contributory pension under the General Old Age Pensions Act, and the resulting benefit to businesses of a definite end-point irrespective of individual circumstances.

Bill leaves room for the social partners to agree on a higher (but not a lower) age in particular contexts, by virtue of which employees can continue working after they have turned 65.[36]

The Bill also leaves room for special regulations permitting dismissal on ground of age in case of specific professions, such as airline pilots or fire-fighters. However, these regulations also need to be objectively justified, and they are not exempted from the application of the legislation. Enforcement of the legislation is vested as with other discrimination grounds in the Equal Treatment Commission, which is authorised under the Bill to investigate cases of alleged unequal treatment on the ground of age.

As the first Bill designed to implement the Directive, the Dutch legislation is obviously of great interest. Its adoption of the open-ended objective justification defence in place of the more specific approach taken in 1998 may leave the law in a very uncertain position, as in Finland. Essentially, the Dutch legislation adopts the Directive, without trying to remedy the defects inherent in the Directive's approach discussed elsewhere in this book. It adopts a loose approach to when 'objective justification' can be shown, and has a restricted scope. Again, utilitarian concerns about socio-economic and demographic factors seem to be driving age policy, rather than an active engagement with a rights-orientated approach.

AGE EQUALITY IN IRELAND

The Irish experience of age discrimination is particularly interesting from a UK perspective. Ireland not alone has a comparable common law legal system and labour market structure to that of the UK, but also is the only EU country to have introduced comprehensive age equality legislation covering much of the scope of the Directive and also extending to goods and services.[37]

As with many other EU states, as noted above, Article 40.1 of the Irish Constitution provides a general guarantee of equal treatment, but has also proved to be of limited use in the context of age discrimination. In applying this test in the context of age discrimination in its judgment on the constitutionality of the first comprehensive employment equality bill introduced by the Irish

---

[36] The social partners in contrast had called for the legislation to provide that that a general dismissal age lower than 65 is objectively justified as long as it is established in a collective agreement, an example of the frequently problematic effect of collective agreements in this area. The Dutch Government however was of the opinion that this was not possible within the terms of the Framework Directive.

[37] The background to the new legislation was very different from the conditions underpinning the development of age discrimination strategies in the rest of the EU. Ireland has the highest proportion of its population under the age of 25 in the EU, and therefore has little of the same concerns about a declining contribution base prevalent throughout other EU states. In addition, massive economic growth throughout the 1990s had substantially reduced youth unemployment. Report on the Republic of Ireland, *Industrial Relations and the Ageing Workforce: a Review of Measures to Combat Age Discrimination in Employment*, European Industrial Relations Observatory (EIRO) 2000, at www.eiro.eurofound.ie/2000/10/study/TN0010201S.html

Government in 1996,[38] the court followed the approach of the US Supreme Court in treating age discrimination as a less problematic category than other forms of discrimination.[39] A rational justification will therefore again be sufficient to demonstrate sufficient objective justification for constitutional purposes. Nevertheless, pressure from age and disability NGOs and the influence of the US and Canadian legislation led to the decision to include age, which was already a protected ground in the law governing dismissals,[40] within the scope of comprehensive new single equality legislation.[41]

The new legislation was designed to prohibit discrimination on the grounds of any of nine equality strands, race, sexual orientation, gender, religion, gender, family status, disability, membership of the travelling community and age. Two separate Acts apply, with the Employment Equality Act 1998 (EEA) prohibiting discrimination in the employment context on the nine grounds, including age,[42] while the Equal Status Act 2000 (ESA) prohibits discrimination by goods and service providers on the same nine grounds. The provisions of the ESA have caused considerable political controversy, centred round the refusal of publicans to serve members of the travelling community,[43] but the age provisions in both pieces of legislation have proved relatively unproblematic. Most of the initial equality cases arising under the age ground have concerned discrimination in access to goods and services, indicating the ongoing existence of many prejudicial age-based assumptions that are discriminatory in effect and yet will remain unchallenged if age equality legislation is confined to the employment context. This clearly signals the limitations of an approach centred upon the scope of the Directive alone.

Discrimination in Employment

The Employment Equality Act (EEA) covers much of the scope of the Framework Equality Directive, and its provisions are similar to the well-established model of UK anti-discrimination legislation, with the basic features of existing Irish, UK and EU sex discrimination law applied across the nine prohibited grounds which are set out in section 6 of the Act. Therefore, direct and indirect discrimination within the scope of the Act on any of the nine prohibited grounds is prohibited, subject to specific exceptions, some specific to certain of the grounds, others of a more general nature.

---

[38] *In the Matter of Article 26 of the Constitution and in the Matter of the Employment Equality Bill, 1996* [1997] 2 IR 321(SC).

[39] *Massachusetts Board of Retirement et al v Murgia* 427 U.S.307 (SC).

[40] The Unfair Dismissals Act 1993, as amended by the Unfair Dismissals (Amendment) Act 1997.

[41] See H Meenan, 'Age, the Individual and the Law' (2002) 20 *Irish Law Times* 10, 154.

[42] For a good summary of the Act, see H Meenan, 'Age Discrimination: Law-Making Possibilities Explored' [2000] 4 *International Journal of Discrimination and the Law* 247, 271 275.

[43] See *Irish Times*, 13 August 2002.

In the age context, the approach of the legislation is to exempt particular professions and activities from the scope of the Act, and to specify particular areas where an objective justification defence will apply. It does not adopt the general objective justification test provided for in the Dutch legislation, arguably providing a greater degree of clarity and certainty. However, the sweep of the Irish legislation has resulted in particular exemptions in the age context being drafted in exceptionally broad terms that substantially reduce the efficacy of the legislation, and which will in all probability need adjustment to comply with the Directive. It therefore in its scope and structure adheres to the 'rights' approach, but in the framing of its specific exemptions preserves areas where the 'minimal' standard applies. In addition, the remedies it adopts arguably fall short of what an approach directed towards the full vindication of the right to equal treatment would require.

Exemptions Within the Scope of the EEA

Section 37(2) provides for a general 'occupational qualification' defence, similar to Article 4 of the Directive in applying across all nine grounds. Section 37(3) however, without prejudice to the generality of 37(2) sets out a specific occupational qualification defence relating to age when, on the grounds of physiology or on the grounds of authenticity for the purposes of entertainment, the nature of a post requires a person of a particular age. While not closing off the possibility of other genuine occupational qualifications being identified, it is noteworthy that the only one specified is also noted in the UK consultation paper.[44]

Other exceptions relate specifically to age, and close off the application of the legislation to particular groups. Section 6(3) carves out a major exception, providing that the less favourable treatment of persons younger than 18 and older than 65 not to be treated as discrimination on the grounds of age for the purposes of the Act, imposing a cut-off point similar to that in the Canadian legislation. This exemption was upheld as constitutional when the original Employment Equality Bill 1996 was referred to the Supreme Court.[45] The age

---

[44] The UK consultation paper *Towards Equality and Diversity: Implementing the Race and Framework Equality Directives* (London, Cabinet Office, 2001) cited the example of child actors playing the title role of 'Oliver' as an example of a genuine occupational age requirement required for the purposes of authenticity for the purposes of entertainment, the only specific type of genuine occupational requirement referred to. See *Towards Equality and Diversity*, 5:15, p 55.

[45] The age restrictions were unsuccessfully challenged on the basis that they were a discriminatory provision without rational justification and accordingly in violation of Art 40(1), the constitutional equality clause. As a result, the Supreme Court held that the aged and young are entitled to protection against laws which discriminate against them, unless the differentiation is related to a legitimate objective and is not arbitrary or irrational. Since the age limits chosen (18 and 65) reflect the ages at which significant numbers of persons enter and leave the workforce they could not 'plausibly be characterised in the view of the Court, as irrational or arbitrary.' See, *In the Matter of Article 26 of the Constitution and in the Matter of the Employment Equality Bill, 1996* [1997] 2 IR 321(SC), 348.

restriction could be argued to comply with Article 6(1) of the Framework Directive, as it could be objectively and reasonably justified by the legitimate aim of regulating and clearing access to the labour market, while preserving the state social security and pension net.[46] While the lower age limit can arguably be justified by the need to protect younger persons, the upper age limit is obviously more contentious, retaining as it does mandatory retirement and exempting the over-65s from any protection, even if they are permitted and choose to carry on working. There has been little debate on this in Ireland as yet.

While the age limits apply to specific age groups, section 37(6) of the Act provides that the age discrimination provisions shall not apply at all to employment in the defence forces, police or prison services. The Irish Supreme Court in hearing the constitutional challenge to the equality legislation held that given the distinctive mental and physical fitness requirements required in the context of these professions, the exemption of the police and the other units was related to a permissible legislative objective.[47] However, the exemption for the police and prison services appears wider than permitted under Article 3(4) of the Framework Directive, which permits member states to provide that the provisions regarding age discrimination shall not apply to the armed forces only.[48] The Dutch Bill, as noted above, does not exempt the police and prison services. Therefore, the EEA may have to be amended to apply to the police and prison services, and any relevant age limits will have to be objectively and reasonably justifiable. (The Canadian experience shows that the courts are generally quite lenient in applying this requirement when public safety and security is at stake).[49]

Other exemptions relate to particular kinds of discriminatory treatment, rather than applying to particular age groups. Sections 8(6) and 13 permit age discrimination with respect to terms of employment that relate to pension rights, and section 34(4) likewise provides that it shall not constitute age discrimination to fix different ages for the retirement of employees. This

---

[46] Similar arguments have been made in relation to the upper limit in The Netherlands, and the content of Recital 14 of the Directive with its statement that the Directive does not alter national retirement age is relevant here.

[47] It was also argued before the Supreme Court that s 37(6) constituted unjustifiable discrimination between employees in the public and private sector (for example, employees of a security firm, who are protected against age discrimination) and therefore was in breach of the constitutional equality guarantee, Art 40(1). Hamilton CJ accepted that at first sight it was difficult to defend on constitutional grounds the wide-ranging exclusions from the Bill. However, as the Court accepted that age-related discrimination fell into a different and lesser constitutional category from sex or race, the decision not to extend it to the public service was justifiable on the grounds of due deference to the legislature. See [1997] 2 IR 321, 349 (SC).

[48] Recital 18 to the Directive does provide that its provisions do not require the armed forces, the police, prison or emergency services to recruit or maintain in employment persons without the necessary capacity, when required by the legitimate objective of preserving the operational capacity of those services. This however does not confer an absolute exemption: it indicates that objective justification will apply here.

[49] See *Ontario Human Rights Commission v Etobicoke* (1982) 132 DLR (3d) 14 (SCC); *MacDonald v Regional Administrative School Unit No 1* (1992) 16 CHRR D/409.

exemption of pension rights was intended to permit differential treatment of various age groups to preserve employer flexibility in pension provision. Article 6 (2) of the Directive as noted above permits states to exempt age distinctions relating to access to retirement benefits: it remains to be seen whether the scope of the Irish exception exceeds that of the Directive, though it would appear that the broad sweep of section 8 (6) is generally compatible with Article 6 (2).[50]

Section 34 (7) creates an exception that permits pay to be linked with seniority, while section 34(5) provides that it shall not constitute age discrimination to set a maximum age for recruitment which takes account of any cost or time involved in training a recruit. Both these exceptions allow objective justification to be shown within narrow grounds, and appear to come within the 'labour market' category of exceptions permitted in Article 6 of the Directive. A stricter approach would have replaced the seniority exception with one that explicitly deemed greater experience and duration of service to be justifiable criteria for determining pay and promotion. This would secure pay scales based on these criteria from indirect age discrimination challenges while prohibiting reliance on age alone as a simple differentiating factor.

The major exception in the legislation is provided for in section 34 of the EEA, in particular section 34(3). It provides that it shall not be unlawful discrimination on the age ground where 'it is shown that there is clear actuarial or other evidence that significantly increased costs would result if discrimination were not permitted in the circumstances.' This exemption is extremely broad, resembles that initially provided for in the Dutch 1998 Bill and is much more permissive than even the open-ended 'objective justification' test in Article 6(1) of the Directive. Differential treatment under this clause on the age ground will still be required to satisfy the proportionality requirement, but the extent of the permissible legitimate aim, the avoidance of 'significantly increased costs', has the potential to nullify much of the impact of the EEA.

Other exceptions are less controversial. Section 16 provides that the Act does not protect individuals who do not have the capacity to fulfil the duties relevant to their position, while section 17 exempts necessary compliance with specified legislative provisions such as the redundancy payments legislation. Section 12 of the Act permits differential treatment on the ground of age in relation to scholarships, bursaries, financial support and educational fees in the context of vocational training, with the ESA making similar provision in respect of education in general. Section 34(6) is a transitory provision, designed to allow for the adjustment of collective agreements that involve age differentiation outside of the permitted exceptions. It provides that any age-related pay arrangements in force on 18 October 1999 must be brought to an end within three years. The EEA also in line with Article 7 of the Directive provides for the possibility for positive action on age grounds, but only when directed towards facilitating the

---

[50] See *Law v Canada* [1989] 1 SCR 143 for a discussion of the justifiability under the Canadian Charter of Fundamental Rights of age distinctions in pension entitlements.

integration into employment of those over 50 years of age. The rather arbitrary cut-off point of 50 years was upheld by the Irish Supreme Court.[51]

Employment Litigation under the EEA

The EEA cases that have arisen in the context of age have so far concerned relatively straightforward factual circumstances. Helen Meenan has noted that the majority of successful employment cases so far have involved ageist language, indicating the extent to which age discrimination remains deeply rooted.[52] In *A Firm of Solicitors v A Worker*,[53] a legal secretary in her fifties was dismissed so the firm could 'take on a young girl who could be trained to do her job': the Labour Court found a causal link between this remark and her dismissal, and awarded her £6,000 IR.

The advertising provisions of the EEA have given rise to the most prominent age case under the Irish legislation so far, and are especially important in the context of age: other forms of prohibited discrimination rarely appear in public adverts, whereas age discrimination in advertising is still very prevalent, and contributes to a culture of 'normalising' ageism.[54] Section 10 of the EEA prohibits the publication of an advertisement relating to employment and which indicates an intention to discriminate or might reasonably be understood as so indicating. In *Equality Authority v Ryanair*,[55] the airline had advertised for a particular position, with the advertisement indicating that 'a young and dynamic professional . . .' was sought and that 'the ideal candidate will be young and dynamic.' The Equality Authority, having the authority to bring actions in respect of potentially discriminatory adverts, brought an action for age discrimination. Ryanair argued that since the advertisement did not refer to actual age limits but was allegedly only referring to characteristics such as enthusiasm, passion and ambition that were associated with a 'young and dynamic' state of mind, no issue of actual age discrimination arose under the Act.

---

[51] The positive action provisions in the original Bill were considered by the Supreme Court on the referral of the Bill. It was argued that while it was a legitimate objective of the state to seek to reduce long-term unemployment, it was not an objectively justifiable ground for discriminating between those aged between 18 and 50 on the one hand and those aged between 50 and 65 on the other. It was also argued that this objective could have been more reasonably achieved by using the length of time for which a person was registered as unemployed as a more appropriate ground for exempting him/her from the effects of the anti-discrimination provisions, rather than using the arbitrary age limit of 50. However, the Supreme Court held that the Oireachtas (the Irish Parliament) was entitled as a matter of social policy to choose between fixing the relevant age at what was an reasonably appropriate level, or employing another more flexible but possibly less practicable yardstick, such as the length of time unemployed; [1997] 2 IR 321, 344 (SC).

[52] For a detailed discussion of these cases, see H Meenan, 'Age, the Individual and the Law' (2002) 20 *Irish Law Times* 10, 154, 171.

[53] Labour Court determination EEDO11, 21 May 2001.

[54] Ibid.

[55] Equality Authority, DEC-E/2000/14, 29 December 2000.

This rather desperate defence proved unconvincing, and the Equality Officer found for the complainant, finding that the use of the word 'young' clearly indicated or might reasonably be understood as an intention to exclude applicants who were not 'young' in chronological terms, and was therefore contrary to section 10. The Equality Officer emphasised that discriminatory advertising is 'overt and public discrimination' and must be countered in the strongest possible way. Ryanair were ordered to pay compensation of £8000 and directed to take a specific course of remedial action.

Equal Status Act 2000

The ESA prohibits discrimination on any of the same nine prohibited grounds in the provision of goods and services, advertising of such goods and services, housing, private clubs (unless specifically aimed catering for a particular group) and education. Again, certain key exceptions are carved out in the context of age. Section 5(d) permits differential treatment in relation to the provision of pensions, insurance policies and other actuarial calculations where it is reasonable to rely on data obtained from a reasonable source or based on relevant commercial or underwriting factors. Actuarial calculations in the context of pensions are exempt under Article 6 (2) of the Directive, and this clause in the ESA extends this across the spectrum of actuarial activity. The Irish Equality Authority have vigorously emphasised however the reasonableness requirement in section 5(d), and have launched a high-profile public campaign against unjustified and unsupported age distinctions in car and other forms of insurance, arguing that age alone is an irrelevant factor for determining insurance risk.[56]

Section 5 also provides for differential treatment on the age ground in the provision of sporting events or facilities when reasonable and necessary, in entertainment for reasons of authenticity and in age requirements to become adoptive or foster parents. Section 5(2)(l) provides for a catch-all exception, where the goods and services in question can only be regarded as suitable for provision to a particular group of persons, while section 5(2)(h) permits differential treatment to bona fide promote the special interests of a category of persons. This last exception would arguably protect over-65s holiday schemes and other specialist services directed at older persons, as well as special young services. Differential treatment in respect of the allocation of places to mature students is permitted by section 7(3)(e).

The major cases that have risen under the ESA have involved door policies in bars, with the travelling community in particular challenging many of the restrictions imposed on them. Similarly, the two major age cases under the ESA so far have involved the exclusion of people being turned away from Dublin

---

[56] See C O'Cinneide, *A Single Equality Body: Lessons From Aboard*, Appendix B (Manchester Equal Opportunities Commission December 2002).

bars. In *O'Reilly v Q-Bar*,[57] a 72-year-old was turned away, and the Equality Officer held that the complainant had established prima facie evidence that his exclusion was based on age, and while bars were entitled to have a door policy, they could not discriminate on the grounds of age. In *Scanlon and Ryan v The Russell Court Hotel*,[58] two 18-year olds were turned away from an event to which they already had tickets on the grounds that there were 'too many young people here already'. The Equality Officer again found that they had made out a prima facie case of discrimination, and awarded them £1,000 IR each.

In many ways, the most obvious impact of the ESA in age terms has been the elimination of age bars to access to pubs, bars and hotels, a not-insignificant achievement given Ireland's cultural attachment to these locations. The ESA in extending protection against age discrimination to goods and services has sent out an extremely clear signal of the unacceptability of age discrimination, and is firmly rooted in a rights-based approach, recognising the full scope of the entitlement to equality.

Enforcement and Remedies

A complainant can take an employment case under the EEA to either the Director of Equality Investigations (the 'Director'), or the Labour Court (an equivalent body to an employment tribunal) if the claim relates to a dismissal. Complaints under the ESA go to the Director, and the procedure is similar. The possible compensation that can be awarded by the Director is limited, with plaintiffs discriminated against in the course of their employment being able to claim up to 104 weeks' salary, but non-employees, such as the job applicants in Ryanair that have suffered discrimination individual's compensation can only be awarded up to £10,000 IR. This is a serious limitation, demonstrated by the meagre sum of £6,000 IR that was awarded to the dismissed legal secretary in one of the first age cases.[59] There is a real possibility that this could be deemed an inadequate remedy under the Directive. The Director can also make an order requiring a specific course of remedial action on the part of the discriminator, as was made in *Ryanair*.

The two acts also establish the Equality Authority (the 'Authority'), a single equality commission with overlapping responsibilities across multiple equality strands. The Authority has been very active in emphasising the importance of age discrimination, best illustrated by the high profile of their campaign against ageist assumptions in insurance. This highlights the central importance of a proactive enforcement authority with responsibility for age. The Framework Directive, unlike the Race Directive does not require the establishment of an

---

[57] Equality Officer Decision No. Dec—S2002-013, available at http://www.odei.ie/Equality%20Caselaw.htm

[58] Equality Officer Decision No Dec-S2001-013.

[59] See n 53 above.

enforcement body: this is unfortunate, and leaves a significant gap in the enforcement mechanisms required under the Directive.

A Rights-based Approach

Much of the political and legal response to age discrimination across the EU has been driven by a utilitarian approach, with the emphasis being on patching up problems in the labour market rather than adopting a rights-based approach. This has contributed to the flawed, patchwork and minimalist legislation that currently exists in most EU states. The Directive constitutes the first major step in genuinely combating age inequality. However, it remains very limited in scope and effect, in particular due to the wide scope of the activities specifically listed in the Directive as potentially justified, which may prove problematic by in turn justifying a permissive application by national governments and the courts of the Directive's objective justification test.[60] In addition, as its scope is confined to employment and employment-related activities, the Directive does not require that age discrimination in goods and services be prohibited, despite the Irish experience showing that such a prohibition is both possible and effective in combating deeply-rooted, irrational age prejudice.

In framing legislation to comply with the Directive, the UK can adopt a similarly permissive approach to that adopted by The Netherlands, which makes full use of the differences of treatment on age grounds permitted by the Directive and confines itself to the employment-related activities covered by its limited scope. Alternatively, the UK could introduce much more extensive and far-reaching legislation, similar to the approach taken in some respects by the Irish. Whichever choice is made will demonstrate the degree of seriousness with which the UK Government chooses to address the problem of age inequalities.

In making this choice, basing policy on the individual rights of citizens to equal treatment and self-realisation offers a coherent principle for framing age equality legislation and policies. International and domestic jurisprudence has consistently required that exceptions to such fundamental human rights principles as equality must be narrowly construed, and that any such deviation be proportionate to the objective sought to be achieved.[61] Exemptions to prohibitions on discriminatory treatment, whether to satisfy social needs or the need to protect individual dignity, must be shown to be clearly necessary and have strong justification.

---

[60] See Eurolink evidence to House of Lords Select Committee on the European Union, 'EU Proposals to Combat Discrimination' (HL Paper 68, 16 May 2000).

[61] See *General Comment 18, Non-Discrimination*, UN Human Rights Committee (1989).

Only a clear demonstration of the necessity of making age-based distinctions should therefore justify exceptions to the scope of age discrimination legislation. This approach is similar to the 'necessity' test adopted by the US Supreme Court in *Western Airlines v Criswell*,[62] and in particular to the strict test adopted by the Canadian Supreme Court in recent sex discrimination cases such as *British Columbia (Public Service Employee Relations Commission) v BCGSEU*.[63] A similarly rigorous approach is needed in implementing the permissive provisions of the Directive, and should be adopted by member states in introducing their own age equality legislation.

Comparative Lessons

If this approach is adopted, then what comparative models should guide the UK in framing age discrimination legislation that takes age equality seriously? The Irish approach of listing specific activities which are exempt from the legislation, which was also initially adopted by the Dutch in the 1998 Bill, arguably provides more precision and legal certainty than the open-ended test adopted in the Directive and in the Dutch and Finnish legislation. However, the Irish legislation and the initial Dutch proposal both made provision for broad exemptions that considerably reduced the effectiveness of either, and the courts in applying an open-ended justification test may apply a 'necessity' standard, as the Canadian courts have done. Therefore, either an open-ended justification test or a specific list of exceptions may be compatible with a rights-based approach to upholding age equality, provided that a strict test of 'necessity' is applied by either the courts in applying the open-ended test or by governments in framing specific exceptions.

However, the Irish comparative experience in particular demonstrates that a rights-based approach directed towards the elimination of unjustified age inequalities has to also target age discrimination in education, health and access to goods and services. The examples of legislation enacted in Canada and in several Australian states and that of Ireland demonstrate that extending the scope of age legislation to these areas can work, and produce real results in combating in-built age prejudice. Limited exemptions may have to be carved out for actuarial industries and other particular services. However, the 'necessity' test would require the justification for these exceptions to be clearly demonstrated, and not just founded upon casual assumptions based on ageist attitudes. The 'objective justification' test developed in EC case law is a flexible tool, and capable of dealing with the complexities of service provision by balancing the requirements of ensuring effective equality with those of social utility. A failure by the UK or other member states to extend legislation to cover services would

---

[62] No 83-1545.
[63] [1999] 3 SCR 3.

leave a gaping hole in the scope of anti-discrimination law, and would be questionable in the light of the Irish experience.

Making Enforcement 'Bite'

A rights-centred approach involves more than applying the 'necessity' standard in framing and applying legislation. Applying the lessons from experience of other jurisdictions and other forms of anti-discrimination legislation, successful rights-based age legislation will have to be effective, be capable of strong enforcement and be directed at achieving meaningful cultural change. The Directive does not require the establishment of a Commission exercising investigative and support functions such as the Commission for Racial Equality. Any UK legislation should establish an equivalent age body with expanded powers of initiating cases, or better still, move towards the merger of the existing equality commissions and extend the remit of the merged body to include age.[64] One of the main problems of the theoretically strong US age discrimination law model is that it relies on mainly individual claims.[65] In contrast, the Irish Equality Authority as noted above has enforced age discrimination legislation with vigour, demonstrating the importance of such an enforcement body.

A coherent response to age inequality also requires that proactive action be taken to eliminate illegitimate age distinctions on the part of public and private bodies. This may include the adoption of positive duties to promote age equality, the mainstreaming of age equality concerns in the formation of policy, and rigorous monitoring of the persistence and justifiability of age differentiation.[66] A meaningful equality response requires that such positive action measures can be taken to ensure substantial equality, and this should be regarded as integral to a rights-based age equality policy. Valuable experience can be gained from Finland's approach of combining age discrimination legislation with a national strategy for enhancing the role and rights of older workers. As part of this process, a critical evaluation and review of existing age distinctions in the public service and in legislation should be adopted in tandem with the introduction of age equality legislation. As noted above, the Dutch have carried out a similar review pending the introduction of their legislation.

No matter how rigorous, legislation introduced in isolation from a coherent overall policy approach and lacking adequate enforcement will inevitably prove disappointing. The Irish experience shows that even flawed legislation can be

[64] See C O'Cinneide, *A Single Equality Body: Lessons From Aboard*, Appendix B (Manchester, Equal Opportunities Commission, December 2002).

[65] See Z Hornstein (ed), *Outlawing Age Discrimination: Foreign Lessons, UK Choices*, Transitions after 50 Series (York, The Joseph Rowntree Foundation) July 2001, see http://www.jrf.org.uk/knowledge/findings/socialpolicy/711.asp

[66] For proposals on extending positive duties in the public and private sectors, see B Hepple, M Coussey, and T Choudhury, *Equality: A New Framework*, The Report of the Independent Review of the Enforcement of UK Anti-Discrimination Legislation (Oxford, Hart Publishing, 2000).

effective if implemented vigorously and well, while the Finnish approach demonstrates the potential effectiveness of a coherent and unified approach by government and social partners directed at supplementing antidiscrimination legislation with social change. All forms of discrimination legislation can only contribute to achieving equality: the symbolic effect of age legislation is considerable, but more is needed.

CONCLUSION

Critical and ongoing scrutiny of age inequalities, affecting young and old, should be central to any policy designed to end age inequality. The Ontario Human Commission has noted that age discrimination seems not to give rise to the sense of moral opprobrium that other forms of illegitimate discrimination attract.[67] However, by centring the debate around the entitlement of age equality and the right of each individual to equal respect in the absence of compelling circumstances justifying discriminatory treatment, a principled approach based on human rights principles can give coherence and force to age equality legislation and policy. Comparative experience from other EU states demonstrates both what is possible and what is effective, and provides valuable lessons for the UK to rise to the challenge of achieving age equality.

---

[67] See *Discrimination and Age: Human Rights Issues Facing Older Persons in Ontario* (Ontario Human Rights Commission, 2000), available at http://www.ohrc.on.ca/

Index